Interior Design Law and Business Practices

D1480659

Interior Design Law and Business Practices

C. Jaye Berger, Esq.

John Wiley & Sons, Inc.

NEW YORK / TORONTO / CHICHESTER / BRISBANE / SINGAPORE

To Jack and Maren.

Library of Congress Cataloging in Publication Data:
Berger, C. Jaye.
   Interior design law and business practices / C. Jaye Berger.
     p. cm.
   Includes index.
   ISBN 0-471-58342-1 (cloth : acid-free paper) :
    1. Interior decorators—Legal status, laws, etc.—United States.
   2. Interior decoration firms—United States—Management. I. Title.
   KF2930.I58B47   1994
   729′.068—dc20   93-36090

Printed in the United States of America

10 9 8 7 6 5 4 3 2 1

Preface

As an attorney who specializes in representing interior designers and architects, I have had the unique opportunity to lecture to groups of interior designers across the country, as well as give legal counsel to many interior designer clients. Each time I speak in public about contracts or litigation, people in the audience ask, "Where can I read more about that?" This book was written to answer that question.

I have addressed all the key issues that design clients have come to consult with me about over the years. I have also invited some highly regarded colleagues to contribute chapters about the areas in which they have expertise.

I have found that as the practice of interior design has evolved into a profession, interior designers have become increasingly concerned with business and legal issues. They want to maintain high standards for themselves and the industry as a whole. One way to do that is to learn more about how to negotiate and draft contracts, organize a business, purchase insurance, and protect against litigation. Increasingly they seek legal counsel for advice before they actually have problems and attend seminars to increase their business skills and awareness of the issues facing them. Similarly, many architects do a great deal of interior design work and need to know more about this aspect of their practice.

Whether you are just starting out in the business or already have your own firm, you will learn new things from this book that will enhance your practice.

C. JAYE BERGER, ESQ.

New York, New York
December 1993

v

Contents

1

Starting an Interior Design Business

FORM OF THE BUSINESS

One of the questions I am most frequently asked by new clients is "What options does an interior designer have in setting up a business?" There are three basic forms in which a designer can do business. If you are an individual, you can operate as a sole proprietorship or a corporation. If two or more people want to be in business together, they can form either a partnership or a corporation. There are also a couple of variations on these basic formats, such as a joint venture and a professional corporation.

SOLE PROPRIETORSHIP

Anyone can go into business as a sole proprietor with little formality. Since many sole proprietors in the design industry use variations on their names or totally different names, usually a Certificate of Doing Business Under Assumed Name must be filed by your attorney with the local County Clerk. This lets the public know that Jane Smith, for example, is doing business as "Creative Designs." The individual and the business are one and all income will be taxed on the designer's individual income tax return.

Although most sole proprietors keep separate bank accounts for their businesses, all liability remains theirs personally. The funds for any settlements or judgments arising out of litigation come out of their personal assets. This is one reason that many people decide to incorporate. This does not mean that you should not be a sole proprietor, but it certainly is something to think about when you are setting up your business and trying to decide on its structure. Many people start their businesses as sole proprietorships and later incorporate.

You will need to establish a bank account for the business. The bank may ask to see the Certificate of Doing Business before they open the account. This assures them that this is a business account and also tells them who is authorized to transact business on behalf of the firm.

The designer will have to register the business with the state agency handling sales taxes. This applies to most, but not all, states, so the designer should check on the sales tax laws in all the locales in which he may be doing projects. The company must apply for a "resale number," by which it is identified.

A number of other issues must be addressed when starting a business. The designer must allocate funds for legal and accounting services, for purchasing letterhead and business cards, for rent, if he works outside of the home, for insurance, and for cash flow to tide him over until projects and project payments start to come in.

The more time and effort you put into organizing your business *before* you get business, the more likely it is that you will succeed and prosper. Once work comes in, it is harder to make the time to go and get legal advice and have a good contract drafted. You don't have the time to set up systems for tracking time spent on projects and money spent for the business. Before you know it, you are overwhelmed with paper and not enough time to sort through it. So use your time before the work starts to flood in to get your office organized.

If you get some fundamental systems in place early and have a team of consultants in place before you go into business, things will run more smoothly once you are busy. You can then call your attorney and ask her to have a contract drafted. You can have your accountant set up your books. You can call your insurance broker and easily obtain more insurance if a client requests it. You have bookkeeping systems already in place so that the quarterly and end-of-year tax filings can easily be done.

PARTNERSHIP

A partnership can be formed by two or more individuals who want to be in business together and share profits and losses. The profits and losses do not necessarily have to be shared equally in order to be partners. It can be 60/40, 70/30, or any other combination you agree on.

Many states have statutes that govern many aspects of the partnership relationship. Since not all areas of the relationship are covered by such statutes and because you may want to handle certain areas differently, it is highly recommended that you have an attorney draft a partnership agreement. This should be done *before* you begin doing business as partners. If you wait until the business is underway, there may be disagreements as to how profits should be shared, as well as other aspects of the relationship. I have seen many partnerships end in less than a year and if there is no partnership agreement and many issues are unclear, there is generally a lot of anger and litigation is likely to result.

A Certificate of Doing Business as Partners may also have to be filed by your attorney with the local municipality. It gives the names of the partners, their addresses, and the name of the partnership. It lets the public know who is in the partnership and is similar to the filing discussed for sole proprietorships.

Partners can be personally liable for the partnership and for each other. This is called "joint and several liability." This means that innocent partners who never worked on a particular project can be liable along with the negligent partner, if there is a lawsuit. If the partnership were to file for bankruptcy, the creditors could then proceed against the partners' personal assets to satisfy debts. Many people start off as partners to share expenses and to see if the relationship will work and later incorporate.

The idea of a partnership is appealing because you can share the burden of the work and business development and also collaborate on projects. However, before you enter into one, you should be sure you are doing it for the right reasons.

All too often I see partnerships being formed because one or both parties are afraid to try being in business alone. This is not a good enough reason to form a partnership. You must have a clear understanding of what each of you is contributing to the relationship and a clear understanding of your potential partner's limitations. For example, if your potential partner is good at getting new clients, but not good at producing work, do not be disappointed when you have a deadline and find they are not there to help out. If your understanding is that one of you will get the work and the other one will do the work, problems may arise if one of you is not holding up your end of the bargain. Be realistic in your expectations.

If you feel that there is an imbalance in what you are each contributing, consider hiring someone as an employee or consultant. You can always form a partnership later on.

PARTNERSHIP AGREEMENTS

This agreement is essentially a contract between the partners discussing how the partnership will be run.

The agreement will discuss issues such as how partners will be treated if they retire, die, withdraw, or are expelled from the partnership. It will describe the voting procedures, how banking will be handled, and how partners will be paid. Of course, it will also describe how profits and losses will be divided. Some partners share these equally, others have elaborate formulas depending on who brought in a project, who managed it, and who worked on it. These are just some of the subjects that should be addressed.

The need for partnership agreements becomes most clear when a dispute develops. At that point, it is too late for discussions about who contributed what to the business, how they should be reimbursed, and what percentages of the profits and losses they are entitled to. If the partners do not have a partnership agreement, their affairs will be governed by the state partnership laws, which may not be the same as what the partners want or thought they agreed to when the partnership was formed.

The agreement is between all the partners and they all must sign it. Managerial positions can be assigned and described in the agreement. It will state how issues will be voted on, for example, whether each partner will have one vote, will vote by their percentage interest in the partnership, or some other method.

When a partner contributes cash to the business, will that be construed as a loan? Will there be interest on it? When will it be paid back? If one partner contributes cash and another partner contributes time to the partnership, how will that be credited? How will profits and losses be calculated, by whom and when?

Voluntary and involuntary withdrawals and expulsions of partners from the business must be addressed. The agreement describes under what circumstances a partner may be forced out. For example, if a partner becomes ill, how many months can he be out sick and still be paid, before he is required to withdraw from the partnership? If a partner declares personal bankruptcy, can he remain in the partnership? If a partner is forced out, what will he be paid?

If the entire firm dissolves, how will the firm's assets be liquidated and distributed? How will projects in progress be completed and distributed?

Can partners participate in any business outside of the partnership? Can a partner in a design firm do small projects outside of the partnership? Does he have to contribute those earnings to the partnership? It may even discuss what would happen if a partner divorces. Can his wife be entitled to some interest in the business?

Partnerships do not have to be created to last forever. The agreement can state how long the partnership will last.

Partners tend to focus more on the notion of sharing profits, rather than on sharing losses. However, in a partnership, you share the good and the bad. If business is slow and more funds are needed, there must be an agreement on where these funds will come from. Each partner is liable for contributing his share. Subsequent contributions can be mandatory or optional.

They can be in whatever sum is needed or they can be based on the initial capital contributions provided by each partner. If the contribution is mandatory, the agreement will have to state what will occur if one partner fails to pay his share.

Partners receive a share in the profits or losses, known as a "draw," and not a salary. This can be handled several different ways. It can be shared in the same proportion as their respective capital contributions bear to the total capital. It can be shared equally regardless of other factors. It can be shared according to stipulated percentages.

An alternative is to allow this decision to be made by designated partners. This is typically done when someone becomes a partner in an already established partnership. When this method is used, the agreement may enumerate the criteria used to make this determination. It may include the amount of business development, involvement with management issues, and time spent on outside work, such as teaching. In a long-established partnership which is adding new partners, it is not unusual for the founding partners to retain veto power over major decisions such as borrowing funds over a certain amount, allowing new partners into the firm, and signing new contracts.

Partners need to agree on whether all their time must be devoted to the business and what other activities they can be involved in. Can a partner teach at a design school one or two days a week? May he keep his salary from teaching or must he contribute it to the firm?

Banking and access to books and records are important. The agreement should state that all funds in the partnership shall be deposited in the partnership's account and who can sign checks. Will two signatures be required on checks over a certain amount? It usually states where the books and records will be kept and that all partners will have access to them.

The ramifications of a partner's death can be serious in a small business and must be addressed in the agreement. The firm may pay for life insurance on each partner so that the proceeds can be used to pay the deceased partner's heirs for his interest in the firm. Otherwise, his heirs may own his interest and be entitled to be involved in the business. The surviving partners may be required to purchase his interest and make payments over a period of time.

There may be an indemnification clause stating that a partner who breaches the partnership agreement, or any fiduciary duty owed to any other partner, must indemnify the partnership for the resulting damages, expenses, and legal fees. Without such an agreement, the partnership may be required to indemnify each partner for any reasonable expense incurred in the ordinary and proper course of the partnership's business.

There may also be an arbitration clause so that any disagreements over the terms of the agreement can be resolved in that fashion, rather than by going to court. Arbitration is discussed at greater length in Chapter 11. Often partnerships end with a great deal of anger and little money in the bank to use for litigation. To the extent that potentially problematic issues can be ironed out, there will be fewer issues to be concerned about should the partnership end.

INCORPORATION

An individual or a group of individuals can incorporate. This means that a separate entity is being formed, distinct from the individuals who organized and will own it. This process should be handled by an attorney to ensure that it is done correctly, but can be done by the designer himself. The process varies from state to state. In New York, a Certificate of Incorporation must be filed with the Secretary of State. It contains information such as the name and address of the incorporator, the location of the business, and how many shares of stock are being issued. There is only one incorporator, even though several individuals all intend to be shareholders.

After this certificate is filed, the shareholders will usually receive a corporate outfit, which is a book containing, among other things, necessary forms for corporate resolutions, proposed by-laws, stock certificates, and a corporate seal. Of course, the designer's attorney can draft new documents or modify them as required.

By incorporating you are forming a separate entity. It is no longer you, but rather a company. Its owners are called "shareholders" and all the people who work for the company are employees. Many people incorrectly refer to their fellow shareholders as "partners." This is a different form of business organization.

The shareholders can each own different numbers of shares. All of the stock may be distributed, or only some of the stock, with the rest being held in reserve (unissued) for potential investors or employees who are allowed to buy stock in the company. The corporation will also have a Board of Directors to make major policy decisions and officers who run the day-to-day affairs. One individual may wear a number of different hats and be an officer, director, shareholder, and employee all at the same time. The actual stock certificates should be given to the shareholders so that they have tangible evidence of their ownership in the company. The shareholder will need this if he ever has a falling out with the company.

It is important to never lose sight of the fact that you and the corporation are not one. This may happen when there is only one shareholder. When the line between the corporation and the individual blurs, an adversary may use this as a basis in a lawsuit for going after your personal assets, rather than just the corporation's, on the theory that the corporation is really just you.

This is called "piercing the corporate veil."

When the lines are kept separate, only the corporation can be sued for corporate matters. This is why some people describe corporations as offering "limited liability," which means that only the corporation's assets are at risk if there is litigation. Your personal assets and those of other shareholders cannot be touched to satisfy a court judgment or arbitration award.

Liability can be expanded if the corporation takes out a bank loan and the major shareholders are required to personally guarantee the loan. However, this does not change the corporation's limited liability.

Corporations can issue and sell stock to attract investors or other shareholders who can contribute to the business. Corporations are of indefinite duration, so that they do not end if one shareholder dies or becomes disabled.

The ability to incorporate is a major advantage designers have over architects. The ability to limit liability is a major advantage of incorporation over other forms of doing business and is the reason most designers eventually consider it.

Your contracts, your letterhead, and the way you run your business should make it clear to others that they are dealing with a company. If you incorporate and use letterhead with only your name on it or order furniture in only your name, you run the risk of being considered a sole proprietor rather than a corporation in your dealings with clients and manufacturers. An adversary may use this as a basis for suing both the company and you personally, if there is a problem on a project. This as a common occurrence with small design firms.

It is important for the shareholders to have an attorney draft a shareholders agreement for them which describes how the business will run and they will work together. It is similar to a partnership agreement as far as the topics covered. A number of topics can be covered in the agreement, such as the conditions for issuing additional stock, selling stock, voting, and the number of hours a day each shareholder/employee will devote to the business.

CHOOSING A NAME

There are generally no restrictions on what name a company may use. Most often design firms choose to include the names of one or more shareholders or principals and some reference to interior design, for example, "John Smith Design, Inc." If the firm is incorporating, the name is rejected only if it is too similar to or the same as another corporation and might cause confusion. If you have a particular name in mind and are not ready to incorporate, the name can sometimes be reserved.

SUBCHAPTER S

Subchapter S status is a tax election available to corporations. It is elected by many interior design firms. In typical business corporations, there are two levels of taxes. First the corporations pay taxes on earnings. Then the shareholders pay taxes on their salaries. As a Subchapter S corporation, earnings are not taxed on the corporate level. They are only taxed once. Any deductions, credits, profits, and business losses are passed through to the owner's personal tax returns. It eliminates the need for two separate tax returns.

Since corporate tax rates are higher than individual tax rates, S corporation status is very desirable. Some people mistakenly think they can take advantage of the lower individual tax rates by paying large salaries to stockholders before paying corporate taxes. However, dividends in a regular C corporation must be paid out of after-tax dollars. So paying large salaries in lieu of dividends may violate tax laws concerning unreasonable compensation.

The S corporations can eliminate accumulated earnings tax problems which C corporations face because for them, all earnings, whether they are distributed or not, are taxed to stockholders each year. Stockholders in S corporations can apply their deductible personal losses against their pro rata share of the company's taxable income. They can also deduct their pro rata share of the S corporation's net operating loss from their personal gross income.

In some states which levy corporate income taxes, S corporations are exempt from corporate tax. The stockholders pay personal income taxes on the corporate earnings passed through to them.

There are some disadvantages to S corporation status. Taxable income is taxed to stockholders even if the income is not actually distributed to them. Certain items that are tax deductible for a C corporation, such as costs of certain fringe benefits, are not deductible for an S corporation.

To qualify for S corporation treatment, certain requirements must be met:

- The corporation must be created under the laws of one of the fifty states.
- There must be 35 or fewer stockholders.
- All stockholders must be individuals, decedents' estates, bankruptcy estates, or certain types of trusts. Corporations, partnerships and certain types of trusts may not hold stock.
- The corporation must have only one class of stock issued and outstanding.
- All shareholders must consent.

These requirements are easily met by most interior design firms. In order to receive this status, certain forms must be filed with the IRS. These can be filed by your attorney or your accountant.

LIMITED LIABILITY COMPANIES

Another type of corporation, the limited liability company (LLC) is only available in certain states. They are:

Arizona	Maryland
Colorado	Minnesota
Florida	Nevada
Georgia	Oklahoma
Illinois	Texas
Indiana	Utah
Iowa	Virginia
Kansas	West Virginia
Louisiana	Wyoming

Georgia and Indiana statutes allow only foreign LLCs to conduct business in the state, subject to applicable registration requirements.

Some other states have introduced legislation to allow LLCs. They are:

Hawaii	Pennsylvania
Indiana	Rhode Island
Missouri	South Carolina
Nebraska	Tennessee

Although this type of corporation resembles a partnership, it is a legal entity distinct from its members. It has the same rights as any corporation does to sue, be sued, and sell property. However, it must be formed by two or more members. Also, its life span cannot be more than 30 years, but it can be renewed. This is unlike a corporation, whose existence is perpetual. In Florida, the company name must end with "limited company" or "L.C." In Wyoming it must end with "limited liability company."

Limited liability companies are governed by articles of organization and regulations. They offer the tax benefits of a partnership and the liability protection of a regular corporation.

It is one more possible form of business organization which should be considered in those states where it is allowed and should be discussed with an attorney and an accountant to see if it is right for you.

JOINT VENTURES

Joint ventures are a popular form of doing business. They are often formed by contractors and design professionals when a firm is doing business in a locale other than their home base, when a small firm needs a larger firm to tackle a big project, or when a minority firm joins forces with a majority firm for a public project. Majority and minority contractors often do this so that minority firms can develop expertise on large projects which they might not otherwise be able to work on. They can also use the majority contractor's larger bonding capacity.

Essentially the two firms come together to form an entity like a partnership, but only for purposes of working on one project. The joint venture can be formed by any type of business: that is, corporations, partnerships or sole proprietors. It is run by an executive committee like a Board of Directors. It has its own name, which usually includes the words "joint venture."

The parties must negotiate all the other terms. They are not usually 50/50 arrangements. Sometimes the percentages are dictated by governmental agencies for their projects. For example, when a majority firm joint ventures with a minority firm, a governmental agency may state that the minority firm must own at least 60% of the joint venture. Other times it is based on each party's contributions.

They must decide how many employees from each firm will work for the joint venture. The firms must agree on a principal-in-charge so that they have a representative who can answer questions.

The financial aspects require careful planning, especially banking. The joint venture will have at least one bank account. It is separate from each company's other businesses. Two signatures should be required for checks—one representative from each firm. Separate books and records will be kept and be available for review by either firm. Depending on the size of the project there will be monthly reports of expenses and payments which will be reviewed at executive committee meetings.

The percentage of profits and losses to be shared must be negotiated. Profits are what is left when expenses and salaries have been paid.

The joint venture will last until the project is complete or for a specified period of time, such as 120 days from final payment or for the period of the longest applicable statute of limitations.

Each firm can be liable for the other's mistakes. However, certain changes can be negotiated such as liability up to certain percentages.

As with any contract, the parties should consider in advance how they will handle disputes. Since the issues can be complex and costly to litigate, I often recommend arbitration. Generally disputes can be resolved quickly and less expensively than in the courts. However, certain tools such as injunctions are only available through the courts.

The importance of contracts detailing the agreement between the parties to the joint venture cannot be minimized. It is a complex form of doing business and many issues need to be negotiated, resolved, and drafted into legal language before work begins to avoid future problems.

ARCHITECTURAL FIRMS WITH INTERIOR DESIGN DEPARTMENTS OR ALLIED COMPANIES

In the last few years many architectural firms have taken more of an interest than ever in cultivating interior design business. This may, in part, be due to the decline in new construction. Whatever the reason, it is a widespread phenomenon.

Basically, there are two ways in which this has been done. Either a new department can be set up or an entirely separate interior design corporation can be formed. Many firms choose to set up separate corporations so that there can be an interior designer in charge of this work and it will not contravene any state licensing laws. In most states, an interior designer cannot be a partner in the architectural firm.

This setup can be a good marketing tool if clients tend to only think of the firm in terms of doing architectural projects. It can make it easier in terms of paying sales tax and separating out architectural from interior design services.

CONSULTANTS AND EMPLOYEES

Many firms rely heavily on consultants as a way to augment their staff and to bring in expertise that may not otherwise be available. It can also be used as a way to determine if you want to be in business with someone before you actually commit to do so.

Consultants are in business for themselves. Even though they may come to your office to do some of their work, they have separate businesses. This means that they pay their own taxes, usually quarterly, and purchase their own insurance and benefits.

By contrast, employers are required by law to withhold certain sums from their employee's salary and to pay it to the government for unemployment and disability. If someone is called a "consultant," but really is an employee, the employer can be subject to penalties such as 1.5% of the wages paid for purposes of income tax withholding; 3% of wages if the employer did not file 1099s; and 20% of the employee's share of FICA taxes. Thus it is important to understand the difference between employees and consultants and to observe the proper formalities.

The following are criteria used by the Internal Revenue Service (IRS) to determine whether someone is a consultant or an employee:

1. Is the person providing services required to comply with instructions about when, where, and how the work is to be done?
2. Is the person provided training to enable him to perform a job in a particular method or manner?
3. Are the services provided integrated into the business' operation?
4. Must the services be rendered personally?
5. Does the business hire, supervise, or pay assistants to help the person performing services?
6. Is the relationship between the individual and the person he performs services for a continuing relationship?
7. Who sets the hours of work?
8. Is the worker required to devote his full time to the person he performs services for?
9. Is the work performed at the place of business of the potential employer?
10. Who directs the order or sequence in which the work must be done?
11. Are regular oral or written reports required?
12. What is the method of payment—hourly, weekly, commission, or by the job?
13. Are business and/or traveling expenses reimbursed?
14. Who furnishes tools and materials used in providing services?
15. Does the person providing services have a significant investment in facilities used to perform services?
16. Can the person providing services realize both a profit or a loss?
17. Can the person providing service work for a number of firms at the same time?
18. Does the person make his services available to the general public?
19. Is the person providing services subject to dismissal for reasons other than nonperformance of contract specifications?
20. Can the person providing services terminate his relationship without incurring a liability for failure to complete a job?

This is not a test that requires a score of 100%. These factors are examined and weighed to form a picture of what is being done in the particular situation.

The key factor is the common law principle that a worker is an employee if the person for whom he works has the right to direct and control the way he works, both as to the final result and as to the details of when, where, and how the work is to be done. The employer need not actually exercise control. It is sufficient that he has the right to do so.

Thus, if someone truly is or wants to be considered a consultant, they should consider doing the following:

1. Incorporate or use a fictitious name (file a Certificate of Doing Business Under An Assumed Name).
2. Secure business cards and stationery.
3. Set up an office, even if it is in a home.
4. Advertise and market services.
5. Join professional organizations for the type of consulting work done.
6. Secure appropriate insurance (general liability for office and projects, disability, health and automobile).
7. Negotiate and sign contracts with clients.

HIRING AN ATTORNEY AND LEGAL FEES

When you are starting a business, working with an attorney knowledgeable in the design industry is essential. It is easier to find such specialists in major cities than it is in small towns. Some of the ways to locate an attorney specializing in interior design include:

- A local Bar Association
- ASID, IBD, or another industry organization
- Industry publications
- Colleagues who have worked with attorneys

Most attorneys charge for their time on an hourly basis. Generally speaking, this is how the designer will be charged for consultations, general advice, and drafting of agreements. Certain attorneys will work on a contingent fee for collection matters only. This means that they are paid a percentage of what they recover by way of settlement or a judgment, but are not paid at all if nothing is collected. This type of arrangement does not usually work well with a design case, since there are often complicated counterclaims and the typical collection attorney will not have the expertise or financial incentive to prosecute such a case as vigorously as may be required.

It is perfectly acceptable to ask an attorney to give you some idea of how much the work will cost before you hire him or her. An attorney may ask for a retainer before he or she begins working with you.

A retainer has a couple of different meanings. One meaning is that a sum of money is paid in advance for services and it is billed against as work is done. The other meaning is that a sum of money is paid every month whether or not you require any services in order to retain the firm as your legal counsel so that they are not hired by an adversary. The first meaning is what is typically encountered with design attorneys. A retainer agreement is used to confirm the terms of payment.

HIRING OTHER PROFESSIONALS

An accountant is also essential for any business. There are any number of issues for which both an attorney's opinion and an accountant's are essential. For example, when a designer is weighing the pros and cons of incorporation, there are legal and tax considerations. The accountant can help you to review the tax implications as they pertain to you. Colleagues are probably the best source for locating accountants who have experience working with designers.

An insurance broker is also very important. There are some that specialize in the needs of the design industry. Colleagues and your professional organizations are the best sources for finding them.

INSURANCE

Having appropriate amounts and types of insurance is important for any business. There should be general liability insurance for your office to cover any damages should someone be injured on the premises or should there be water damage or a similar disaster.

You must have a thorough understanding of what is covered and not covered. For example, if there is water damage and desks are soaked, the desks themselves may be insured, but not the contents. Also, will you be insured for the amount you paid to purchase them several years ago or for the current replacement value? Often people do not find out the answers to these questions until they have occasion to use the policy and then it is too late to improve the coverage.

When a disaster occurs you may find that you are underinsured. You also may not assume that you will be covered by your landlord's insurance policy, especially if the damage is caused by another tenant.

There are various kinds of insurance that you may be required by law to maintain, such as workers compensation. Health insurance is generally optional.

Then there is insurance related to your projects. Clients may require that you provide professional liability insurance to cover any errors and omissions in your work. They may also require general liability insurance naming them as an additional insured. Sometimes the contractor will provide general liability insurance and name both the client and the design professional as an additional insured.

Thus it is recommended that you meet periodically with an insurance broker to review your insurance needs, since they may change.

LEASING AN OFFICE

Many new design firms begin in people's homes. If you work out of an apartment, you should inquire as to whether this is allowable by law. As the firm expands, eventually it may become necessary to rent an office. Depending upon which city and part of the country your office is in, this may be very complex.

In New York City, for example, the base rent is the smallest part of the total rent. Additional sums may be due periodically for building operating expenses, porters' wages, and real estate tax escalations. The calculations for these sums can be complex and they can add a substantial amount to your rent.

There may be restrictions on when services are available, such as air conditioning after hours or on weekends and elevator service. You may want to renovate the premises. The landlord's approval may be required before any work is done and he may or may not contribute toward the expense of renovation.

These and many other issues must be discussed and drafted into the final lease. It should always be reviewed by an attorney before it is signed. Business people are expected by the courts to understand the ramifications of signing agreements which are not reviewed by an attorney. Naivete is not an excuse. In other words, if you sign a lease and later find out that you did not understand the ramifications of a particular term, you will still be bound, unless the term is against the law.

CONTRACTS FOR PROJECTS

When you are starting your business some time should be spent examining the contract you intend to use for your projects. It is best to do this when you have no projects so that you have plenty of time to really think about how you want it to be organized. Unfortunately this is the time when many designers feel least inclined to do this, because they are unsure about future revenue. However, the designer should have funds put aside for various start-up costs and this is one. The terms of such contracts are discussed in detail in Chapter 7.

When a client calls you will then be able to hand him a well-drafted, carefully thought out, professional contract. Even if some terms are negotiated, you will be able to use this agreement for future contracts with changes as necessary.

2

The Business of Interior Design

Neville Lewis

The process of starting and running a business has all the elements of an army "obstacle course" or the perils and adventures of seeking the Holy Grail, with success and riches (hopefully) at the end of the quest.

Most startup enterprises fail after the first year of operation. The odds for success increase with each year of operation. Generally the rule of thumb says that if you can survive at least three years, you're going to make it. In other words, these are the foundation years. The better you plan and build, the more likely your company will be to survive. Of course, you should factor in the local and national business climates, political effects, recessions, and depressions that are hard to predict.

The above-mentioned "obstacles" are all in the future. First you will have to decide whether or not you should go into business.

What are your motivations for starting a business? Are they practical? Emotional? Born out of necessity? Impulsive? Or carefully planned? The rationale for beginning a business is generally the first element in your success or failure and should be carefully considered.

There are people who seem destined to be leaders; others are not. Many of us have no idea what our capabilities are and many others overstate their capabilities. They're going to be in for a surprise when things don't work out as planned. The safest approach is not to have any illusions, although I think that if we knew all the problems that we may encounter, there would be far fewer new business startups. So maybe a little naivete is a help.

Neville Lewis is an interior designer with over 40 years experience in design, planning, and management. He now divides his time between teaching, consulting, and gardening.

The complexities of starting a new business are not for everyone. If you're looking *only* for security, it's not for you. To begin, look to yourself and decide if this is really what you want to be doing for possibly the rest of your career, for you're going to be making a commitment that will affect you, your family, and your friends. Starting your own business will enhance your capabilities and your talents will be stretched. You'll see things in yourself that you didn't know existed and regardless of what happens, it's an experience you'll never forget. Most important is that at the very least you tried.

In this chapter I will discuss some of my personal reflections and experiences on starting a new business.

WHAT ARE THE RISKS AND REWARDS?

Starting a business is full of risks, rewards, infinite details, and hard work. Unfortunately most of the rewards don't show up until your business is established, and even then, the prudent owner puts everything back into the business until there is a solid financial base to build upon. These are material rewards—the abstract rewards can be there the day you "open up for business." You're your own boss; the problems and decisions are yours alone, so there's no one to blame or look to but yourself. You should be aware of all the risks involved, discuss them with your spouse, companion, lawyer, accountant, or someone whose experience and advice you trust. Will you be able to deal with the strain of the financial and logistical pressures that will be there on the first day, such as finances, rent, payroll, clients, and all the people who will be relying on you? It's a great responsibility which does not let up. In fact, it increases exponentially. Some people thrive on it! Do you? Do you have enough capital to last for six months? Assuming that you have no income, do you have enough personal savings and insurance (medical, etc.)? Can you take care of the general obligations, such as rent? Can you support a staff and how far will your resources go?

My decision to start my own company in 1976 was a combination of all the factors discussed above. I was 48 years old (certainly over the normal age to start). We had three children in college, a house, the usual expenses that all families have, and not much of a cushion financially. We only had a dream and the realization that if I didn't do it *now* I never would. After all, we were in the middle of the recession of the mid-1970s. I figured that it couldn't get worse than it was, so my prognosis was that the only way to go was up. Furthermore, the timing was right: I had a potential client.

All of these items were discussed with my wife and sons. The positive outcomes were enumerated as well as the potential risks: possible failure, loss of savings, and how long we could exist without totally jeopardizing our capital. These were short- and long-term concerns. Over the years I had worked for and studied other firms, their operations, problems, and successes. I realized that the best chance I had for success would be to try not to make the same mistakes, while emulating their successes.

Generally the past mistakes were basic, such as lack of attention to details, being too extravagant with too little capital, having egos that were out of line with reality, over- and underdesigning projects, and running out of fees. But the most telling error was the lack of ability to face issues, postponing distasteful decisions and then making them too late. Many companies did not treat their staffs well and, as a result, these employers engendered no staff loyalty. Many principals I had seen over the years never realized that their success was because of unrecognized staff members.

I was at a point in my career that I no longer wanted to take orders from people whose business and design concepts I did not agree with. There had to be a way that I could more effectively control the direction of my life and put into practice some of the ideas I had regarding business and the business of design.

Luck and timing have to play a part in anyone's future. At that point in my life I was determined to leave my job and possibly change careers—get into education or work independently doing design and interior illustrations/renderings. There was an opening for a Department Head at an upstate college and several other design firm offers, so fortunately I had job potential. I wasn't doing what I felt was my best work and over the years I had learned every facet of the interior design profession. What better time for a change? Changing careers or resigning from a job doesn't happen on the spur of the moment—it usually has been a seed growing for some time. At the time of my resignation, one of my old clients was merging with another large firm, thus creating a large investment banking complex with all the resultant facilities management problems. As a result, there was a need for a consultant and this was my chance. I had a potential client and my teaching plans were forgotten.

Once I realized the scope of work involved for this merged client, it was apparent that consulting was not the answer, but rather it was the development of a *facilities group* for my client and a major project for a new design firm. In reality our first project was to help set up and establish an "in-house" facility staff for our client.

Having a client reduced the initial investment for me as I could count on some initial income; however, there was a need for cash to start up, money for phones (deposits), petty cash, supplies, services, and so on. I had a start; the rest was up to me. My preliminary plans had been made so nearly everything was ready for the startup.

If you're thinking of going in this direction, study how to make a smooth transition before you leave your present job. Remember it's possible that your employer may not be happy about your plans, so if you can, try to exit in a clean and friendly manner without burning your bridges. Some considerations are:

1. Never discuss your plans with any of your clients while you are still employed, especially with the idea of soliciting their future business. If you do, you may be sued.

2. Make your plans—but privately.

3. Retain an attorney and accountant, and discuss everything with them. They will guide you through all the steps required such as budgets, corporate structure, legal and financial obligations, and tax requirements.

4. Stay on good terms with your clients, employers, and suppliers. It's conceivable that even your past employer could be your client.

5. Have a detailed plan and schedule of all the things you're going to do the day you leave your present job. Here is a list of just some of the items:

   a. Send out announcements (*after you leave your job*)
   b. Call important contacts
   c. Retain a lawyer or accountant
      (1) Incorporate
   d. Bank
      (1) Checking
      (2) Credit if possible
      (3) Bookkeeping procedures
   e. Supplies
   f. Office space
      (1) Furniture and equipment
      (2) Phones
      (3) Lease
   g. Staff (if any)
      (1) List of possible employees
   h. Budgets
   i. Client list
   j. Insurance

When I left my job and started Neville Lewis Associates (N.L.A.), my previous employer's company was part of a large conglomerate and their lawyers wrote to me that I was not to approach their clients. I discussed this in detail with my attorneys. Since I had not solicited any clients while still employed and made no overt moves, such as announcements, until I had resigned, my counsel told me I was free to solicit any clients I wanted. I had never signed a noncompete or contractual agreement, therefore, there was nothing to bind me to them. My attorneys wrote back to the company stating the case and telling them not to harass us. That was the last we ever heard from them.

When N.L.A. was opened, we had a client with an enormous potential for work. Here we were with three people, including my wife, answering the phone and managing everything else while trying to sell, draft, design, and convince a client that we could handle their business. We then grew to four people (my secretary came with us and was later to become my associate in charge of purchasing, expediting, furniture, and furnishings). Over the next 10 years we grew to 160 professionals with offices in New York, Denver, Dallas, and Los Angeles and satellite offices in Pittsburgh and Seattle.

In the beginning no one knew what type of firm we wanted to be. We knew that N.L.A. would produce "corporate interiors" and that we would do the best possible planning and design for our clients. Doing large corporate interiors does give you a direction and specialty and does have the potential for large staffs due to the project size.

There are smaller firms of between 1 and 20, mid-sized, and large companies who are all successful and profitable. Size does not necessarily mean large or small profits. Knowing what you want to be, whether small and specialized or larger and more general, is important because it affects the types of clients you go after and the personnel you hire. It also affects your financial needs and the business approach and concentration.

The same planning should go into the product you are selling, be it furniture design, specialized facility consulting, residential interiors, institutional or corporate interiors, or as with us, all of them. Ideally you should have a professional staff that knows the business before selling it to a client. Clients today are far more sophisticated in the selection of design firms; they want to know who is going to work on their job and what their qualifications are and they want them securely tied to their project. Trying to cover all the market areas is a mistake. The best bet is to focus on what you want to do and what you do best.

Now you have a client, you know the direction you're going in, and the type of work that your company will produce. You're now ready to put all those plans into action. The following is a partial list of the basic items you will need to set up shop. These are probably repeats of items you considered before you made your move, but without them you don't have the necessary tools.

1. Budgets
2. Office space

3. Staff/salaries
4. Clients—potential and actual; cash flow
5. Accountants, lawyers
6. Insurance: health, accident, medical and general
7. Office supplies
8. Stationery and business cards
9. Photos and slides of past work
10. Staff resumes
11. Bank
12. Marketing contacts; public relations
13. Phones, fax

BUDGETS

Budgets should list all the items you can think of that will have a financial impact on your business. These budgets will give you an idea of projected overhead costs; in other words, how much it will cost to keep running weekly, monthly, and yearly. These are items you should develop from your own experience and knowledge of the field and with the help of an experienced bookkeeper and your accountant. Don't be too conservative—it's easier to cut back than to add on.

Once you have a budget, relate it to the amount of money you can afford or the limit of a bank loan that you can support. It will let you know how much you must bill to break even and to make a profit. Your budget will have to factor in estimated taxes, startup costs, and consultant fees. All of these items should be discussed with your accountant. Your budget can be adjusted up or down depending on the funds available. Try to be realistic financially. Most of your clients will respect your prudence and enjoy helping you grow.

OFFICE SPACE

You'll need a place to work and it should reflect your present needs with some growth built in. Choosing the right office is extremely important and can cause the downfall of a new company. Don't get saddled with a huge rent. Keep in mind that you see most clients at their offices in the beginning. What you need is a clean, comfortable space that is good for your staff to work in. You're a designer so you'll make it look good and if you're smart, you'll be innovative. Remember rents do not go away until your lease is up and if you are paying too much, it can be a millstone around your neck. Don't rent space just for show.

We rented our first office from our first major client. It worked well for us and them. We were doing all their work and were always on call. We also were able to piggy-back many services, thus reducing our respective overheads. As this client represented at that time the bulk of our work, it was an ideal relationship. This arrangement lasted for almost three years until we finally outgrew the space, but by then we had established ourselves, had banking relationships, were a known quantity, and had clients.

We were fortunate to have a client who not only had work for us, but delighted in the fact that we were growing and becoming a strong independent business. This is a very fortunate situation for any startup firm and is very rare.

You may not have the option we did, but the principle is still the same. Try to keep expenses as low as possible. Put your money into salaries and get the best people available. Staff who are well paid and well treated don't care about fancy uptown spaces. They want to be productive and creative in a nice working atmosphere and to make a decent living.

Your accountant, attorney and real estate broker will determine your needs and what you can afford. A sublet or shared space to start is not a bad idea as you don't know what's going to develop over the next 6 months to a year and this will give you a chance to plan in more detail. Rent and salaries are the largest expenses and can be the ruination of any company. So select the space that you can *afford* and see that it is flexible enough to expand or contract.

STAFF

Think very carefully about who you want for your staff and/or partners.

Generally, whoever goes with you is probably someone that you've known and worked with over the years. Select people who have the talents that are needed to run a business and don't be emotional. Try to be objective. Select people who can do it as well or better than you can. Your staff will be your eyes, ears, and talent. You can't be everywhere at once.

Selecting a good staff is the most important aspect of any new business. They can assure your success or failure. Treat them well—like family. Pay them well—at least at a rate comparable to your competition and, if possible, more. It will benefit you in the future.

Try to create an atmosphere that is pleasant for people to work in, one where your staff feels secure and is confident that they can be creative. I'd rather have a smaller group of experienced professionals who can handle all the jobs and keep busy. A smaller core group reduces the need to constantly hire and fire, which seems so endemic to our industry. This formula goes for large as well as small firms.

If you have a partner or are contemplating having one, remember that it's like a marriage and the best partnerships are the ones where there are specific areas of responsibility. Trust is an important component and flexibility in dealing with each other is essential. Make sure that you have legal agreements so that all contingencies are covered—such as partner insurance, buy/sell agreements, stock arrangements, and so on. It can be as complex to sever a partnership as it is to divorce a spouse.

If you can do it on your own, the easiest way is to be a sole proprietor. Hire people, pay well, and eventually sell or give stock to your key personnel. However, if you want control, then you have to retain at least 51% of the voting shares. The amount of stock you sell or give is based solely on you and your perception of what your new stockholder will contribute. It also depends on your age and ability to be productive—or when you want to get your money out of the company. It is one of the most difficult decisions for an owner to make.*

There are so many different ways to give someone equity in a company and it's based on people being able to pay for the stock in one way or another and your judgments as to whether they will help your company grow. It's also a way to keep the very best people around when you want to slow down, then your proportionate share of the business can change, thus, allowing younger and more energetic people to keep the company going. This is sometimes easier said than done. There are other options such as direct sale and outside investor partners. Each option is different with separate sets of problems and rewards.

GENERAL HOUSEKEEPING ITEMS

Every business, large or small, must consider cash flow, insurance, accounting procedures, and contracts. All the mechanics of running a business are in addition to the job at hand. The better the systems you put in place, the better you will know how you're doing both in production and financially.

IN BUSINESS

Your business has now started, you're incorporated, and you have cards and stationery, an office, phones, office equipment, a staff, and, we hope, a client and project to work on in order to pay for all of the above. Now is the time to

---

*Be aware that when you grant stock or ownership, you have partners (even at 1%) who have opinions, so make sure that you select well.

start your marketing program and sell your services in order to build a backlog of work. I was always selling and worrying when I had plenty of work. That's the time to worry—when there's no work it's too late and then you're not selling from strength. A good sales manager should constantly monitor the work in house, backlog, and bring in new prospects. The larger your company becomes the more you must concentrate on sales and have someone who will be responsible for marketing.

Another area that helped me was public relations. I hired a PR consultant on the advice of a colleague, and I asked him "Why do I need a PR consultant? I've just started and have hardly any staff and one project." His reply to me was "That's just when you need one!" It was the best advice I've ever had. My relationship with my PR consultant, E. Siroto, over the years was so productive that it put us on the map, introduced us to editors and the public, and gave us a direction and a personality. Our PR person helped to get our work published, got us involved in seminars and industry panels, put us in places where we could be visible, and teamed with me and my staff to show us off at our best advantage. She arranged openings, presentations, and parties for our clients and the press, but most important, it was always done with taste and never cost more than our budget would allow.

I thought carefully about the staff that we would require and how to fill the gaps with professionals who would be multitalented, thus giving us the potential for covering each other. These people would be the core of the business in the areas of Design, Production, Marketing, and General Management. These managers would be the nucleus and would hire and organize the staff according to the work in house. This core staff became the heart of my company. They did the respective hiring for their specialties, always communicating with each other so there were no redundancies. A general rule was don't hire and fire—keep the staff lean and multitalented and grow when there are the projects to support additional staff.

The following section outlines topics that are crucial to the success of your business.

EXPANDING YOUR BUSINESS

Businesses expand when there are capital and projects to support expansion or the potential for new clients or additional work for existing clients. A manager should always look to the future and plan expansion based on *real potentials*. My expansions were generally client driven. If we opened an office in another city, it was generally based upon a real project in that area or the potential for other client work. In times of slow business, it is best to be conservative and not risk diluting your existing staff. Studied growth is always safest and growth should respond to need. Ideally funds should be put aside to support key staff during lean times.

ATTRACTING NEW CLIENTS

Every firm that wants to expand and grow has to attract new clients. This is achieved by doing excellent work and having the best references and the public relations activity to advertise your firm's accomplishments. Having all your staff assist in marketing also helps.

Study your competition. See how they do it and then do it better. Send out brochures. Speak on panels. Be visible. We attracted business by showing potential clients our finished work and using our existing clients as examples of what we could do for them. Aggressive marketing and careful study of how to approach new clients and package our presentations also helped. We worked hard on our reputation and always stressed excellence in design, planning, and creating appropriate spaces for our clients. The most important selling tool was that the majority of our clients kept coming back to us. That is the best recommendation of all.

PRESENTATIONS TO PROSPECTIVE CLIENTS

Good presentations don't just happen; they're well planned, organized, and concise. At all of our presentations the first item of business was to figure out what our competition was doing and then plan accordingly. The prospective clients needs were always considered so the presentation was geared to them. We would do as much research on the client as possible and interweave this with our presentation. It was also important to show off our staff and have them present their own areas of expertise. Show relevant work that the client can relate to and talk about how you do your work, budgets, schedules, and so on. Remember that all the competition is *supposedly* as competent as you—your job is to convince them that you're much better. Assuming that the competition is equal, you will be selected because the client likes your group and wants to work with them—that's chemistry!

MANAGING A STAFF

Always try to understand that everyone is an individual who has cares and aspirations and wants to succeed. Motivating people to get the best out of them requires time and effort.

Delegate responsibility and take chances on your staff. If anything goes wrong, you can usually fix it and move on, but this helps you to see who you can rely on and who you can promote. If your staff knows that a firm offers advancement and a career path, responsibility, and independence, you'll be amazed at how the word will spread and the right people will want to work for your firm. Walk through your office. Speak with the staff. It takes time and effort, but it pays off. Have a sense of humor, be accessible, and try to listen.

MANAGING TIME

If you're the boss, get a good secretary/assistant, an excellent bookkeeper, and plan out your days, always leaving enough time to think and plan. Managers are supposed to use their brains and delegate responsibility. Most of my time away from the office, at home, and in planes was spent thinking and planning for the present and future, so much of a manager's time should be spent in dreaming and then making these dreams a reality.

SETTING UP PROJECT TEAMS

Teams for projects should be set up so as to utilize the best talents for the project, even though many times you won't have the available staff to assign. However, this should be the responsibility of a staff member. You have other things to worry about. Even though you have your management groups assign the teams for projects, be very sure that you know their decisions and approve of them. Don't change things *after the fact* (this goes for all decisions, whether in business, design, or production). Changing things after the fact is costly both in personnel confidence and in fee time, so always try to be aware of what is going on.

SHOULD YOU GET INVESTORS OR A PARTNER?

There are many reasons for finding a partner or investor. Generally it's financial, but it could be that you need someone to share the work load—physically, emotionally, and financially. Partners and investors cost you control, which you give up in proportion to the investment. Partnerships are like a marriage—easy to establish and hard to break up. Like a good marriage, they are built on trust, communication, and love. It also helps if you have separate areas of expertise and do not get in each other's way—ideally, one inside and one outside.

Outside investors, depending on their financial input, also want a say in the running of your firm and I can guarantee that regardless of their experience, they know (or think they do) how to run your business better than you.

My experience with a partner was difficult and did not work as I had expected—my extrication was expensive, but I had good legal counsel and was therefore well protected. I personally do not recommend partnerships. Good ones are hard to find and generally work better if you start out that way. Successful partnerships require lots of work on both sides.

My decision to sell my business was born out of the need for greater capital, a chance to really grow and meet new challenges and to get out and try other endeavors. Also, I received an offer I couldn't refuse! My advice is, "If the offer is too good to refuse—get out, don't look back, and don't have any regrets."

No one can tell you when to sell. You must weigh both the costs and benefits and hope that there is someone who wants to buy your business. If that's what you want, then position your business for a sale, that is, make it desirable to a prospective buyer. But selling may not be for you. You have to factor in many items—your age, the money, the prospect of losing control, and so on.

FINANCING EXPANSION AND GROWTH

Financing expansion and growth must be done very carefully. You need to have a good relationship with your bank and have a well-prepared business plan and projection of business. It helps to have some capital and a record of repayment to your creditors and bankers and it should be backed up with work in hand. Unfortunately, when banks are less than eager to lend money, firms look for partners or investors, and the price they pay is diminished control.

Most design firms are cash poor and generally don't have much work backlog—as a result most banks are wary of your prospects because you deal in services, not product. Your inventory is your professional staff.

I'm not against investors or partners, as long as they are carefully considered and working relationships are carefully delineated in a written agreement. Sometimes it is the only way you can fund your exit or retirement from the company. It is then that you should consider your key personnel. Unfortunately, in our business they usually can't afford the price; however, there are ways to do make some financial arrangements these should be discussed with your accountant and lawyer.

SUMMARY

No one can tell you how to run your business. The assumption is that you know your profession and the decisions that made you start a new business were valid. The mechanical aspects of business, legal, accounting, and production, we can get from books and experience; however, there is an abstract part of any successful business that one can't quantify. This may be more important than all the textbook items and it's called "mystique." All the successful companies have it, especially the ones people want to work for. There are some simple rules for success and I list them in no specific order, but they helped me and I found that most of the companies that I respected, and that were successful, had these qualities:

1. Use common sense.
2. Treat people with dignity.
3. Share your successes with the staff.
4. Give clients value for their money.
5. Do appropriate work.
6. Establish a profit sharing plan.
7. Have a good medical plan.
8. Give people a chance to grow.
9. Don't be afraid to give people responsibility.
10. Always do the best designs.
11. Do not compromise your ethics.
12. Keep your sense of humor.
13. Have fun.

3

Running the Business

Learning to be a good business person and to run a business takes time, but it is certainly something to strive for from day one. Being good at business means knowing what is going on in all aspects of your business, including when to take a firm stand and when to yield if a dispute arises. It means making informed decisions on such issues as: whether to sign a contract with a new client or let them pass; whether to admit to a client that you have made a mistake and offer to fix it; and whether to sue a client or settle.

One of the most fundamental things lacking in business today is good business skills. Something as simple as returning telephone calls can make a tremendous difference in your relationships with your clients and vendors. It shows clients that you care about their project and that you are well organized. It shows vendors that you are not avoiding paying them. If for some reason you cannot return a call as quickly as you may like, you should have a staff member return the call to see how they may be of assistance. The client then knows that you are on top of things.

Designers often come to me for advice and they tell me that they feel taken advantage of by their clients. They feel that they have provided services above and beyond what is called for in the contract and they are not being paid enough. It does no good to feel this way if you do not share your feelings and communicate them to the client. It also does not help if your contract does not allow you to charge for these services. The only person you should be angry at is yourself. The next thing you should do is meet with an attorney who knows this area of the law to discuss revising your contracts.

COMMUNICATION

Communicating effectively with others is a skill one constantly has to work at improving. Most people aren't born being good at business. They become good business people over time. They learn from their mistakes and are constantly honing their skills.

When people are shy or afraid to confront difficult subjects, they tend to avoid them. This may mean anything from postponing meetings to not returning telephone calls promptly and not answering critical letters. This *always* leads to misunderstandings and problems.

For example, if a client gives a designer large deposits for ordering furniture and the designer does not return calls and is unavailable, the client may start to fear that the designer will misuse those funds. This may not actually happen, but I have seen problems arise from such conduct over and over again.

My advice is to try to talk things out as much as possible. If you are unavailable, have someone from your office call the client and let them know when you will be available to talk. Set up a meeting with your client to address any concerns they are having.

The minute you avoid clients, or seem to, they will panic, assume the worst, and act accordingly. One couple called me because their designer was never in when they called and deliveries were late. They panicked and tried to call manufacturers to find out if orders had actually been placed. They had been placed, but later than the clients were led to believe. In this instance, it took getting both parties' attorneys involved to get firm delivery schedules and to reassure the clients. Once the schedule was agreed on, the designer adhered to it. The client, however, was quite upset, the relationship was ruined as far as future projects, and the client had to incur legal fees.

I have also encountered similar situations in which the client's fears turned out to be justified. The designer had serious financial problems and simply kept the money. So communication and reassurance is extremely important.

INTRAOFFICE COMMUNICATIONS

The owners of a business must know what is going on in all aspects of their business, even though certain responsibilities are delegated to others. If employees are signing contracts because the owners are busy and they are in total control of the project, problems will occur.

Owners must have systems in place for maintaining control over their offices. In small offices this may mean having coffee together a few mornings a week to discuss and review the status of projects. In larger firms it may mean formal meetings with many individuals present.

Staff may also be required to prepare written status reports of varying length.

RECORDKEEPING AND TIMEKEEPING

Since design work primarily involves creativity, not all designers tend to think as much about office matters as perhaps they should. Yet these matters can be equally as important as designs. A designer should always be thinking, "If anything went wrong on this project, would I have adequate documentation to show my side of the story?"

It is quite common during installation and construction of a project for a client to feel that the designer has not visited often enough. Thus it is essential that the designer have some systematic routine method of keeping track of when the project was visited, how much time was spent, and what was done on the visit. In a small firm, this might mean something as simple as keeping a daily pocket diary. In a larger firm, it might mean that each employee prepares and submits daily timesheets.

This can be extremely useful if there is ever litigation. But it is useful for other purposes as well. If you find that you and your staff are working overtime and not making a profit, you may want to examine how productive your office is. Maybe your staff is spending too much time drawing and redrawing. They may be using their time inefficiently. Maybe you are shopping a lot, but not being asked to buy anything for clients and thus not being paid.

Examining time slips may show you areas in which your staff can make more efficient use of time. It may cause you to call an attorney and revise your contract so that (1) you are compensated for unusually large amounts of time spent shopping for a client who doesn't purchase anything or (2) you can put limits on the amount of time spent shopping when no purchases are made.

Other types of records must be kept as well. You will want to keep a folder of photographs or catalogue cuts of items you have shown to the client for consideration. This shows how much work you did for the client. It can also be useful if you are terminated and another designer orders the same things for the client and you are not paid a fee. All purchase orders should be kept in a separate folder for each project. You must keep scrupulous records of how much money the client has given you for deposits and how it was spent so that you can always account for the funds.

If there is a particularly difficult episode on a project, you should write down your recollection of the details of what happened and just keep it in the file. This can be helpful to your attorney if there is ever a legal dispute.

CORRESPONDENCE

Keeping a correspondence folder is very important. Letters from the client and your responses thereto can help to win or lose litigation. Always keep copies of letters you send to clients. If you send things by certified or registered mail, keep the receipts attached to the file copy of the letter. If you deliver drawings to a client, have a confirming letter or a transmittal sheet which accompanies them to show when this occurred. It is better to be able to pull out a cover letter than to say to a client, "You remember I gave the sketches to you, don't you? It was the day you were in a hurry to leave."

This is a very underutilized form of communication and one which should be used more. Correspondence should be used to confirm delivery dates and the status of orders for furniture, to answer any questions the client may have, to confirm discussions, and to voice concerns. It creates a written record concerning the issue and helps to reconstruct events if there is ever a problem with the client down the road.

Of course, you do not want to flood your client with correspondence and you should balance written correspondence with verbal communication.

Needless to say, copies of all correspondence should be kept in a labeled folder in the office in chronological order.

DELEGATING AUTHORITY

One person cannot do everything. In those firms that have employees, the owner(s) must strike a balance between trying to continue to do everything himself and delegating too much authority.

It should always be made clear to clients who your employees are and what their role is. Clients should not be under the mistaken belief that an employee is an owner of the business. Clients may demand that the owner of the firm be primarily responsible for his project. If employees are assigned to a project, the designer should discuss this with the client. I have seen instances in which an unhappy client sues both the designer and his employee because the employee appeared to be a partner in the firm. You do not want such confusion to arise. This can also occur if employees sign contracts with clients on behalf of the firm.

It is also important to determine how much responsibility to delegate to an employee concerning money matters. If an employee makes bank deposits for the firm, it should be clear to the bank that the individual is only an employee and he only has authority to make deposits in the firm's business account. I have seen situations where employees were able to embezzle client funds because the bank employees believed the individual was an owner of the company and the records did not state otherwise. The employee deposited clients' checks into his own account. He later made restitution to avoid criminal prosecution.

EMPLOYMENT AGREEMENTS

Sometimes design firms hire key employees who are given special perks and bonuses. Often these employees have written employment contracts detailing the terms of their employment and scope of their responsibilities.

The agreement can discuss anything from bonuses to when the person will be eligible for partnership or to purchase shares.

Other topics may include having an expense account, a company car, vacation time, and insurance benefits. Such agreements can reassure employees of their long-term future with the firm.

CONSULTANTS

A written contract with a consultant is very important in order to distinguish him from an employee. It is a business relationship in which the consultant is retained to provide certain services, for a period of time, for an agreed upon fee.

Although a consultant may provide these services at your office, they must be able to show that they have an independent business. As will be discussed below, it is important to have a contract for tax and copyright purposes and to establish the terms of the relationship.

EMPLOYEES VERSUS CONSULTANTS

Design firms should have agreements with employees and consultants explaining their responsibilities and level of involvement with the work. This is particularly important when a designer or a design firm is working on developing ideas for furniture or products.

For example, I have had design clients who had an employee develop designs and then the employee came to believe that they would be partners in this venture. Often the employee may have done a lot of the design work and may rightly or wrongly come to believe that it was he who really did all the work and that he is more than an employee.

Ordinarily an employee is not entitled to copyright work he has done in the course of his employment since it is owned by the firm. But he may try to claim that there are some special circumstances entitling him to that right.

However, it can be very messy if a design firm is negotiating a licensing agreement with a company and the company gets a letter from a disgruntled employee claiming that the designs are really his.

Relationships with consultants should also be examined when they are working for you on copyrightable issues. They have independent businesses and they very definitely can claim coauthorship of work they do for a designer or a design firm, if not an exclusive copyright. Thus there should always be an agreement with any consultant stating, among other things, that any designs they work on for the company will be owned by the company and not by them.

MAKING EMPLOYEES SHAREHOLDERS OR PARTNERS

In certain design firms, especially some of the larger ones, long-term employees will be offered an opportunity to have an ownership interest in the firm. In corporations they may be offered some shares of stock which they can purchase over time. In partnerships they may be offered a percentage interest in the partnership. In smaller firms, an employee may even be groomed to take over the business when the owner retires.

Depending on how many principals there are and how old the business is, this offer will be more or less meaningful. In other words, in a well-established firm with many principals, being a shareholder may give the employee a sense of advancement in the firm, but not much say in how the firm is run. In a smaller firm with two founding partners who may want to retire, partnership may mean being groomed to take over the business eventually.

The employee is usually asked to make a financial contribution to the firm. This sum can be negotiated and in some cases eliminated. The terms of such agreements are generally confirmed in writing.

BANKRUPTCY AND MISUSE OF FUNDS

In troubled economic times it is not unusual for a manufacturer to go out of business or to file for bankruptcy during a project or for the designer to do this. A client may be left in limbo. If the client has paid a lot of money in deposits to the manufacturer, he may not be able to recover this money and place the order with another manufacturer. If the designer has filed for bankruptcy, the money may not have even reached the manufacturer.

Designers and clients in this situation should work with an attorney to endeavor to eliminate some of these situations, if possible and to learn what can be done so that the damages are minimal.

Occasionally a designer may divert project funds from their intended use and then not be able to do whatever work is necessary or replace the funds. This is a very serious situation which can result in civil as well as criminal litigation. Once again, legal counsel should be sought. Sometimes restitution can be made and criminal charges can be avoided.

DESIGNER REFERRAL SERVICES

Designer referral services provide another source from which design professionals obtain work. These services act as the middle men in introducing clients to designers who may be able to service their design needs. Generally the referral service's fee is paid by the designer from his project fees.

As with any business arrangements, there should be a written agreement between the referral service and the designer so that the arrangement for the payment of fees is clear.

Any designer referred by such services should be separately interviewed by the client to ensure that they are the right firm for the client and that their references check out.

4

Marketing Interior Design Services

Roslyn S. Brandt

Interior design and architectural firms must rely on a steady flow of new business, from existing as well as new clients, if they are to maintain a healthy practice and meet their goals for future growth. The most successful firms today are those that, in addition to producing good design and providing quality service, have the commitment of the partners to a strong marketing program to help them attract new clients and new projects. Without effective marketing, the most talented and capable designers will be unable to fulfill their potential.

Marketing is the umbrella that covers all the things that need to be done to obtain new work. The marketing process covers three areas which are explored in detail in this chapter: planning, supporting, and executing. Marketing is interactive. It is a series of individual processes which depend on each other to be effective.

PLANNING

This includes conceptualizing and developing strategies for attracting the types of clients and kinds of projects you want as well as setting your goals for future growth. It involves creating a marketing plan based on these

Roslyn Brandt is a founding principal of Barnes and Brandt Inc., a New York based marketing consulting and executive search firm to the design community that she formed with Diane Barnes in 1988. She works extensively with architecture and design firms and facilities managers to broaden their business opportunities. Ms. Brandt was formerly a Senior Vice Principal and Managing Director of the HOK Interiors Group.

strategies, as a part of the firm's overall business plan. Careful planning will help the firm's principals to be proactive—to initiate creative approaches to marketing their firm.

To begin with, each firm must have the commitment of at least one partner whose primary responsibility is the development of new business. In a sole proprietorship, it is very clear where that responsibility lies. In larger firms, the role should go to the individual with natural instincts for marketing and a clear vision for the future of the firm. This vision must be articulated to all members of the firm and everyone must support that focus. Marketing activities should occupy at least one third of this person's time, although this will increase for larger firms.

The planning phase is the time for the firm's partner(s) to be very intro-spective about strengths and weaknesses—of individuals and the firm at large. Coming to grips with management style, abilities of the staff, and goals for the future is not an easy process, but it is a very necessary and important one. In fact, the development of a meaningful marketing plan can only be undertaken once there is a general agreement amongst the partners about these issues as well as the unique features that set the firm apart from its competition.

The *marketing plan* will outline the financial resources, people activities, space growth, and project types to which the firm will commit. It creates the benchmark for daily marketing tasks and activities. The purpose of the plan should be clearly understood, frequently discussed, and often looked at. It is intended to stimulate thinking about the strategy for running a consistently stable and professional company, now and for the years to come. It should include the following components:

- Mission statement
- Image statement
- Analysis of existing conditions
- Analysis of current market trends
- Preferred target markets
- Strengths and weaknesses of the firm
- Goals and objectives
- Action plan
- Marketing budget

It should begin with a definitive *mission statement* which describes what business the organization is in, the purpose or function that the organization is attempting to fulfill in society or the economy, and for whom the firm is providing their services.

An *image statement* should be included to describe the creative focus of the firm. Define *what makes you different* from your competitors, both in terms of design philosophy and delivery of service, and find a way to articulate it to potential clients so they can understand it as a strong benefit to them. For example, one architectural firm describes themselves this way: *XYZ Architects provides creative solutions based on a strong belief in history and tradition, interpreted in a contemporary idiom. Our solutions relate directly to solving our clients' problems, but are always based on our bold interpretation of a strong concept unique to each specific project.*

Image is the credibility established by all the impressions that a firm conveys. In order to get an objective viewpoint, many firms find it valuable to commission an outside consultant to conduct an *image survey.* This can be done both internally and externally. An internal survey will determine your employees' perceptions of the firm, including their views of how the outside world sees them. An external survey, conducted amongst past, present, and potential clients, as well as suppliers and peers, will reveal how they perceive your firm. The goal is to find out if the firm's principals have the same view of the firm as do their clients and competitors, and if not, it will provide the incentive to make necessary changes.

The marketing plan should include a summary analysis of *existing conditions*—who are your clients, what disciplines are practiced, what is your firm's financial history, what are your company's strengths, what is the firm's current project experience by market sector and in what markets have you been successful and unsuccessful, what is the competition like, what are the economic conditions, how effective is your marketing effort, how is your marketing budget spent, what is the real quality of your company's services, and what is its reputation. It should also outline the status of your firm's marketing tools including brochures, reprints, prospective client mailing list, and a public relations program.

The next step involves analyzing *current market trends.* You must understand the state of the economy and which businesses and companies are growing the fastest in your market. Information is readily available by reading daily newspapers, business publications, trade publications, and value-line industry reports. Then, based on the acknowledged strengths of your firm and current market conditions, you need to determine the preferred market directions or *target markets* you will pursue. Companies frequently segment the market by geography, project type, client type, or project size, although other bases may be used. The selection of target markets is, together with establishing goals, the most powerful decision made in the marketing planning process. It determines where you will direct your marketing efforts and dollars. Many firms find it helpful to retain the services of an independent marketing consultant to assist them through this in-depth market analysis.

Based on all the information established to this point, the next step will be to *define the goals and objectives* for your firm, both short- and long-term, as well as an *action plan* to accomplish these goals. Goals are rather general statements of direction, such as: *To establish the perception of XYZ firm as a leading hospitality design firm in the industry.* Objectives are more specific, qualifiable statements, the attainment of which should lead to attainment of the goals. For example: *Develop and implement a publicity plan to create a visible image for the Principals and key staff of XYZ firm in the marketplace.*

A series of action steps should then be articulated for each objective, such as: *Retain the services of a PR consultant by January 15.* The overall action plan must clearly list all the tasks that must be accomplished to reach the objectives, including the name of the individual responsible for each and target dates for completion of each item. Exhibit 4.1 is an example of an action plan.

The final step in the planning process is the development of a *marketing budget.* A general rule of thumb is that marketing expenditures should range from 6 to 10% of gross revenues. (For example, the annual marketing budget might be $80,000 or 8% of an annual gross revenue of $1,000,000.) Personnel expenditures (time spent by all individuals involved in the marketing process) should range from 75 to 85% of the total marketing budget, and direct expenses (brochures, photography, public relations, etc.) should range from 15 to 25% of the total marketing budget. (In our example, therefore, personnel expenditures would be approximately $64,000 and direct expenses would be about $16,000.)

Task	Individual	Date
Create a firm database	Tom	June 1
Complete brochure	Bill	June 1
Organize a PR program	Alice	May 1
Submit five design awards	Mary	April 15
Contact associations	Ed	May 1
Representatives for:		
IFMA		
AIA		
ULI		
IBD		
Target market research	Mary	May 1
Presentation skills training	Ed	June 1
Slide library creation	Alice	July 1
Computer education	Tom	July 1
Warm and hot calls to potential clients	Everyone	50 by March 1

Exhibit 4.1   *An example of an action plan.*

SUPPORTING

This includes promoting the firm and its capabilities among prospective clients. It also involves developing an organized process to support the marketing efforts of the firm.

To manage an effective marketing program, professional design firms must have well-organized resources with which to work. Tools and processes must be in place, staff must be well-trained, and a system of ongoing market research must be maintained.

Marketing Resources

All firms should dedicate a specific area within the office for marketing-related activities. In large firms this may be an entire room, while in small firms it may be confined to a single file cabinet. In this area should be stored all *marketing tools*, including archive photography and slides, brochures, information organizers such as covers and dividers, pre-printed project case histories, and magazine reprints. Graphic and publication support via desktop publishing aids should also be available in this area. Physical equipment should include a binding machine, paper cutter, laser printer, and large table for collating. The area must be maintained on a daily basis and this is important no matter the size of the firm.

A *strong graphics program* which includes a firm logo and distinctive letterhead, consistently presented on all literature issued by the firm, is an important way to increase market awareness by potential clients. Even small firms should allocate a portion of their annual marketing budget to the firm's graphics program. Many firms will amortize the cost of a firm brochure or individual mailers over a two- or three-year period. Specialized services, announcements of staff promotions, celebrations of completed projects, and other significant occasions can be emphasized through the development of a specific mailing piece which is then distributed to a targeted mailing list.

It is equally important that completed projects are properly *photographed* and *project descriptions* are written. Selecting a good photographer is extremely important if you wish to get your projects placed in trade publications. Many designers have attempted to save money by taking their own photographs, only to be disappointed when rejected by magazine editors because the quality of the photography is substandard. Qualified photographers will charge a per diem fee ranging between $1500 and $2500 plus approximately 10% for expenses, including an assistant, film, processing, and travel. They can be expected to take four to six shots per day. Many designers seek to share these costs with suppliers of furnishings or materials who may wish to use the photographs for their own marketing purposes.

The best people to provide information for *project case histories* are the hands-on designers and project managers who can write the "story line" while it is fresh in their minds. This is important both for use in future marketing efforts as well as for submission to trade publications.

Other standard tools that should be well organized and updated on a regular basis include a comprehensive *mailing list* of existing and potential clients, *slides* of completed projects, *magazine reprints, brochures, market research studies,* and *marketing files.* One individual should be designated with the overall responsibility for organizing and updating these tools and for maintaining all data-base information.

The marketing efforts of the principals of the firm must be supported on a weekly basis by the development of a *weekly marketing status report.* It can be prepared by the marketing coordinator or by the Principal in charge of marketing. It includes a prioritized list of all prospects and potential leads, the individuals responsible for following the lead, the status of each, and any action to be taken. This becomes an effective communication tool and a reminder to all those involved about calls to be made, proposals to be sent or follow-up tasks to be accomplished. See Exhibit 4.2 for an example of a weekly marketing status report.

Date Prospect	Resp.	*	Status
ABC Company 212-543-2121 Carl Jenson, Sr. VP	Jane	1	Waiting for decision, expected June 1
XYZ Corp. 212-298-1313 John Eng, Facil. Mgr.	Bob	2	Needs a proposal by May 11 3 firms short-lived
Ballinger's 212-333-1221 Tom Anthony, Pres.	Al	3	Send qualification statement to Tom Anthony. Al will see him at lunch meeting Wednesday
Place Elegante Boutique 404-5500 Donna Smith, Manager	Mary	4	Call Joe at Turner to ask him to recommend us. Send qualification statement and letter of interest to Donna by Tuesday

*1 = high potential (80%)
 2 = medium potential (50%)
 3 = low potential (25%)
 4 = new lead (0%)

Exhibit 4.2   *An example of a weekly marketing status report.*

Boilerplate Information

Normally there is a very short turnaround time allotted for submission of proposals for new projects. It is very important that firms have well-written *boilerplate information* describing the firm, its services, and its staff. *Staff biographies* should be consistent and informative, pointing out unique capabilities and experience. *Outline proposals* should be on file for each project type practiced by the firm. Data for *U.S. Government standard forms 254 and 255* should also be kept in the files of firms wishing to pursue public projects. The 254 form contains an overview of the firm's project experience over a five-year period and is intended to be updated annually as a statement of the firm's qualifications. The 255 form is the actual application for a specific project listed in the Commerce Business Daily (CBD), the primary publication through which all federal agencies solicit design services. Having this information readily available will allow the marketing staff to spend the bulk of their time on *tailoring the proposal* response to the specific needs of the client.

Presentation Skills Training

Another key area of preparation is a training program to improve *presentation skills* of both principals and staff. Today, more than ever, with intense competition and high expectations on the part of clients, the quality of a presentation can make the difference between success and failure in winning a new commission. Once the basic techniques are learned, it is equally important that rehearsals occur prior to each client presentation. This helps each team member feel comfortable with their role in relation to others and allows a more spontaneous atmosphere in the actual presentation. Clients are very savvy today and react most favorably to teams that are well prepared.

Market Research

Market research is a critical activity in a comprehensive marketing program, both in terms of target markets as well as specific client companies. For instance, if a firm determines, through the planning process, to explore opportunities in a new market sector, research should be undertaken to provide important information about all aspects of that particular market. An understanding of social, economic, and political conditions affecting that particular market sector, names of specific companies, trade and professional associations, and so on can all be gained through careful market research. It is also critically important that marketing staff and principals keep up to date by voraciously reading daily newspapers and business and trade publications.

In the April 1991 issue of *Modern Office Technology* magazine, Roger Sullivan, Vice President of BIS Strategic Decisions, advises "If you don't understand my business, you won't get my business." All clients react most favorably to consultants who show a genuine interest and understanding of the client's business. There are many sources that professional services firms can use to gain important information about a specific client firm or business type, including the public library, published guides to businesses in specific cities, Chambers of Commerce, annual reports, trade and professional associations, real estate brokers, suppliers, and other professional associates.

Public Relations

There is one additional support resource that is most important to a successful marketing program, and that is *public relations.* All firms, no matter the size, must take advantage of all opportunities to raise the awareness of potential clients to the capabilities of the firm. There are many ways to do this, including the following:

1. Getting completed projects published and articles placed in both the trade and business press is an important step in the process. This effort can be initiated by someone within the firm or by a PR consultant acting on behalf of the firm. In either case, it is extremely important that an ongoing effort be made to produce newsworthy information.

2. The principals and key staff members should also participate in design juries, professional seminars, trade association activities, and community events. Each such event also provides opportunities for follow-up articles for the press.

3. Receiving design awards for completed projects will further reinforce the firm's image and reputation and provides another excellent public relations opportunity.

4. Staff promotions, company anniversaries, and special exhibitions held at the firm's offices can all be used to promote the firm's image and to keep clients aware of the firm.

EXECUTING

This includes all the efforts involved in identifying specific prospective clients and persuading them to retain your firm. It involves the action steps delineated in the marketing plan, and is often referred to as "selling."

Generating Leads

Once the overall marketing strategy has been established, it is time to identify specific clients and projects to pursue. Leads can be generated in a number of ways—through referrals from past clients, from networking with respected colleagues, consultants, and suppliers in the industry, or by initiating a cold calling campaign to a targeted list of potential clients.

Once any of these efforts yields information about a specific project, the first step is to determine if the project meets the firm's business and marketing goals.

- Is it in keeping with the firm's expertise?
- Who are the competitors and what are the firm's chances of success?
- What will be the cost of pursuing the project and does it fit within the firm's marketing budget?
- What will be the consequences of NOT pursuing the project?

This is the time to make the "go/no go" decision. If all the responses are positive, begin by submitting a letter of interest along with a qualifications statement and the firm's brochure to establish credibility.

Many clients will issue a *request for proposal* (RFP) when an actual project is identified. Generally, once a firm reaches a short list, any of the firms included are technically qualified to perform the services. The quality of the response and the ability of the firm to set itself apart from its competitors are usually the major criteria in determining which firm will be awarded the commission.

The Proposal

The *proposal* may include a cover letter, boilerplate information about the firm, a team organization chart with resumes, a description of similar project experience, client references, a well-defined scope of services, and, if requested, a specific fee. Your approach to the project presents your best opportunity for serious consideration. Always respond to questions exactly as they are stated in the RFP. Here's where the importance of client research will pay off. Be sure that all questions are answered in terms of value-added benefits to the client and are directed at resolving the client's specific concerns. Give examples of similar successful projects and your innovative solutions. Describe your approach in such a way that it recognizes an understanding of the client's business.

You may choose to separate basic services from additional services. In a competitive situation, your understanding of the basic services required and your ability to definitively describe those services so that the client has a complete understanding of the extent of your involvement, can be the creative difference between success and failure in being awarded the contract. Those services which you feel are desirable, but may be questionable in the mind of your client, should be listed as additional services, not included within the proposed fee. Leave the door open for incorporating such services if the client requires them. The actual proposal is a tremendously effective marketing tool. The client *must* feel it addresses his specific needs and that it is not just a standard form proposal.

Once the scope of services is well defined and once you have a general understanding of a schedule, you can determine what your fee should be (always include the schedule with the fee proposal so the client realizes there is a time limit involved). It is best to determine a fee by cross checking yourself in several ways:

- Project the man-hours per task to determine total manpower requirements. Then multiply by an average hourly billable rate to arrive at a total fee.
- Estimate a fee cost per rentable square foot based on your past experience on similar projects.
- Estimate the fee as a percentage of what you think the project will cost.

Each of these methods can be used as a guideline only to assist you in determining what range your fee will be in. Final determination of fee depends on many other factors:

- What do you think your chances are, weighed against those of the competition?
- What method of expressing your fee is most comfortable to your client? Hourly? Percentage? Fixed fee? Each of these methods requires variations in the way you propose your services. Be sure to carefully consider all aspects in order to protect yourself as the project progresses.
- How badly do you need the work? You may decide to lower your fee in order to get the job, just to keep your staff busy or to give the firm exposure to a new project type.

Do not discount your basic "gut feeling" about what should be the correct fee. Sometimes such feelings, which are based on past experience, can outweigh any logic.

Remember to note that all reimbursables will be billed separately. These include travel, reproduction, messenger, facsimile, and telephone costs which are usually billed on a monthly basis at actual cost.

The Presentation

As a professional, one of your major responsibilities is to communicate effectively. A thought or idea may never become reality unless it is brought to life and effectively shared with others so that they can respond and, hopefully, support it enthusiastically. This is equally important for both marketing and design presentations.

Short-listed firms whose proposal is favorable are usually invited to make a *formal presentation* to the client's selection committee. The interview is an important part of the selection process. It is important that confidence is established during the presentation, not only in the service and the approach, but also in the firm's representative and in the firm itself. You want to walk away from a presentation leaving the client feeling comfortable that "These people will be good to work with."

In preparing for a presentation there are three specific areas that must be addressed:

1. Understanding the client and his key project concerns
2. Preparing for the presentation
3. Delivering the message—effective techniques

Understanding the Client and His Key Project Concerns There are many sources you can investigate to help you understand the client's industry, organizational structure, and key decision makers. For corporate clients, you can read the company's annual report, which discusses the business of the firm, or the Prospectus (if the company is publicly held), which deals with personnel matters, rate of growth, and problems of the firm. Additional information about the client's industry can be found in SEC sector analyses, Moody's, or Standard and Poor's, value-line industry analyses, or the company's 10K form (if publicly held). Industry-specific reference guides are available at public libraries for health care, retail, hospitality, or other project types. In the case of a private residential client, your best reference may be the client.

For additional information, talk to other designers or suppliers who may have worked with the individual client representatives in the past. Determine the authority structure of the firm, both the financial authority (to understand the funding process for the project you're pursuing) and the facilities authority (to understand the structure regarding design issues).

Take a tour of the client's facilities and speak with people on the client's staff to gain valuable insights about the company. You can get important clues by observing how clients work, how they dress, their personality traits, and their existing environment.

To understand the requirements for the specific project you are pursuing, there are a number of key questions to be asked:

1. What does the client want to accomplish in the presentation and what is the actual problem they want to be solved? Master the ability to listen to what the client is telling you about his or the company's concerns so that you can effectively address these needs. Keep an open mind, don't jump to conclusions and concentrate on the information being delivered. By doing your research carefully, you will have a significant body of information with which to formulate a carefully tailored presentation.

2. What is the proposed schedule? You can use this information to describe how you would do the job within that predetermined schedule, if there is one.

3. Who will attend the interview? How many people? This information is useful so you can have the appropriate number of copies of any pertinent information and so that you can address any introductory letters to the appropriate people. A general rule of thumb is that your team should never exceed the number of people in the audience. If there are four of them, your team should include two or three, and all of your team members should be prepared to participate in the presentation.

4. Where are you in the sequence of the process? Remember that reviewers go through a learning curve. First presenters can be "educators." The first person to introduce a subject gets the credit for it even if subsequent presenters do the same thing. So you must have a very thorough presentation including presenting more alternatives. Last presenters can presume that their audience is already educated in the basics and can make the greatest impact by providing new information. So go over the "general" information quickly, then concentrate on details and uniqueness.

5. Who are your competitors? Ask your client who else is being considered and network with your industry resources and consultants to discover what they know about these competitive firms. See if anyone on your staff worked for these firms previously and can give you some valuable information about their philosophy, style, process, people, and so on. Assuming you know the strengths and weaknesses of your competitors, you can gear the presentation accordingly. You should never knock your competition, but knowing what they can't do that you can do may guide you in stressing these points. Effective research should also reveal if the job is "wired" to any given firm, how "hungry" is the competition, and who they will likely bring to their presentation.

6. Where will the presentation take place? If the interview could take place in your office instead of theirs, it will allow you to take them on a tour of your facilities and to have ready access to additional materials you may need during the presentation. It is also a great way to get your office cleaned up! If the meeting is at your client's office, be sure to survey the room in advance for size, availability of audio-visual aids, tack-up space, location of outlets, adaptability of lighting, and controls for air-conditioning and ventilation.

7. How will the interview panel rate you? This will help you direct your presentation toward those criteria.

8. When do they expect to award a contract? This is important to determine manpower assignments.

Don't be embarrassed to call up your client to ask these questions. This is a businesslike approach and the client expects you to come to a presentation prepared.

Preparing for the Presentation   Formal presentations are normally limited to a specific period of time, often one hour with a half hour for questions. In preparing for your presentation, it's important that you determine the message you want to deliver about your firm and your approach to the project. Focus on two or three main points that you want your audience to remember after your presentation is over since too many messages in a presentation weaken them all. Prepare a prioritized list of the client's goals and objectives, then gear your presentation to addressing the primary goals. Supportive or detailed information should be presented in written form, as a leave-behind for your client to review after the presentation.

Establish the team, internally as well as consultants. Team members should be selected on the basis of technical capability, prestige factor (reputation, image, rank), and presentation skills. Try to match the rank of your team members with those of the client team. Key members of your team should attend and participate in the interview. The client isn't interested at this point in meeting only the marketing professionals. He wants to see who he'll be working with on a day-to-day basis.

Prepare a team organization chart and a project work plan and schedule to describe exactly the scope of services you will provide, who will be responsible for what task, and what the overall schedule will be.

Plan on spending a brief amount of time introducing your firm, your design philosophy, and your special characteristics. The bulk of the time should be spent on addressing the client's specific concerns and your unique approach to solving his problems. Always structure your presentation toward *relevancy* to that client and be sure to constantly build impact, beginning with the least and ending with the most impressive information.

Be sure that every member of the presentation team is thoroughly familiar with the information to be presented, and be sure that they rehearse, both individually and as a team. Each team member should be prepared to introduce himself/herself, explain educational background, relevant experience, and project role. Be responsible for knowing your material so well that you can present in a natural manner, without nervous mannerisms, and without sounding as if you have memorized a script. If it will help, summarize the key points you wish to make and write down some key words on index cards to remind you of each point. Once each individual knows his/her "part," the team should rehearse so that the overall presentation will be smooth and effortless. In a successful presentation, the interaction between team members will be well-coordinated, information will be organized, and each subsequent presenter should be able to refer to what came before or what is yet to come.

The client must perceive that the team is comfortable working together and that they all have a complete grasp of the project. Your chances of success will be much greater if you are enthusiastic and if you have clearly articulated the unique characteristics that set you apart from your competitors.

Delivering the Message—Effective Techniques   The logistics of a presentation must be carefully dealt with. One team member should be charged with the responsibility for planning the presentation to fit the room. Be totally self-sufficient by having extra bulbs for slide projectors, extension cords, push pins, tape, and other necessary supplies. Close doors to shut out interruption. Always present at a right angle or better to the client (no acute-angle relationships). The thermostat should be set to cooler than normal (warm rooms tend to make people sleepy). You have the right to control seating arrangements. In large, formal presentations, hand out an agenda at the beginning.

Restrict the use of visual aids to those projects that directly relate to the client's needs. Always give the reason for showing each slide. If the lights are turned out for too long, you may put the interview panel to sleep. *Do not* completely darken the room to show slides. Never start the presentation with slides.

Plan for progressive disclosure of information. Never disclose information before you've verbalized it. Since clients can read faster than presenters can speak, firms that expose all their presentation boards at the start of the presentation risk "losing" their audience.

Remember to maintain eye contact with members of the audience. Pay attention to each person, pick up their eye contact and "close on them" if it appears that their attention is wandering. They cannot avoid acknowledged eye contact under that circumstance.

Vary the speaking voice to avoid monotony. Lower your voice for impact for very important information. Raise it to give impact to less important information. Pause after making an important point to emphasize the point. If you need to recapture wandering attention, pause before making the next point.

There should be a minimum of two "links" forward (references to information yet to come) and one "link" back (reference to information already delivered) in a presentation. The links are what keep you from having several mini-presentations that seem disconnected. For instance, a designer might say "In a few moments, John will explain to you how we propose to manage the various phases I've just discussed, so you'll be able to move in on schedule."

Be sure to stay within the allotted time schedule. Always leave enough time for questions and answers. If you have one hour for a presentation, it should last no more than 45 minutes with 15 minutes for questions.

Be enthusiastic and keep the client's attention focused. Don't use buzz words or jargon. Encourage interaction, particularly during the question and answer period since a healthy dialogue with the client produces the best results. Be sure to remain flexible and adapt where necessary to demonstrate your responsiveness to the client.

Distribute leave-behind materials only at the end of your verbal presentation so that you don't risk "losing" your audience. And remember to maintain a sense of humor. You may need it!

After the presentation is over, the first thing to do is DEBRIEF. Get out of the client's environment and recap/reassess the situation immediately. If someone on the team sensed a frown or disconnection on an important point, you can get back to the client suggesting that you may have inadequately communicated that point and asking for the opportunity to clarify it.

Set the strategy for the interim period until the selection is made. You should consider this period an important part of your overall presentation strategy and never let more than seven (7) days go by without sending some pertinent information or keeping in touch. "Thank you" should be a part of another communication, not a stand-alone communication suggesting closure or the end of the relationship.

SUMMARY

By executing a well-planned marketing program as outlined in this chapter, you will help to support and perpetuate the ongoing efforts of your firm to provide quality service and design for your clients.

5

Accounting for Interior Designers

Joseph P. Beck, CPA

INTRODUCTION

An interior designer about to start a new firm should possess a foundation of good business knowledge. Some knowledge of accounting and tax matters is an essential component of good business acumen.

   The information that follows is not intended to replace the services of an accountant. It is intended to provide the interior design firm owner with basic knowledge of some of the important accounting and tax issues that relate to the interior design industry.

BUSINESS PLAN

Every interior designer should have a business purpose and a company philosophy. A purpose will enable the business owner to focus on the goals of the company and to communicate the goals of the organization to the employees. Employees that are given clear direction as to the designer's goals will work harder in trying to achieve those goals. Adoption of a business plan will enable management to monitor results of the company's efforts to achieve its goals.

Joseph P. Beck is a licensed CPA in New York City, specializing in accounting for design firms.

In uncertain economic times, most businesses are either slow to react to a changing marketplace or they overreact. This can cause new problems rather than provide a solution to an existing problem. For example, assume an interior design firm has just completed a large project. The firm has several proposals with prospective clients but no contracts have been signed. In an effort to cut expenses, the owner lays off one or two of his assistant designers. Two weeks later the owner has two signed contracts and not enough personnel to assist him in completing the projects. He attempts to rehire the assistants only to discover that they found new employers and they are unwilling to take a chance of being laid off again. The owner of the interior design firm must now hire two new assistants within a short period of time.

Key employees should occasionally be retained through slow periods if there is a reasonable likelihood that these employees will be needed for an expected increase in business. However, this policy, if taken to an extreme could result in financial suicide. Sound business judgment is necessary to make the correct decision on this important issue.

An analysis must be made of the environment in which the design firm operates and of the strengths and weaknesses of the firm itself. The firm will want to build on certain strengths and try to reduce or eliminate disadvantages. Does the firm want to concentrate on commercial or residential work or does it want to do both? What is the strength of the owner(s) with regard to design? Do the location of the firm and the local economic conditions dictate that there will be more of a demand for one type of work than the other? These factors should be taken into account in a business plan.

ORGANIZATIONAL MATTERS

No matter which type of organization one selects for his or her business, the owner should apply for a Federal Identification Number. A Federal ID Number, also called an Employer Identification Number (EIN) can be obtained by filing Form SS-4, Application for Employer Identification Number, with the Internal Revenue Service (IRS). In the past, it usually took about six weeks after mailing Form SS-4 to receive the EIN. However, about two years ago the IRS set up a special telephone number through which EINs are issued immediately. After completing Form SS-4, the designer calls the IRS and is asked to provide some of the information from the completed Form SS-4. The IRS will then issue the EIN to the designer. Form SS-4 is then sent to the IRS by facsimile. This facilitates the opening of a business bank account since most banks require a design business to have its own federal ID number before allowing it to open a bank account.

CAPITALIZATION

A business must be adequately capitalized to compete in the marketplace. Capitalization is the investment of money into the business by its owners. A shortage of capital will prevent the business from making the proper investment in inventory and fixed assets such as leasehold improvements, furniture and fixtures, and office equipment. Capital will also be required for an organization's start-up costs and expenses. Organization costs are the expenses of organizing the business, such as professional fees and printing expenses. Start-up costs are expenses incurred by a business prior to the start of the business and may include items such as advertising and promotion.

The capitalization of a sole proprietorship or partnership is known as the "owner's equity" or "partners' capital," respectively. Corporate shareholders must assign a value to their initial investment in capital stock. They may also assign an additional amount to paid-in capital.

In addition to the capital requirements previously discussed, the interior design firm usually will need some financing to start the business. Some overhead expenses, such as rent and insurance, must be paid in advance. Salaries must be paid regularly. Office furniture and equipment, such as computers and printers, may be necessary. Once the firm begins to earn profits from its design work it should not require regular financing if it plans its expansion wisely.

Many design firms require a client to advance a "retainer" which may be either nonrefundable or applicable to open items at the end of the job. This common industry practice provides the design firm with a good "cash flow" at the onset of a new project. Although the traditional industry practice of "COD" at the end of a project seems to be an exception these days, if the firm closely monitors its accounts receivable it should not have regular cash flow problems. Even so, additional financing may be periodically required to meet the cash needs of the business.

Many small business owners and designers have had to make personal loans to the business or borrow from a bank to meet cashflow needs. A bank loan to a small corporation will almost always require the personal guarantee of the stockholder(s). This is because small corporations present a much higher risk to a banker than do large corporations owing to the high rate of small business failures. The business environment in which the small corporation operates can be extremely volatile. Many small businesses have a few "key" clients. A loss of one or more of these clients can cause the small business to have operating problems from which recovery may not be possible.

CONTRIBUTION OF PROPERTY

The most common investment that a business owner makes to his business is cash. However, property may also be invested or contributed to the business. Contributions of property to a sole proprietorship are relatively simple. The value of the property on the books of the business is the cost of the property to the individual less any depreciation previously deducted. Contributions of property to a partnership are treated similarly. No gain or loss is recognized either by the partnership or any of its partners upon a contribution of property to the partnership in exchange for a partnership interest.

For example, two partners make initial contributions to a partnership. One partner contributes $5000 in cash. The other partner contributes a computer with a fair market value of $5000. Each partner would have an equal capital account of $5000. Upon dissolution of the partnership, any distribution to a partner in excess of the partner's basis would be treated as income to the partner.

The general rules for a contribution of property to a corporation from a shareholder call for any gain to be recognized by the shareholder. However, this does not apply where the property is contributed to a "controlled" corporation. A "controlled" corporation as it applies to property transfers is one in which a shareholder owns 80% or more of the stock of the corporation. No gain or loss is recognized when a person transfers property to a controlled corporation solely in exchange for its stock. The term "controlled" corporation that is used here should not be confused with a "closely held" corporation where more than 50% of the corporation's stock is owned by one individual.

If a shareholder owning less than 80% of the stock of the corporation makes a transfer of property to the corporation in exchange for its stock, the basis of the property to the corporation is the fair market value of the stock. Since the stock of most closely held corporations has no established market value, the value of the stock will be considered to be equal to the fair market value of the property contributed to the corporation.

Assume two individuals form a corporation and intend to own 50% each. If one shareholder makes a contribution of property with a fair market value of $5000, the other shareholder must contribute any combination of cash and property valued at $5000 in order for the shares to be distributed equally.

If a shareholder owning all the shares of a corporation were to sell 50% of those shares to another designer who would become an equal owner, the original shareholder would most likely realize a profit on the sale. A capital gain would result along with a tax liability on the gain. This can be avoided if there are unissued shares of stock of the corporation. Any excess paid over par value to the corporation would be known as "paid-in capital" and would be treated as an investment into the corporation. Accordingly, if the 100% shareholder of a newly formed corporation might someday consider selling some shares to another individual, it would be wise to issue less than all the authorized shares of stock to the founding shareholder upon the initial capitalization of the corporation. These shares would remain unissued until a potential investor comes along.

STAFFING

The large interior design firm will have one or more owners who also manage and design, one or more assistant designers or project managers, possibly an office manager, a full-time/full-charge bookkeeper, and possibly an assistant bookkeeper. The smallest of interior design firms will consist of the owner and a part-time bookkeeper. A small interior designer may utilize a part-time bookkeeper anywhere from one or two days per week to one or two days per month as required. Whether a design firm is large or small, at some point in time it will require the services of a part-time employee. The small interior design firm will make greater use of part-time employees, especially in the area of bookkeeping.

PERSONNEL FILES

An employee or personnel file should be maintained for each employee of the firm. The file should include such information as the employee's name, address, telephone number, social security number, and the date that the employee started working for the design firm. Personnel files should also contain Form W-4, which indicates the withholding allowances claimed by each employee for payroll withholdings. It can also contain information such as beneficiaries of insurance policies. Personnel files may also contain any review summaries, the salary history of each employee, and attendance records, including vacation and sick days for each employee. If there are employee contracts or noncompete agreements with employees, a copy should be kept in the employee's personnel file.

COMPENSATION/BENEFITS PLANNING

As with any industry, compensation should be commensurate with experience and the current market conditions. The old rule of thumb that employee benefits approximate 15–20% of annual compensation is no longer utilized. Because of the tremendous increase in recent years of hospitalization and major medical insurance costs, the percentage of annual compensation used to estimate the cost of employee benefits is closer to 20–23%. In addition to hospitalization and major medical, employers are also required to pay federal and state unemployment insurance and the FICA expense (which is social security and Medicare) at the current rate of 7.65% of gross salaries, subject to limitations. There is also disability insurance required by state laws as well as workman's compensation insurance. The existence of a retirement plan can increase the cost of employee benefits by as much as 15% of annual compensation.

RETIREMENT PLANS

Retirement plans are not required by law to be offered to employees as a benefit. However, many large firms currently provide some type of retirement benefits to their employees in order to compete with other interior design firms in attracting the best personnel. Another reason to institute a pension plan in any company is to save or defer taxes for the owner or owners of the business. However, a retirement plan which covers the owner(s) must also cover the employees. Most plans require that the employee have one year of service and be 21 years of age to be eligible to participate in the plan.

Pensions are administered by a bank, a brokerage firm, a pension plan/ benefits company, or a life insurance company. The administration will depend on the type of pension plan. Several different types of pension plans are currently used by interior design firms today. To determine the correct plan for your particular firm requires some investigation and some discussion, usually with your accountant. Your accountant or attorney may be able to recommend a plan or a pension consultant.

ACCOUNTING SYSTEM

An accounting system required by interior designers, similar to any other business, is a chart of accounts and the standard set of five books or journals as they are known in the bookkeeping and accounting world. The standard bookkeeping system uses double-entry bookkeeping. A chart of accounts is a listing of all titles of each account and a numerical code assigned to each account. Exhibit 5.1 shows a typical interior designer's chart of accounts. These five journals are the cash receipts, cash disbursements, payroll, sales, and the purchases journals.

These five books of original entry are posted on a monthly basis to a general ledger. The general ledger is the focal point, to which all the information is posted. The general ledger is then used to prepare a "trial balance." The trial balance is a debit and credit listing of the amounts in each of the accounts of the business and is adjusted by the accountant to come up with an adjusted balance sheet and income statement.

Let us take a look at the five books of original entries. The first is the cash receipts journal. The cash receipts journal used by an interior designer is the standard cash receipts journal used by almost any other business. There is nothing particular to interior design firms in regard to the cash receipts journal. As you can see in Exhibit 5.2, there is a column for the date, the source of the funds received, the amount, and then several other categories for which to spread the amount. These may be accounts receivable, client deposits, or any one of several other categories, and a "general" category in the last column which has room for the item and the amount.

The second book of original entry is the cash disbursements journal. As with the cash receipts journal, the cash disbursements journal is a standard journal that is not customized when used by an interior design firm. As you can see in Exhibit 5.3, the cash disbursements journal shows the date, the payee of the check that is being written, the amount of the check, and several columns in which to spread the category for which the check is being paid. These may include accounts payable, petty cash, sales tax, and any number of other items. As with the cash receipts journal, a general column is provided at the end to indicate the item and the amount of miscellaneous cash disbursements.

Exhibit 5.4 shows an example of a sales journal. The sales journal of an interior design firm must show a little bit more information than the standard sales journal used by general industry. The additional information is largely due to the requirements of tax authorities for sales tax to show taxable sales, other taxable items, and the amount of sales tax on each of those items. A sales journal also requires standard information such as the date, name of the client, invoice number, amount that is due as an account receivable, and the total. Other columns include sales, sales tax, freight, fees and/or commissions, and always a "general" column which shows the item and the amount of miscellaneous items.

The sales columns should be divided between Taxable and Nontaxable to facilitate the preparation of the sales tax returns. In some localities, fees and commissions are also taxable. In these cases it may be wise to create taxable

CHART OF ACCOUNTS

SPEC ACCT	ACCT NO.	ACCOUNT TITLE	ACCT TYPE	D/C BAL	PCT	SUM YTD	PR CD
	102.00	Petty Cash	AA	D		N	
	104.00	Cash—Chase Checking	AA	D		N	
	105.00	Cash—Chase MM	AC	D		Y	
	111.00	Bank Transfers	AA	D		Y	
	113.00	Payroll Exchange	AA	D		Y	
	115.00	Certificates of Deposit	AA	D		N	
	121.00	Accounts Receivable	AA	D		N	
	153.00	Inventory	AA	D		N	
	160.00	Prepaid Expenses	AA	D		N	
	163.02	Other	AA	D		Y	
	163.00	Loans and Exchanges	AA	D		Y	
	165.00	Loan Receivable—Officer	AA	D		Y	
	167.00	Prepaid Taxes	AA	D		N	
	168.00	Vendor Deposits	AA	D		Y	
	207.00	Office Equipment	AF	D		N	
	208.00	Accum Deprec—Office Equip	AD	C		N	
	209.00	Furniture and Fixtures	AF	D		N	
	210.00	Accum Deprec—F & F	AD	C		N	
	211.00	Automobiles	AF	D		N	
	212.00	Accum Deprec—Auto	AD	C		N	
	271.00	Leasehold Improvements	AF	D		N	
	272.00	Accum Amort—LHI	AD	C		N	
	283.00	Refundable Deposits	AA	D		N	
	302.00	Notes Payable	LL	C		N	

Account	Description			
313.00	Accounts Payable—Trade	LL	C	N
325.00	Accrued Expenses Payable	LL	C	N
327.00	Accrued Profit-Sharing	LL	C	Y
331.00	Client Deposits	LL	C	Y
333.01	SS	LL	C	N
333.02	FWT	LL	C	N
333.03	SWT	LL	C	N
333.04	CWT	LL	C	N
333.05	Medicare	LL	C	Y
333.00	Payroll Taxes Payable	LL	C	N
350.00	Sales Tax Payable	LL	C	N
354.00	Income Taxes Payable	LL	C	N
367.00	Loan Payable—Stockholder	LL	C	Y
411.00	Preferred Stock	R1	C	N
413.00	Common Stock	R1	C	N
416.00	Other Paid-in Capital	R1	C	N
426.00	Retained Earnings	R1	C	N
501.00	Sales—Taxable	I1	C	Y
503.01	NJ	I1	C	Y
503.02	CT	I1	C	Y
503.03	FL	I1	C	Y
503.04	MS	I1	C	Y
503.05	MA	I1	C	Y
503.00	Sales—Nontaxable	I1	C	Y
517.00	Less Sales Returns and Allowances	I1	D	N
651.00	Inventory Change	E1	D	N
653.01	Stock	E1	D	Y
653.00	Purchases	E1	D	N

Exhibit 5.1 Typical interior designer's chart of accounts.

CHART OF ACCOUNTS

SPEC ACCT	ACCT NO.	ACCOUNT TITLE	ACCT TYPE	D/C BAL	PCT	SUM YTD	PR CD
	654.00	Purchase Discounts	E1	D		Y	
	655.00	Drafting	E1	D		Y	
	751.00	Advertising	E1	D		N	
	755.00	Automobile	E1	D		N	
	759.00	Commissions	E1	D		N	
	761.00	Customs and Duty	E1	D		Y	
	763.01	Taxable	E1	D		Y	
	763.02	Nontaxable	E1	D		Y	
	763.00	Delivery	E1	D		N	
	771.00	Entertainment & Business Meals	E1	D		N	
	775.00	Gifts	E1	D		Y	
	779.00	Promotion	E1	D		N	
	785.00	Storage—Clients	E1	D		Y	
	787.00	Travel	E1	D		N	
	803.00	Amortization Leasehold Improvements	E1	D		N	
	809.00	Bad Debts	E1	D		N	
	811.00	Bank Charges	E1	D		N	
	812.00	Bookkeeping	E1	D		Y	
	813.00	Books	E1	D		Y	
	815.00	Computer Service Charges	E1	D		Y	
	817.00	Contributions	E1	D		N	
	823.00	Depreciation	E1	D		N	
	825.00	Dues and Subscriptions	E1	D		N	
	826.00	Employee Benefits	E1	D		Y	
	829.00	Equipment Rental	E1	D		N	

830.00	Film and Developing	E1	D	Y
831.00	Interest	E1	D	N
833.00	Insurance	E1	D	N
839.00	Legal and Accounting	E1	D	N
841.00	Licenses	E1	D	N
843.00	Maintenance and Repairs	E1	D	Y
844.00	Messengers	E1	D	N
845.00	Miscellaneous	E1	D	N
847.00	Office Expense	E1	D	N
849.00	Office Salaries	E1	D	N
851.00	Officer Salaries	E1	D	N
852.00	Outside Labor	E1	D	Y
853.00	Postage	E1	D	N
854.00	Penalties	E1	D	Y
855.00	Officer Life Insurance	E1	D	N
856.00	Profit-Sharing Plan	E1	D	Y
857.00	Professional Fees	E1	D	N
859.00	Rent	E1	D	Y
861.00	Storage	E1	D	Y
865.00	Taxes and Licenses	E1	D	N
867.00	NYS Corp. Tax	E1	D	Y
868.00	Taxes—NYC Corp.	E1	D	N
869.01	FICA	E1	D	N
869.02	NYSUI	E1	D	N
869.03	FUI	E1	D	N
869.04	Disability	E1	D	N
869.00	Taxes—Payroll	E1	D	N
873.00	Taxes—NYC Comm. Rent	E1	D	N

Exhibit 5.1 *Continued*

CHART OF ACCOUNTS

SPEC ACCT	ACCT NO.	ACCOUNT TITLE	ACCT TYPE	D/C BAL	PCT	SUM YTD	PR CD
	875.00	Telephone	E1	D		N	
	877.00	Travel—Local	E1	D		N	
	879.00	Utilities	E1	D		N	
	901.00	Interest Earned	I1	C		N	
	903.01	Taxable	I1	C		Y	
	903.02	Nontaxable	I1	C		Y	
	903.00	Commissions	I1	C		Y	
	905.01	Taxable	I1	C		Y	
	905.02	Nontaxable	I1	C		Y	
	905.00	Design Fees	*R	C		N	
	980.00	Earnings Before Taxes					
	981.00	Less Federal Income Taxes	E1	D		N	

Number of Accounts: 118

Exhibit 5.1 *Continued*

66

JOHN DOE DESIGNS
CASH RECEIPTS JOURNAL
JANUARY, 1993

DATE	SOURCE	CASH	BANK DEPOSIT	ACCOUNTS RECEIVABLE	CLIENT DEPOSITS	LOAN PAY-OFFICER	GENERAL ITEM	GENERAL AMOUNT
Jan 11	George Smith	5000.00	5000.00		5000.00			
12	John Doe	10000.00	10000.00			10000.00		
25	Robert Johnson	300.00	450.00		300.00			
	Blue Cross Blue Shield	150.00					Refund of empl benefits	150.00
29	George Smith	5825.00	5825.00	5825.00				
	TOTALS	21275.00	21275.00	5825.00	5300.00	10000.00		150.00

Exhibit 5.2 Cash receipts journal.

JOHN DOE DESIGNS
CASH DISBURSEMENTS JOURNAL
JANUARY, 1993

DATE	PAYEE	CHECK NUMBER	CASH	ACCOUNTS PAYABLE	PETTY CASH	SALES TAX PAYABLE	GENERAL ITEM	AMOUNT
Jan 03	XYZ REALTY, INC.	101	1500.00				RENT	1500.00
08	JANET JONES	102	355.00				NET PAYROLL	355.00
12	SUSAN FURNITURE CORP.	103	3333.00				VENDOR DEPOSIT	3333.00
29	ABC TRUCKING CO.	104	200.00	200.00				
	SUSAN FURNITURE CORP.	105	3333.00	3333.00				
	TOTALS		8721.00	3533.00				5188.00

Exhibit 5.3 *Cash disbursements journal.*

JOHN DOE DESIGNS
SALES JOURNAL
JANUARY, 1993

DATE	CLIENT	INVOICE NUMBER	ACCOUNTS RECEIVABLE	CLIENT DEPOSITS	SALES TAXABLE	SALES NON-TAXABLE	FEES & COMMISSIONS TAXABLE	FEES & COMMISSIONS NON-TAXABL	SALES TAX PAYABLE	REIMBURSEMENTS FREIGHT	REIMBURSEMENTS TRAVEL
JAN 22	GEORGE SMITH	1001	5825.00	5000.00		10000.00			825.00		
	TOTALS		5825.00	5000.00		10000.00			825.00		

Exhibit 5.4   Sales journal.

fees and commissions and nontaxable fees and commissions columns, again in order to facilitate preparation of the firm's sales tax returns.

The sales journal of an interior design firm will normally have, as in the example above, an accounts receivable column which is the balance owed to the designer upon the invoice being sent to the client. It will also show a client deposit column representing the amount of the client's deposit that is being applied against the sale plus any other charges, including freight and sales tax, billed to the client on that particular invoice.

The payroll journal is used to record a breakdown from gross to net of the wages being paid to each employee on a weekly, biweekly, semimonthly, or monthly basis. Exhibit 5.5 shows an example of a standard payroll journal. The payroll journal will have columns for gross wages, wages taxable for social security purposes, wages taxable for medicare purposes, federal withholding tax, state withholding tax, local withholding tax (when applicable), state unemployment (when applicable), state disability withholding (when applicable), and the net payroll amount, which represents the amount of the check paid to the employee. The payroll journal is used to post the salary expense to the general ledger as well as the withholding of taxes for each

---

JOHN DOE DESIGNS
PAYROLL JOURNAL
1993

NAME: Janet Jones
ADDRESS: 123 Main Street
Anywhere, NY
PHONE: (123)456-7890
S.S. #: 123-22-4567

FIRST QUARTER

Payroll Period	Gross Wages	Social Security	Medicare	Federal Withholding	State Withholding	City Withholding	Disability	Total Deductions	Net Paid
1/8/93	500.00	31.00	7.25	71.15	25.00	10.00	0.60	145.00	355.00
TOTAL 1ST. QUAR	500.00	31.00	7.25	71.15	25.00	10.00	0.60	145.00	355.00

SECOND QUARTER

Payroll Period	Gross Wages	Social Security	Medicare	Federal Withholding	State Withholding	City Withholding	Disability	Total Deductions	Net Paid
TOTAL 2ND. QUAR	0.00	0.00	0.00	0.00	0.00	0.00	0.00	0.00	0.00

Exhibit 5.5 Payroll journal.

locality. It is also used to prepare quarterly payroll tax returns, as well as workmens' compensation and state disability premiums. Payments to outside consultants will be entered in the cash disbursements journal.

The fifth and final book of original entry is the purchase journal. The purchase journal in Exhibit 5.6 shows columns for the date of the purchase, the vendor, the account payable, which is the amount owed to the vendor, client purchases, and also a column for other purchases, leaving room for the item and the amount. Depending on the interior designer's business and requirements, the purchase journal may further break down client purchases between residential and nonresidential or contract purchases. The purchase journal may also show job costs by client. Exhibit 5.6 is a simple purchase journal using basic information which may be expanded as desired.

Each of these five original books of entry are summarized on a monthly basis and posted to the general ledger. The posting to the general ledger and the write-up of the journals are generally considered bookkeeping functions. Depending on the size of the design firm, the services of a bookkeeper may be required on a daily, weekly, monthly, and very rarely, an annual basis.

The smallest interior design firms will often not keep a purchase journal, due to lack of volume or in an effort to keep bookkeeping costs low. When a purchase journal is not utilized, entries in the cash disbursements journal will be classified to expenses rather than to an accounts payable column. An open "Payables" file will be used to prepare an "Accounts Payable Schedule" periodically. The disadvantage is that there is no control total to tie into. If a vendor's invoice is misfiled, the Accounts Payable Schedule will be understated, unbeknownst to management. Therefore, it makes good business sense to maintain a purchase journal whether your firm is large or small.

There are a few subledgers, or subsidiary ledgers that should be kept by the design firm to provide important information on an ongoing basis. These are the accounts receivable ledger, the accounts payable ledger, and the inventory ledger.

JOHN DOE DESIGNS
PURCHASE JOURNAL
JANUARY, 1993

DATE	VENDOR	ACCOUNTS PAYABLE	PURCHASES	FREIGHT	BLUEPRINTS	GENERAL: AMOUNT	ITEM
JAN 04	BLUE CROSS BLUE SHIELD	550.00				550.00	EMPLOYEE BENEFITS
19	SUSAN FURNITURE CORP.	3333.00	6666.00			-3333.00	VENDOR DEPOSIT
	ABC TRUCKING CO.	200.00		200.00			
	TOTALS	4083.00	6666.00	200.00		-2783.00	

Exhibit 5.6 Purchase journal.

The accounts receivable ledger shows all of the funds received from a client, as well as all of the invoices billed to a client. It shows a balance at any given time of what is owed to the designer or what is collected from the client in terms of client deposits. By matching payments received against invoices billed to clients, in the accounts receivable ledger, an accounts receivable schedule and an open client deposits schedule can be prepared.

The larger design firm will want these schedules prepared on a monthly basis. Not only are these schedules compared to the accounts receivable and the client deposits amounts in the general ledger, but they also provide the design firm with important information regarding the accounts receivable and client deposits at any given time. The design firm's accountant will request these schedules at least annually and perhaps on a quarterly or even monthly basis, depending on the agreement with management as to the accountant's frequency of reporting.

The accounts payable subsidiary ledger shows all amounts owed to a particular vendor, as well as all amounts paid to a particular vendor either for vendor deposits or for payments on vendors' invoices. As with the accounts receivable subsidiary ledger, the accounts payable subsidiary ledger is kept on an ongoing basis wherein items are keyed off in order to prepare monthly schedules of vendor deposits and accounts payable. These schedules are then compared to the general ledger for accuracy, as well as utilized by management in its decision-making processes. For example, prior to placing a new order with a particular vendor the accounts payable subledger may be examined for outstanding invoices from that vendor.

The inventory subsidiary ledger shows the date, the item purchased for stock, and the amount of the item. It should also show a detailed description of the item, perhaps even a purchase order number. This ledger keeps track of all purchases for stock inventory. A small design firm must be very careful not to overbuy inventory because of the possibility that the items may not be sold within a reasonable period of time. Many designers will want to purchase an item or several items with the idea that they will be sold to an existing or future client at a relatively large profit. While this may happen quite often, it is also possible that an item of inventory may not be sold for a long period, thereby tying up valuable cash which then cannot be used in the normal operations of the business. The balance in the inventory subsidiary ledger should be compared to the balance in the inventory account in the general ledger as often as on a monthly basis to insure accuracy in recording and posting items.

As stated previously, the monthly totals in each of the five journals will be posted to the general ledger. The general ledger is then used to prepare a trial balance. The accountant will make adjustments to the general ledger for items such as depreciation, income taxes and accrued expenses in order to prepare financial statements for the design firm. The financial statements consist of a balance sheet, an income statement, a statement of cash flows, and footnotes.

The balance sheet lists all of the assets, liabilities, and equity of the design firm. It groups assets such as cash, prepaid expenses, accounts receivable, and inventory as "current" assets because of their short-term realization into cash. These assets are the most liquid. It groups assets such as land, buildings, office equipment, leasehold improvements, and furniture and fixtures together owing to their long-term nature and nonliquidity.

On the liability side of the balance sheet, liabilities such as accounts payable, accrued expenses, accrued taxes, and payroll withholdings will be grouped together as "current" liabilities because of their maturity within one year. Liabilities having maturity of more than one year will be grouped together as long-term liabilities. Examples might include mortgages, security deposits, and possibly other bank loans. The equity section of the balance sheet will show the capitalization of the company as well as the retained earnings or owner's capital of the design firm. The retained earnings or owner's capital represents the amount of past and current earnings that remain in the business. The owners equity or capital represents the excess of total assets over total liabilities. When total liabilities exceed total assets, owners equity or capital will be a negative amount, representing a deficiency.

The realization of income increases the capital or retained earnings of the business. The advances or draws of a sole proprietor or partner, as well as the salary of an officer of a corporation, will decrease the owner's capital or retained earnings of the business.

SYSTEM FOR A SMALL ENTERPRISE

An accounting and bookkeeping system for a small or even a one-person design firm does not have to encompass every one of the journals and ledgers discussed above. It is important to maintain enough information to comply with the requirements of governmental authorities in terms of sales tax and corporate tax, and also to provide management of the firm with enough information to make intelligent decisions regarding the operation of the business.

Questions about which vendor to pay and at what time, the firm's sales tax liability that is due on the twentieth of the current month, and the amount and timing of payroll tax deposits are common and must be addressed regularly. For example, small design firms may decide not to keep a purchase journal, but rather to hold all unpaid invoices in a file and record them as accounts payable at the end of each month or quarter. While this requires some adjustments to be made in recording the cash disbursements journal, it facilitates the record-keeping requirements of the small or one-person firm. In the one-person firm, the payroll journal may consist of one employee's payroll card.

SEGREGATION OF DUTIES

The accounting industry strongly recommends the segregation of accounting duties among various employees in order to keep the record-keeping function separate from the personnel who are actually making the transactions. This is to hold employees responsible for particular job functions and also to help prevent misappropriation of assets of the firm. For example, the person opening the mail, preparing the bank deposits, and taking the deposits to the bank should not be the same person who prepares the bank reconciliation. Similarly, the function of sending out sales invoices (billing) should be separate from recording those invoices in the sales journal (accounting). However, most interior design firms will find this to be impractical and impossible because of small staff size.

SELECTING AN ACCOUNTANT

Selecting an accountant and an attorney to advise the interior designer are perhaps two of the most important decisions the designer will make at the onset of his or her new venture. Each of these professionals should have at least some experience working in the interior design industry.

In addition to preparing tax returns and generally advising the interior designer, one of the accountant's duties is to issue a financial statement at least annually to the designer. The financial statement, which will be discussed in detail later, consists of a balance sheet, an income statement, a statement of cash flows, and footnotes. The statement of cash flows presents detailed sources and uses of cash from operations, investments, and financing.

The financial statement may have three levels of reporting. The first and simplest level is a compilation. When preparing a compilation report the accountant gives no opinion as to the materiality or accuracy of the financial information.

The second level of financial reporting is the review report. The review consists of the same information as a compilation report, but also includes several analyses of financial information, including various ratios, to ascertain the accuracy of the financial information.

The third and most extensive level of reporting is the audit. The audit includes a test of the financial transactions of the business. It is the highest and most prestigious level of service provided by accountants. Only Certified Public Accountants may provide an audited financial statement.

In all three levels of reporting, the accountant's report will state that the financial information is that of management. In the audit report the accountant will attest to the accuracy and to the materiality of the financial information. All interior design firms should periodically consult with an accountant and an attorney.

ESCROW ACCOUNT FOR CLIENT DEPOSITS

When receiving client deposits and depositing those in the design firm's bank account along with other funds, it can be very easy to lose track of how much of the firm's total funds is attributed to client deposits versus profits which can be used to pay overhead expenses. Many design firms use a separate account, usually a savings account or money market account, to hold client deposits. This will help to prevent the designer from using current client deposits to pay past and present vendors for purchases or overhead expenses.

It is fairly easy for an interior designer to unintentionally miscalculate the projected profit on a client's deposit, withdraw the profit as a "bonus," and spend the funds on personal items. This can cause serious financial problems for the design firm. It can put the firm in a financial hole from which it can take months or years to recover. Separating the client deposits that are being held prior to paying vendors will help to prevent this from happening. However, this will not overcome a firm's lack of accurate accounting on a timely basis. The periodic preparation of accurate client deposit schedules is essential to making good management decisions.

SALES, COSTS OF GOODS SOLD, AND INVENTORY

The gross profit of an interior design business is its sales less its cost of those sales. The cost of sales represents the purchases of merchandise from trade vendors and the freight to get the purchases from the vendor to the designer. Fees and commissions should not be a part of the gross margin equation unless the fee or commission is actually a mark-up of an item or service on which the designer computes the fee or commission. Design fees computed on an hourly basis generally should not be entered into the gross margin equation.

The cost of the design fees is usually the salaries of the designers and/or owners. Unless the costs of these salaries is included in the cost of goods sold, the fee income should not be included in the computation of gross profit. When fees and/or commissions are not included in the gross profit, they can be shown "below the line" as other design income. This allows management to get a clear picture of what type of income contributes to the gross profit of the business. The design industry standard gross profit is 33%.

The example below shows how the 33% is calculated. Assume a designer sells merchandise to a client for $15,000, and the cost of the merchandise to the designer is $10,000. The designer uses a standard mark-up for that type of merchandise of 50%. Fifty percent of $10,000 is $5,000, added to the $10,000 gives us $15,000. Taking the sale of $15,000, less the cost of the sale of $10,000, gives us a gross profit of $5,000. The gross profit of $5,000 divided by the sale of $15,000 leaves us with a gross profit of 33%. However, the designer's overall profit will seldom be 33% on the cost of sales of merchandise. Other miscellaneous costs and accommodations by the designer for the client can reduce the gross profit percentage to as little as 15%. In difficult economic times clients will often expect the interior designer to accept less than the normal mark-up.

		%
Sales	$15,000	100.00
Cost of sales	10,000	66.67
Gross profit	$ 5,000	33.33

TAX ACCOUNTING BASIS

All businesses must choose an overall accounting method by which to report their income for tax purposes. The two most common methods are the cash basis and the accrual basis. The cash basis of accounting means reporting income when it is received and recording expenses when they are paid. Reporting income using the accrual basis of accounting means reporting income when earned rather than received and recording expenses when incurred, rather than when paid.

There are advantages to using the cash basis of accounting for income tax purposes. These include ease of use and the fact that it enables the taxpayer, in this case the interior design firm, to avoid paying income tax on income that has been earned but not received. Taxpayers using the accrual basis of accounting must pay income tax on their income when it is earned rather than when it is received. This could cause the interior designer to pay income tax on money that it has earned but may not collect from its clients until months later.

There are some limitations on the use of the cash basis method of accounting. An interior designer who has stock inventory at the end of the year may not use the cash basis of accounting to report income. Since most interior designers do have some stock inventory that is held for resale, most interior designers may not use the cash basis. Another restriction on the use of the cash basis method is the $5 million or less gross receipts test for all prior tax years beginning after 1985. A business meets the $5 million gross receipts test if its average annual gross receipts for the three tax years ending with the prior tax year do not exceed $5 million.

TAX YEAR

Taxable income is computed on the basis of a period called a "tax year." A tax year is the annual period which the designer uses to keep its books and records in order to compute taxable income. A fiscal year or calendar year must be selected by the designer. A calendar year is a period of 12 months ending on December 31. A fiscal year is a 12-month period ending on the last day of any month other than December.

A new taxpayer will most likely not have a 12-month period for its first tax year. For example, assume a design firm began doing business on April 20, 1992. The end of its first tax year cannot be later than March 31, 1993, because a tax year cannot be longer than 12 months and must end on the last day of a month. Virtually all sole proprietorships are required by the IRS to use a calendar year which coincides with the tax year of the owner. Income or loss of a sole proprietorship is reported on Schedule C of an individual's Form 1040. The calendar year filing requirement for individuals results in sole proprietorships also filing their tax returns on a calendar year basis.

Most partnerships have a calendar year as their fiscal year, again to coincide with the tax years of the partners. If the partners are all individuals, tax returns are filed on a calendar year basis. An individual's share of partnership income or loss is reported on Schedule E of Form 1040.

A corporation (except S corporations) may choose any month in which to end the business' taxable year, including a calendar year. If the business is seasonal, a good choice for a fiscal year end would be at the end of the business cycle. The end of the business cycle is the end of a month immediately after the peak of business volume. A corporation must file its annual tax return on Form 1120 or Form 1120S (for an S corporation).

Partnerships and S corporations may, however, elect to file on a fiscal rather than a calendar year basis by making an election on Form 8716 under Section 444 of the IRS tax code. Code Section 444 requires the partnership making the election to make an interest-free tax deposit with the IRS. This tax deposit is required to cancel the tax benefits resulting from the use of a fiscal tax year.

The electing partnership or S corporation must compute and remit the tax that would otherwise be due from partners or stockholders had these entities used the required calendar tax year. The tax payment is due by May 15th after the calendar year in which the election year begins. No payments are due from partners or shareholders individually. The intent of Section 444 is to prevent a business with a tax year ending January 31, for example, from reporting income to its owner(s) who would not have to pay tax on this income until April 15 of the following year. The rules are complicated and should be discussed with an accountant prior to making the election.

S CORPORATIONS

An S corporation is a small business corporation whose status is elected by the shareholders of a new corporation or by an existing C corporation under

IRS Code Section 1362. The significance of the S corporation is that an S corporation pays no taxes at the corporate level. Rather, the income or loss of the corporation "flows through" to the stockholder(s) of the corporation and is taxed at the individual level. Internal Revenue Service Form 2553 is used to elect S corporation status. Form 2553 is filed with the IRS Service Center where the corporation files its Form 1120S.

An S corporation can have no more than 35 shareholders. A husband and wife are considered to be a single shareholder for purposes of this limitation. All shareholders must be individuals, estates, or certain defined trusts. No shareholder may be a nonresident alien. Foreign corporations may not elect S corporation status. Generally speaking, the corporation must not be a member of an affiliated group.

The consent of all shareholders of the corporation is required for election of S corporation status. The S corporation status is automatically terminated if any event occurs that would prevent the corporation from electing S corporation status in the first place, such as having more than 35 shareholders. An S corporation election may be revoked with the consent of shareholders owning more than 50% of the outstanding shares of stock. If an election is terminated or revoked, the corporation may not reelect S corporation status without IRS consent for five years.

The taxation of S corporations is quite complex and management of the interior design firm should always consult with its accountant when dealing with S corporation issues. State and local laws vary as to the acceptance of S corporation status. Form 2553 can be prepared by either an attorney or an accountant. If the incorporating attorney does not prepare the form in conjunction with the corporation's bylaws and minutes, then the accountant will prepare the form after consulting with the designer. The S corporation election must be made by the fifteenth day of the third month of the fiscal year. The IRS is extremely unforgiving regarding the due date for this election.

PAYMENTS TO OWNERS

The character of payments to owners will depend on the type of organization of the business. Payments to owners of corporations differ greatly from payments to owners of partnerships and sole proprietorships.

"Salaries" is not a term used when discussing payments to owners of partnerships and sole proprietorships. As previously discussed, the term "draw" is used. Officer salaries are applicable to corporations only. Because the officer of a corporation is separate from the corporation itself, when an officer takes money out of a corporation, it must be declared as one of three things. Payments to stockholders must be either salaries, dividends, or loans. The significance in tax treatment of each of these is quite different. An officer's salary is similar to a draw of a sole proprietor or partner of funds from the business in that it is the normal compensation method used by the owner. The terms "officer" and "stockholder" are used interchangeably here.

The distinction must be made between the design firm earning income and the firm compensating its owner(s). The owner of a sole proprietorship using the cash basis will be considered as having received the income simultaneously with the earning of the income by the business. This is true even if separate bank accounts are maintained for business and personal reasons, which should be the case anyway. The "drawing" of a check from the business account to the personal account will have no effect on income. The same is true for partners in a partnership. The earning of income by the partnership is an event separate from the partners taking periodic draws of cash. Both sole proprietors and partners are required to make quarterly estimated tax payments to the IRS and to the taxpayer's home state when applicable.

The corporation and its stockholders are treated differently because a corporation is a separate entity. The corporation earning income and the stockholder/officer earning a salary are two separate and distinct events. The officer is given a periodic salary to pay for living expenses. An annual bonus can be declared depending on the projected income of the firm. This can be an effective strategy to minimize the combined income tax burden of the corporation and its stockholder by using the different tax rates that apply to each to the stockholder's advantage. Corporate tax rates for 1992 range from 15% on income up to $50,000 to 39% on income between $100,000 and $335,000. Individual tax rates for 1992, for example, range from 15 to 31%. Reducing corporate income via bonuses to stockholders will increase the income and income tax of the stockholder.

Even though this strategy loses much of its effectiveness on the federal level when the corporation is an S corporation, many states and localities do not accept the S corporation status. The S corporations doing business in areas that do not accept the S status can save thousands of dollars in annual income taxes by paying the officer an amount of salary that will minimize the overall tax burden. This important tax strategy should be implemented by the firm's accountant in those locales where it applies.

The salary paid to an officer will reduce the income of a corporation. Paying dividends to a stockholder of a corporation, who is also an officer, does not reduce income. Dividends are a distribution of profits to stockholders. Dividends are an example of double taxation under the United States tax code. This is because dividends are not deductible for income tax purposes by the corporation, but they are included in taxable income to the recipient of the dividends. Here is where the double taxation effect takes place. The corporation pays income tax on its income. Afterwards, dividends are distributed on the income.

For these reasons, any payment to a stockholder of a closely held corporation should be either a salary or a loan. As was discussed above, dividends are rarely a good strategy for compensating the owner(s) of a closely held corporation. Any loan paid from a corporation to its stockholders in excess of $10,000 should be evidenced in writing. A promissory note should be drawn up, and interest, at reasonable rates, should be paid periodically. The IRS can "impute" interest income and expense between parties to a loan if the loan itself does not call for interest.

In other words, the IRS can determine what the market rate of interest should be and add the calculated amount to the taxable income of the stockholder. In addition, because the corporation and the owner are "related taxpayers," the corporation is on the accrual method of accounting and the owner is on the cash method, a deduction will not be allowed for interest expense payable to the owner until the owner includes the interest in taxable income. This prevents an accrual basis corporation from deducting interest expense to reduce taxable income, but not actually paying the interest to the owner, who is on the cash basis. The interest expense must be paid to the stockholder in order for the corporation to deduct the interest.

The same holds true for *salaries* paid to stockholders of a corporation. Assume a stockholder owns more than 50% of the outstanding shares of a corporation. If the corporation is on the accrual basis of accounting and wants to pay its owner a salary, the salary must be paid within the year that it is received and recorded by the stockholder. This prevents the accrual basis corporation from taking a deduction for salaries paid to controlling stockholders where such salaries are not paid until sometime in the following year.

A sole stockholder of a corporation is entitled to deduct a reasonable allowance for salaries, other compensation, and other services. The IRS may declare extremely high salaries as unreasonable. The concept of "reasonable compensation" as determined by the IRS is an amount that would ordinarily be paid for like services, by like enterprises, in like circumstances. The relationship of salaries to gross income, personal ability, responsibility of the position, and the cost of living and living conditions in the locality are all factors that must be considered.

Once again, because of the complexity of IRS tax rules, it is advisable to consult with one's accountant prior to making payments from a corporation to an officer/stockholder. It is usually wise to set up a base salary for the officer, and upon planning for taxes prior to year end, a bonus may be declared.

Payments from a sole proprietorship to its owner and from a partnership to one of its partners are known as "draws." These payments reduce the amount in the partner's or sole proprietor's capital accounts, and do not in themselves affect income or loss of the business. However, these drawings should closely resemble the income earned by the business, or at the very least, not exceed it, otherwise a cash shortfall may occur.

TAX COMPLIANCE

Federal Income

As discussed briefly in the opening section, income or loss in the design firm is required to be recorded in accordance with the organizational nature of the firm. A corporation will report income or loss on IRS Form 1120, U.S. Corporation Income Tax Return. If a corporation has elected S corporation status, that corporation will report income or loss on IRS Form 1120S, U.S. Income Tax Return for an S Corporation. Both forms are required to be filed with the IRS by the fifteenth day of the third month following the corporation's year end. For most S corporations this will be March 15th. An extension of time to file Form 1120 of up to six months can be obtained from the IRS. A corporation requesting an extension can do so on IRS Form 7004.

A partnership's income or loss is reported on IRS Form 1065. Each of the partner's individual income or loss is reported on Schedule K-1 of Form 1065. The individual partner will report his share of the income or loss, as shown on Schedule K-1, on Schedule E on the individual's IRS Form 1040. Partnership law can also become complicated in some cases, and again, a design firm's accountant should prepare the partnership's tax return.

A sole proprietor will report his or her share of the firm's income or loss on Schedule C of Form 1040. The income or loss is reported on Form 1040 along with all other items of income or loss and deductions that apply to the individual taxpayer. A sole proprietorship is the simplest of the three basic organizational forms for doing business. However, knowing when to report certain items of income and expense can be tricky.

State Income

State and local income tax laws vary as to the treatment of corporate income taxes. Some states and localities recognize the S corporation, whereas others do not. For example, the State of New York accepts S corporation status, the City of New York does not. This can have an enormous impact on tax planning and on corporate tax liabilities. Remember that the major advantage of an S corporation is that it does not pay federal taxes on the corporate level. The taxability of the S corporation on the state or local level will lessen the advantages of doing business as an S corporation. The state and local income tax laws must be familiar to the design firm and its advisors so that they can minimize income tax and take advantage of any situations which may be available to the design firm.

Federal Payroll

Compliance with federal payroll tax laws is very important to any business owner. Failure to withhold and pay the government the proper withholding of payroll taxes can subject the business owner to personal liability for those taxes. Even paying the payroll taxes late can subject the firm to penalties and interest. When a business fails to pay its payroll withholdings and expenses to the government, the most common reason is that the funds are not available because of the weak financial condition of the firm.

Proper capitalization of the firm and current financial reporting will enable any firm to make sound decisions regarding such items as salaries and overhead. While it may be relatively easy to know when to add an additional employee to one's staff, knowing when to lay off an employee is not as simple. Although financial considerations are key, there are other considerations involved. Employees are sometimes kept through slow and unprofitable periods when the possibility is great that they will be required in the near future.

Federal payroll taxes are paid to the IRS via one's commercial bank. Payroll tax deposits are due as frequently as eight times per month or as infrequently as once per quarter, assuming that salaries are paid at least quarterly. The employer's payroll tax returns are filed by the end of the following month after each calendar quarter. Internal Revenue Service Form 941, Employer's Quarterly Federal Tax Return, is due to be filed with the IRS on April 30, July 31, October 31, and January 31. Form 941 pertains to federal withholding taxes and also social security and medicare withholdings which the employer must match.

Employers are also responsible for federal and state insurance contributions. Federal unemployment insurance contributions are payable as often as once per quarter or as little as once per year. Deposits are required when the total liability reaches $100 per quarter. Currently, the federal insurance tax rate is 6.2% with a maximum credit available of 5.2%. The credit is available to all employers who make timely state unemployment insurance contributions.

Federal unemployment insurance contributions are calculated on the first $7000 paid to each employee on a calendar year. Form FTD-8109 is used to make all federal tax deposits for corporation income tax Form 1120, for employer's report of withholding taxes Form 941, and for federal unemployment insurance contributions, IRS Form 940, Employer's Annual Federal Unemployment (FUTA) Tax Return. Annual unemployment insurance contributions must be reported and reconciled on Form 940. Form 940 is due on January 31 following the previous calendar year.

Internal Revenue Service Forms W-2 and W-3 are also due to employees by January 31 following the calendar year. Forms W-2 are wage and tax statements for each employee. Forms W-2 show gross wages subject to federal income tax, social security tax, medicare tax, as well as state and local wages. Each of the appropriate withholding taxes are also shown on Form W-2 for each employee. The employee's name, address, and social security number are also recorded on Form W-2.

The IRS is currently assessing penalties as part of a nationwide program to enforce the compliance with all employer's tax laws. Penalties are being levied for incorrect employee social security numbers. Penalties are also being assessed for the late filing of Forms W-2. The employee's copy of the W-2 is required to be mailed to the employee by January 31 for the previous calendar year. One copy of Form W-2 is required to be sent to the Social Security Administration by February 28 for the previous calendar year.

Internal Revenue Service Form W-3 is a transmittal of income and tax statements which is required to be attached to the front of all copies of Form W-2. Form W-3 shows the total federal, social security, and medicare tax withheld for the entire firm.

Forms 1099-MISC and 1096 must be filed with the Internal Revenue Service for all outside contractors of the design firm who are paid at least $600 for the previous calendar year. Form 1099-MISC is titled "Miscellaneous Income." An exception is made for payments to corporations. However, the IRS has considered extending the Form 1099 reporting requirements to include payments to corporations as well as noncorporations to insure maximum compliance with income tax laws.

The rules for whether an individual or entity should receive a 1099 as opposed to a W-2 are complex and should be fully understood prior to the undertaking of services from an individual to the design firm. After years of warning employers about auditing an employer's outside contractor payments to determine if any should be considered employees, the IRS has recently initiated an audit program to enforce these laws. Form 1096 is titled Annual Summary and Transmittal of U.S. Information Returns and shows the total payments to outside contractors.

Sales Tax

The authority to collect sales tax is given by state governments to vendors doing business in that state. An application must usually be signed by a principal of the vendor. The vendor becomes an agent for the state for the purpose of collecting the sales tax on all applicable sales and services. Failure of the vendor to pay collected sales tax to the vendor's state can result in the state forcing the individual responsible for paying the sales tax to be held personally liable. The client can also be held responsible if the sales tax was never paid to the designer. The fact that an interior design firm is incorporated does not prevent state governments from obtaining a judgment against a responsible officer of the corporation for failure to remit collected sales tax. Sales tax is one of the most complex tax issues that an interior designer will have to deal with. Each state is authorized to charge its own sales tax rate. Many states give individual counties and cities the authority to charge their own sales taxes in addition to the state sales tax.

The budget shortfalls that confront many state and local governments have caused many states and localities to increase their sales tax rates. As rates change, the vendors who are affected must keep abreast of the changes to ensure that they collect the correct amount of tax. And as more states are having budget deficit problems, more sales tax audits are being performed by state and local agents than ever before. Failure to comply with state and local sales tax laws can be very expensive if uncovered during an audit. Most sales tax audits result in an assessment against the vendor. The cost of compliance with sales tax laws has also increased. The typical large interior design firm spends between $2000 and $5000 per year in record keeping and forms preparation. A sales tax audit can easily double this cost.

The Sales Tax Rate Chart in Table 5.1 shows the average sales tax rates charged by each state as well as by counties and cities within each state. The table also shows the taxability of services provided by interior designers as well as the applicability of an exemption of sales tax on capital improvements. Note that New York is the only state which allows for this exemption.

Many states currently levy a sales tax on freight charges when the freight charge is directly related to an event that is itself subject to sales tax. An example would be the freight charge on the sale of a sofa being shipped to the designer's client. Table 5.2 shows those states that charge sales tax on freight charges paid to the seller when the item is shipped by common carrier, FOB destination. When an interior designer purchases materials or tangible personal property for resale, these items are not subject to sales tax if the designer presents a "Resale Certificate" to the vendor. Generally speaking, the sales tax is a "destination" tax and is levied on the ultimate consumer.

One particular problem all vendors should be aware of is when a resale certificate is presented for the purchase of an item that appears to be inconsistent with the nature of the purchaser's business, such as when a fashion retailer purchases a coffee table. The vendor can be held liable for the sales tax if it can be shown that the vendor should have known that sales tax evasion was taking place.

Some states currently charge sales tax on interior design services, such as fees and commissions, that do not relate to the sale of merchandise. This prevents an interior designer from charging sales tax on the sale of merchandise at cost and, on a separate invoice, billing for design fees which were formerly not taxable.

TABLE 5.1   Sales Tax Rate Chart[a]

State	Average Sales Tax Rates			Taxes Interior Designers	Provides Exemption
	City	County	State		
Alabama	2.058	1.721	4	No	No
Alaska	2.946	2.884	None	No	No
Arizona	1.732	0.509	5	No	No
Arkansas	1.125	1.093	4.5	Yes	No
California	1	1.232	6.25	No	No
Colorado	2.659	1.535	3	No	No
Connecticut	None	None	6	Yes	No
Delaware	None	None	None	None	None
District of Columbia	None	None	6	No	No
Florida	None	0.941	6	No	No
Georgia	None	1.535	4	No	No
Hawaii	None	None	4	Yes	No
Idaho	1.5	None	5	No	No
Illinois	0.635	0.437	6.25	No	No
Indiana	None	None	5	Yes	No
Iowa	1	1	5	No	No
Kansas	0.859	0.969	4.9	Yes	No
Kentucky	None	None	6	No	No
Louisiana	1.52	2.869	4	No	No
Maine	None	None	6	No	No
Maryland	None	None	5	No	No
Massachusetts	None	None	5	No	No
Michigan	None	None	4	No	No
Minnesota	0.6	0.5	6	No	No
Mississippi	0.25	None	7	No	No
Missouri	1.215	0.851	4.225	No	No
Montana	None	None	None	None	None
Nebraska	1.088	None	5	No	No
Nevada	2.5	2.39	4.25	No	No
New Hampshire	None	None	None	None	None
New Jersey	None	None	6	No	No
New Mexico	1.272	0.494	5	Yes	No
New York	3.519	3.236	4	Yes	Yes
North Carolina	None	2	4	No	No
North Dakota	1	None	5	No	No
Ohio	0.25	1.002	5	No	No
Oklahoma	2.681	1.057	4.5	No	No
Oregon	None	None	None	None	None
Pennsylvania	1	None	6	No	No
Rhode Island	None	None	7	No	No
South Carolina	None	1	5	No	No
South Dakota	1.493	None	4	Yes	No
Tennessee	1.458	2.16	6	No	No
Texas	1.168	0.526	6.25	Yes	No
Utah	1.079	1.034	5	No	No
Vermont	None	None	5	No	No
Virginia	1	1	3.5	No	No
Washington	1.208	1.123	6.5	No	No
West Virginia	None	None	6	Yes	No
Wisconsin	None	0.5	5	No	No
Wyoming	None	1.263	3	No	No

[a] Courtesy of Vertex, Inc.

TABLE 5.2 Vertex Inc. Product Code—Master List[a]

Vertex Chart Number: 030	Date: 05/18/92
Product Code: FRT-03	Type: Freight
Production Description: Common Carrier, FOB Destination, Paid to Seller	

State		T/E	Note[b]	TDM	State		T/E	Note[b]	TDM
Alabama	AL	E		N	Montana	MT	E		N
Alaska	AK	E		N	Nebraska	NE	T		Y
Arizona	AZ	T		Y	Nevada	NV	T		Y
Arkansas	AR	T		Y	New Hampshire	NH	E		N
California	CA	E	1	N	New Jersey	NJ	E		N
Colorado	CO	T		Y	New Mexico	NM	T		Y
Connecticut	CT	T		Y	New York	NY	T		Y
Delaware	DE	E		N	North Caorlina	NC	T		Y
D.C.	DC	T		Y	North Dakota	ND	T		Y
Florida	FL	T		Y	Ohio	OH	E		N
Georgia	GA	T		Y	Oklahoma	OK	E	6	N
Hawaii	HI	T		Y	Oregon	OR	E		N
Idaho	ID	T		Y	Pennsylvania	PA	T		Y
Illinois	IL	T	5	Y	Rhode Island	RI	T		Y
Indiana	IN	T		Y	South Carolina	SC	T		Y
Iowa	IA	E		N	South Dakota	SD	T		N
Kansas	KS	T		Y	Tennessee	TN	T		Y
Kentucky	KY	E		N	Texas	TX	T		N
Louisiana	LA	E		N	Utah	UT	T		N
Maine	ME	E	1	N	Vermont	VT	E		N
Maryland	MD	E		N	Virginia	VA	E		N
Massachusetts	MA	T		Y	Washington	WA	T		Y
Michigan	MI	T		Y	West Virginia	WV	T		Y

State		T/E	TDM
Minnesota	MN	E	N
Mississippi	MS	T	Y
Missouri	MO	T	Y
Wisconsin	WI	T	Y
Wyoming	WY	T	Y

T/E
T = Taxable
E = Exempt
M = Taxability determined by dollar value

Note = Review corresponding endnote for additional information

TDM
Y = Yes, tax applies
N = No, tax does not apply

[a] Copyright 1993 Vertex Inc.

[b] (1) Taxable if shipped to someone other than the purchaser. (2) Exempt if transportation occurs after the sale. (3) Exempt if property is shipped FOB origin and the transportation occurs entirely within the state. (4) Exempt if the common carrier is regulated by the Public Service Commission. (5) Exempt if transportation is arranged for in a separate contract. (6) Intrastate shipments are exempt. Charges for interstate shipments are taxable unless the charges are paid by the purchaser directly to the carrier.

Sales tax returns and related payments are filed with the state tax department on a monthly, quarterly, or annual basis. Frequency of filing usually depends on the volume of taxable sales or the dollar amount of sales tax collected.

CONCLUSION

We have seen that the accounting and taxation issues, as they relate to the interior design industry, are quite complex. No interior designer can expect to handle all the issues without getting competent professional assistance. It is important to use the services of an accountant at the beginning of the process of starting up a new business. I also have attempted to highlight some of the many potential financial, taxation, and administrative problems that may arise.

6

Professional Liability Insurance for Designers

Joseph P. Monteleone and Bruce M. Eisler

The opinions expressed herein are personal to the authors and do not necessarily reflect any opinion of Reliance National or of any insurance company in the Reliance Insurance Group. Further, the authors, through these materials, do not purport to restate, explain, or interpret any policy of insurance issued by a member company in the Reliance Insurance Group.

While the information contained in these materials is believed to be accurate and authoritative, it is not intended to be a substitute for legal, insurance, or other professional advice. The reader should consult legal and/or insurance professionals for advice or assistance on specific issues of interest.

OVERVIEW OF PROFESSIONAL LIABILITY INSURANCE FOR INTERIOR DESIGN PROFESSIONALS

Introduction

Professional liability insurance for interior designers is a widely available product from a number of insurers who have developed a market specialty in the area.

Joseph P. Monteleone is Senior Vice President and Claims Counsel at Reliance National in New York. Bruce M. Eisler is Assistant Vice President and Claims Counsel at Reliance National. Reliance National is a major underwriter of design professional liability insurance through various companies in the Reliance Insurance Group.

While most of the policy forms in use currently are denominated Design Professional Liability or Architects and Engineers Professional Liability policies, these same policy forms are employed by insurers to provide coverage for interior designers as well as the various architectural and engineering disciplines. If there is a specific aspect to an interior design practice that may cause the insured designer to seek a broader coverage, or the insurer to want to exclude a perceived hazard from the coverage, this will generally be addressed by an endorsement to the policy form. This may occur especially when the practice of the particular firm is multidisciplinary and may involve activities such as data processing and management consultant services. Likewise, design services that may involve activities such as asbestos abatement, nuclear power plant design, or hazardous waste treatment may provoke concern on the part of insurers. Unless the insurer and insured can agree on an increased premium in order to provide the coverage, the activities will generally be specifically excluded from coverage under the policy via an endorsement. Failure to do this may lead to a coverage dispute at a later time if a claim arises involving activity that the insurer never intended to cover, but that the insured believes is covered under the policy issued to it.

In addition to the type of policy discussed in this chapter, an interior designer who is *not* an architect may also be able to purchase an enhancement to his or her general liability insurance that will provide coverage for interior design errors and omissions. Such an enhancement, however, will not usually provide coverage for architectural and/or engineering services other than customary interior design and thus would not be appropriate for the professional whose practice encompasses these other services. A qualified broker will best be able to advise further with regard to the type of coverage available and suitable.

Although it is the authors' intention to provide the reader with a primer and broad overview of the subject, the most critical initial task for the interior designer to undertake in purchasing such insurance is to select an appropriate insurance agent or broker. In this chapter we will generally refer to *brokers* rather than *agents*.

In a brief and somewhat simplistic summary, an insurance broker is an individual or organization that represents the interests of its client (the purchaser of the insurance product) in dealing with a number of potential insurance markets in which to place the coverage. An insurance agent, however, generally represents the interests of only a small number or one insurance company with which it has an agency relationship.

The insurance broker will assist the design professional in determining coverage needs and selecting an appropriate insurer and policy contract. If the particular broker selected does not have substantial experience in design professional liability insurance or does not have direct access to a particular insurer to which it desires to submit an application for a policy, that broker will usually obtain the services of a *wholesale broker* who has the demonstrated expertise and/or access to the appropriate insurance markets. In such cases, the broker who initially and directly deals with the design professional is generally referred to as the *retail broker.*

In addition to advising with regard to the type of coverage needed, the broker should also advise the design professional as to the financial stability of various insurers and their underwriting and claims handling reputations. In appropriate situations, it may be helpful for both the insurer and the potential insured to have a personal meeting wherein various underwriting and claim concerns may be addressed. Such meetings will generally be arranged through and with the professional advice of the offices of the broker.

Determining Insurance Coverage Needs and Selecting Appropriate Coverage

Although this topic is addressed in more detail in the following sections of this chapter, perhaps the three most important aspects of a professional liability policy that should receive the immediate attention of the design professional are premium, limits of liability, and deductible or retention level.

Premium   Obviously, the premium paid for a policy is a very important factor and, between and among a number of insurers with similar financial stability and claims handling reputation, may be the deciding factor in selecting an insurer. It is beyond the scope of this chapter to present a detailed analysis as to how the premium for a particular risk is determined, but there is generally a direct relationship between the premium for the policy and the annual revenue or billings of the design firm. This is because, if for no other reason, experience has demonstrated to insurers that the likelihood and severity of a loss increases with the amount and size of the designer's professional engagements, which are reflected in the firm's annual revenue. Admittedly, this is not always a perfect method of assessing an appropriate premium, but on an overall and long-term basis it is fair to both insurer and insureds.

Limits of Liability   With regard to limits of liability to be carried, there is no easy and general answer as to how much is enough. For the sake of cost efficiency and administrative considerations, many insurers will not consider issuing policies with limits of liability less than $250,000 or for an annual premium less than $25,000. At the other end of the spectrum, limited reinsurance capacity and/or a desire to avoid practices that pose unacceptably high exposures (usually in the structural engineering area), may preclude insurers from offering limits of liability above $10,000,000. The considerations here are in many respects no different from what an individual would have in purchasing personal homeowners or automobile liability insurance protection. Again, the broker is the best source of advice.

Anecdotally, there are instances of insureds who for years carry liability limits of $1,000,000 per claim and in the annual aggregate, or even less, without a history of a claim even remotely approaching the liability limits. On the other hand, the authors were recently involved in a claim against a large engineering firm which resulted in a $42 million verdict against an insured with only $20 million in available policy limits. Interestingly, this matter ultimately settled for the $20 million in insurance limits. Nevertheless, the insured was a large and financially viable engineering firm that came under considerable pressure from the plaintiff to contribute to the settlement in excess of the available insurance. Perhaps only the risk, albeit slight in this particular case, of losing on appeal, convinced the plaintiff that a settlement of less than half the amount awarded at trial was prudent.

This unfortunate case also illustrates the function of an annual aggregate limit of liability in the policy. Although there were other pending claims against the insured at the time this settlement was consummated, the settlement exhausted the available limits of liability. Thus, although there was no reason based upon the insurance policy language why the remaining claims made in this policy year would not be covered, the exhaustion of the aggregate limit renders them uninsured on a practical basis. The lesson to be learned here is to appreciate the importance of purchasing sufficient liability limits to account for the potential of catastrophic exposures.

Retention Level   Deductible or retention levels, like limits of liability, can be structured so as to minimize the premium to be paid for the policy. Because the insured will be responsible in most cases for all amounts, including defense expenses, incurred in connection with a claim that are within the deductible amount, insurers are legitimately concerned with the level of deductible that they will allow an insured to carry. An insured will not be permitted to purchase coverage with a large deductible in an effort to reduce the premium if the insurer believes that the insured will not have the financial ability to "fund" that deductible in the event of a claim. To a certain extent, however, insurers desire maintenance of significant deductibles (typically at least $5,000) to ensure a financial stake for the insured in the litigation and thus enhanced cooperation with the insurer.

Under most policy forms, deductibles apply on a per claim basis without an aggregate maximum. The insurer will carefully review the insured's application to determine if there have been numerous claims against the insured that may be subject to coverage under the policy to be offered. If claim frequency is expected to be a concern, this may be addressed by an endorsement to the policy (for additional premium) that provides for an aggregate cap on the deductible amount to be borne by the insured during a policy year.

As an example, the policy could be written with a $10,000 deductible amount for each claim subject to an aggregate deductible of $25,000 for the entire policy period. Assuming that four separate and unrelated claims are made against the interior designer during the policy period, the first two would each be subject to a $10,000 deductible, but the third would only bear a $5000 deductible (the amount remaining in the aggregate). Since the aggregate deductible would be exhausted by the third claim, the fourth claim would not be subject to any deductible amount. Some policies, however, may be written with a "reinstated" deductible after the aggregate is exhausted. In such cases, once the aggregate is reached, there would once again be an "each claim" deductible. The reinstated deductible amount will be less than the original "each claim" deductible amount, but it is intended nonetheless to ensure that the insured bear some portion of the financial exposure posed by the claim.

Coverage Generally Afforded Under a Professional Liability Policy

As will be explained below, a professional liability policy for an interior designer will generally provide coverage for claims made *against* the designer and which arise from the rendering of professional design services for a fee.

The policy does not afford legal expense coverage for claims which a designer may seek to bring against its client for payment of fees, or indeed against any other party. However, many claims for fees oftentimes, albeit not meritoriously, trigger a counterclaim by the client or other party for design malpractice. This latter claim (including legal defense fees and costs) is precisely what the policy, subject to its various terms and conditions, is intended to cover.

Of course, when the designer is utilizing the same counsel to prosecute its fee claim and to defend against the malpractice or errors and omissions claim, allocating what are covered legal fees and costs and what are not under the policy may be the subject of disagreement between the insurer and the insured.

Such disagreements may unfortunately be difficult to resolve, particularly when the designer's claim for fees and the client's counterclaim for malpractice are part of the same lawsuit. Taking the example of a day-long deposition of the designer in that lawsuit, who can accurately assess how much of the time spent in that deposition was devoted to the fee claim and how much was related to the malpractice counterclaim? Unfortunately, it is not objectively possible to classify each question at a deposition as a "fee" question or a "malpractice" question. Hopefully, any dispute as to the insurer's allocation assessment would be resolved through good faith negotiation. Nevertheless, complex disputes, especially those involving large amounts of legal expenses and other costs, may ultimately become the subject of arbitration or litigation if negotiations fail.

The basic coverage grant of the policy is very broad and, in the case of an interior designer, may be as broad as "all interior design services provided for others for a fee." We shall explore how this broad coverage grant is limited by various policy conditions and exclusions. Exposures arising from other than professional services may be addressed by other insurance policies such as workers' compensation, fire, property, and comprehensive general liability insurance. The latter is briefly discussed in the following section, but a discussion of other insurance coverages is beyond the intended scope of this chapter and should be the subject of informed discussion with a knowledgeable insurance broker.

General Liability Insurance

In a sense, general liability insurance is a more "basic" type of insurance than professional liability insurance. For financial and other reasons, a professional may elect to maintain little or no professional liability insurance, but general liability insurance must almost always be purchased for the same reasons an individual maintains such insurance on his or her home and automobile.

What would be covered under a general liability policy that would not be covered under the professional liability policy?

Generally speaking, the general liability policy provides coverage for accidents that result in bodily injury or tangible property damage. As an illustrative example, a client who slips and falls in the designer's office in the course of a meeting regarding an existing professional engagement would present a claim for bodily injury that is subject to coverage under the general rather than professional liability policy. The insurers, and there may well be different insurance companies for each policy, would more properly consider that claim to be general liability and not professional liability.

Just as the professional liability policy limits its coverage grant to claims arising from professional services, the general liability policy will usually be endorsed so as to exclude coverage for claims arising from the provision of professional services.

Although most situations should be rather clear cut, in some situations there may be uncertainty as to what type of coverage should apply to a given claim. These usually occur in the context of an injury to a worker or other party at a job site at which the design professional has rendered some professional services.

In the event of such nondisclosure, the insurer may deny coverage for any claim that relates to such non-disclosed claims or circumstances or, more drastically, seek a rescission of the entire policy. In the event of rescission, the insurer will generally be required to return the premium paid for the policy and possibly some interest. Of course, the insured is then left without coverage not only for the claim that gave rise to the misrepresentation concern, but also any other claims that may be subject to coverage under the policy.

Not every misrepresentation can give rise to a rescission of the policy or a denial of coverage. This is usually governed by the insurance law of the state in which the insured does business, unless the insurance policy provides for a different governing law provision.

In most states, the misrepresentation must be material, that is, the insurer either would not have underwritten the risk if it had known the true situation or would have done so with a significantly higher premium level. Other jurisdictions require, in addition to materiality, that the misrepresentation be intentional on the part of the insured. In the event of a misrepresentation or any other coverage issue, an insured design professional would be well-advised to consult with legal counsel experienced in dealing with such issues.

THE DESIGN PROFESSIONAL LIABILITY INSURANCE POLICY

Introduction

As it is the authors' intention to familiarize the reader with the Design Professional Liability Insurance Policy, a specimen copy of an Architects and Engineers Professional Liability Insurance Policy is included in this chapter (see Exhibit 6.1). While policy forms vary among insurers, this policy is typical of the policy form utilized for underwriting professional liability insurance for interior designers, architects, and other design professionals.

The Design Professional Liability Insurance Policy, like any other policy of insurance, is a contract between the insured and the insurance company. It is therefore critical for the Design Professional to have an understanding of the terms and conditions of the insurance coverage *before* a claim arises. Since an exhaustive analysis of all the policy terms would be as lengthy as this entire book, this chapter will address some of the more significant policy provisions.

Perhaps the most significant provision of the Design Professional Liability Insurance Policy is the Insuring Agreement, as this provision is essentially the trigger for coverage under the policy. While there are, of course, other provisions in the policy that serve to clarify, define, and in some instances limit and/or exclude the coverage described in the Insuring Agreement, this provision sets forth the coverage afforded by the policy.

RELIANCE INSURANCE COMPANIES
Architects and Engineers
Professional Liability Insurance Policy

Policy No.
Prev. No.
Prod. No.

DECLARATIONS

Item 1. — NAME INSURED:

Item 2. — MAILING ADDRESS OF THE NAMED INSURED:

Item 3. — POLICY PERIOD FROM: _____ **To:** _____
(12:01 AM standard time at the address of the NAMED INSURED as indicated herein)

Item 4. — NAMED INSURED'S PROFESSIONAL SERVICES:

Item 5. — LIMIT OF LIABILITY:

The liability of the Company for the combined total of Damages and Claim
Expenses for each Claim first made and reported during the Policy Period shall
not exceed: $ _____

and subject to that limit for each Claim, the total limit of the Company's liability
for the combined total of Damages and Claim Expenses for all Claims first made
and reported during the Policy Period shall not exceed in the aggregate: $ _____

Item 6. — DEDUCTIBLE:

Shall be applicable to the combined total of Damages and Claim Expenses arising
from each Claim: $ _____

Item 7. — PREMIUM: $ _____

Item 8. — ENDORSEMENTS ATTACHED AT POLICY INCEPTION:

Except to such extent as may be provided otherwise herein, this insurance is limited to
liability for only those Claims that are first made and reported against the Insured during
the Policy Period in accordance with the terms of this Policy. Please review the Policy
carefully and discuss the coverage hereunder with your insurance agent, broker, or
representative.

Countersigned

_____
Duly Authorized Officer or Representative

ALL CLAIMS TO BE REPORTED DIRECTLY TO:
Reliance National Risk Specialists, Inc.
77 Water Street
New York, N.Y. 10005
(212) 858-3600

Exhibit 6.1 *Specimen copy of an Architects and Engineers Professional Liability Insurance policy.*

ARCHITECTS & ENGINEERS PROFESSIONAL LIABILITY INSURANCE
(Claims Made & Reported Basis)
The Company Designated on The Declarations Page
(A stock insurance company, herein called the Company)

In consideration of the payment of the Premium, the undertaking of the Insured to pay the Deductible as described herein, and in reliance upon the statements in the application made part hereof, and subject to the Limits of Liability of this insurance as set forth in the Declarations, and the Exclusions, Conditions and other terms of this Policy, agrees with the Named Insured as follows:

INSURING AGREEMENTS

1. COVERAGE—PROFESSIONAL LIABILITY:

Subject to both the Limits of Liability and Deductible, the Company will pay on behalf of the Insured sums incurred as Claim Expenses and sums which the Insured shall become legally obligated to pay as Damages, both as a result of Claims first made and reported against the Insured during the Policy Period by reason of any act, error or omission in the performance of Professional Services of the type described in the Declarations committed or alleged to have been committed by the Insured or by any person or entity for whom the Insured is legally liable.

2. TERRITORY:

The insurance afforded applies worldwide except:

(a) with respect to any Claim arising out of any project situated in and/or

(b) with respect to any Claim made in;
    Afghanistan, Albania, Algeria, Angola, Arab Republic of Yemen, Bulgaria, Burma, Cambodia, Cuba, Czechoslovakia, Ethiopia, German Democratic Republic, Hungary, Islamic Republic of Iran, Korean People's Republic, Laos, Libya, Mongolia, Nicaragua, People's Republic of China, People's Republic of Yemen, Poland, Romania, Saudi Arabia, Socialist Republic of Viet Nam, Somalia, Syria, Uganda, Union of Soviet Socialist Republics and Yugoslavia.

3. CLAIMS MADE PROVISIONS:
This insurance applies only to negligent acts, errors or omissions which are committed or alleged to have been committed and result in damage or alleged to have resulted in damage provided always that, the negligent act, error, or omission:

(a) Arises out of the Insured's performance of Professional Services as described in the Declarations;

(b) Was committed or alleged to have been committed during the Policy Period and Claim is first made and reported or suit is brought and reported for such Claim during the Policy Period;

(c) Was committed or alleged to have been committed prior to the inception date of the Policy, and Claim is first made and reported during the Policy Period, or if suit for such Claim is commenced and reported during the Policy Period, provided:

   1. the Insured had no knowledge of any such prior or alleged negligent act, error, or omission, on the effective date of this insurance, and

   2. no other valid and collectible insurance is available to the Insured for any such prior negligent act, error, or omission.

4. DEFINITIONS: When used herein or in any endorsement, the following terms shall have the definitions indicated.

A. THE "INSURED"

The Named Insured and also any employee of the Named Insured while acting within the scope his duties as such.

The word "Named Insured" shall mean:

1. If the Named Insured is designated in the Declarations as an individual, the person so designated;

Exhibit 6.1 *Continued*

2. If the Named Insured is designated in the Declarations as a partnership or joint venture, the partnership or joint venture so designated and any partner or member thereof but only with respect to his liability as such;

3. If the Named Insured is designated in the Declarations as a corporation, the corporation so designated and any officer or director thereof while acting within the scope of his duties as such;

4. Any present or former owner, partner, director, officer or employee of the Named Insured but only for Claims arising out of such person's duties conducted for and on behalf of the Named Insured and arising out of Professional Services as described in Item 4 of the Declarations.

In the event of the Insured's incapacity, death, or bankruptcy, the heirs, executors, administrators, assigns and legal representatives of each Insured as defined above, but only for Claims arising out of the performance of Professional Services of such Insured for and on behalf of the Named Insured.

B.   "CLAIM:"

A demand for money or Professional Services made on the Insured arising out of an act, error, or omission in Professional Services as described in Item 4 of the Declarations. A Claim is considered first made against the Insured at the earlier of the following:

1. Receipt by the Insured of notice of Claim from a claimant or his legal representative, or

2. Report by the Insured of a circumstance which might reasonably be expected to give rise to a Claim to any insurer, whether or not such insurer affords coverage for such circumstance or for any Claim subsequently arising out of such circumstance.

Any Claim arising out of any circumstances reported in answer to any question on the application for this insurance or any prior application for insurance shall be considered to have been first made prior to the Policy Period, and shall not be subject to coverage under this Policy of insurance.

C.   "CLAIMS EXPENSES:"

Fees charged by any attorney designated by the Company, all other fees, costs and expenses resulting from the investigation, adjustment, defense or appeal of a Claim, if incurred by the Company; and fees charged by any attorney designated by the Insured with the prior written consent of the Company. The determination by the Company as to the reasonableness of Claim Expenses shall be conclusive on the Insured.

D.   "DAMAGES:"

Judgments, settlements and Claim Expenses excluding the cost of investigation and adjustment of Claims by salaried employees of the Company, but including attorney's fees, arbitrator's fees, pre-judgement and post-judgement interest, court costs, expenses incurred in obtaining expert testimony and the attendance of witnesses and costs incurred in connection with arbitration proceedings against the Named Insured; provided, however, that only those items of expense which can be directly allocated to a specific Claim involving litigation or possible litigation shall be included.

The following shall not constitute Damages as defined above:
Punitive or exemplary damages; any damages which are a multiple of compensatory damages; fines, penalties or sanctions; judgements or awards deemed uninsurable by law; the restitution, withdrawal or reduction of consideration and expenses paid to the Insured for services or goods.

E.   "POLICY PERIOD:"

The period from the effective date of this Policy to the expiration date or earlier termination date, of this Policy.

F.   "POLLUTANTS:"

Any solid, liquid, gaseous or thermal irritant or contaminant, including smoke, vapor, soot, fumes, acids, alkalis, chemicals and waste, including materials to be recycled, reconditioned or reclaimed.

G.   "PROFESSIONAL SERVICES:"

Those Professional Services described in Item 4 of the Declarations.

Exhibit 6.1 *Continued*

H.   "PERSONAL INJURY:"

Bodily injury; false arrest, detention or imprisonment; wrongful entry or eviction or other invasion of private occupancy; malicious prosecution or humiliation; the publication or utterance of a libel or slander or other defamatory or disparaging material, or a publication or utterance in violation of an individual's right of privacy; discrimination.

5.   LIMITS OF LIABILITY:

The liability of the Company for each Claim which is first made and reported during the Policy Period shall not exceed the amount stated in the Declarations for "each Claim", and, subject to that limit for each Claim, the total limit for the Company's liability for all Claims which are first made and reported during the Policy Period, as covered hereunder, shall not exceed the amount stated in the Declarations as "aggregate". The inclusion herein of more than one Insured or the making of Claims or the bringing of suits by more than one person or organization, shall not operate to increase the limit of the Company's liability for "each Claim" and in the "aggregate".

Two or more Claims arising out of a single negligent act, error, or omission shall be treated as a single Claim. Each separate negligent act, error, or omission shall be treated as a separate Claim.

6.   DEDUCTIBLE:

The Deductible amount stated in the Declarations as applicable to "each Claim" will apply to the combined total of Damages and Claim Expenses for each Claim. However, either singly or combined, the total payments requested from the Named Insured in respect of each Claim shall not exceed the Deductible amount stated in the Declarations. Such Deductible amount shall not reduce the Company's Limits of Liability.

The determination by the Company as to the reasonableness of the "Claim Expenses" shall be conclusive on the Named Insured.

7.   DEFENSE, SETTLEMENT, COOPERATION, SUPPLEMENTARY PAYMENTS:

(A)   The Company shall investigate and defend any Claim against the Insured seeking Damages to which this insurance applies, even if the allegations of the Claim are groundless, false or fraudulent. Claims Expenses incurred in investigating and defending such Claim shall be part of and not in addition to the Limit of Liability stated in the Declarations and shall reduce such Limit of Liability. Upon exhaustion of the Limit of Liability through payments of Claims Expenses or Damages or a combination of both, the Company shall not be obligated to continue to defend any Claim or to pay any further Damages or Claim Expenses.

(B)   The Company shall not settle any Claim without the consent of the Insured. If, however, the Insured shall refuse to consent to any settlement recommended by the Company and shall elect to contest the Claim or continue any legal proceedings in connection with such Claim, then the Company's liability for the Claim shall not exceed the amount for which the Claim could have been settled plus Claims Expenses incurred up to the date of such refusal. Such amounts are subject to the Limit of Liability and Deductible provision of the Insuring Agreements. (Items 4&5).

(C)   The Insured shall not, except with the prior written consent of the Company, make any payment, settle Claims or incur Claims Expenses, admit liability, or waive any rights. However, the Insured must take reasonable action within its power to prevent or mitigate any Claim which would be covered under this Policy.

(D)   The Insured shall cooperate with the Company and upon the Company's request, shall submit to examination and interrogation by a representative of the Company, under oath if required, and shall attend hearings, depositions and trials and shall assist in effecting settlement, securing and giving evidence, obtaining the attendance of witnesses and in the conduct of suits, as well as in the giving of a written statement or statements to the Company's representatives and meetings with such representatives for the purpose of investigation and/or defense, and all without charge to the Company.

8.   EXCLUSIONS:

The Coverage of this Policy shall not apply to any Claims, or Claim Expenses for or arising out of, or involving:

(A)   Liability of others assumed by the Insured by agreement under any contract, whether written or oral, unless such liability would have attached to the Insured even in the absence of such agreement;

(B)   Liability of any kind based upon, involving or arising out of, the conduct by an individual, corporation, partnership or joint venture of which the Insured is a partner, officer, director, member or employee which is not designated in the Declarations as a Named Insured or specifically endorsed hereon;

Exhibit 6.1   *Continued*

(C)   Claims by any person or entity (or its subrogees or assignees) that did or now does wholly or partly own, operate or manage the Insured or was or is now wholly owned, operated, or managed by the Insured or any contractor or subcontractor thereof, unless specifically endorsed hereon.

(D)   Bodily injury, personal injury, sickness, disease or death of any employee of the Named Insured arising out of and in the course of his employment by the Named Insured; or to any Claim for which the Named Insured or any carrier as the Named Insured's insurer may be liable under any Workers Compensation, Unemployment Compensation, Employer's Liability, Disability Benefits Law or under any similar law;

(E)   The insolvency or bankruptcy of the Named Insured or any other person, firm, or organization.

(F)   The advising or requiring of or failure to advise or require, or failure to maintain any form and/or amount of insurance, suretyship or bond, either with respect to the Named Insured or any other person, firm, or organization.

(G)   The ownership, rental, leasing, operation, maintenance, use or repair of any real or personal property, including property damage to property owned by, occupied by, rented or leased to the Insured;

(H)   The ownership, maintenance, operation or use, including loading and unloading, by or on behalf of the Insured, or at the direction of the Insured, of watercraft, automobiles, motor vehicles, aircraft or mobile vehicles of any kind;

(I)   The failure to complete drawings, specifications or schedules of specifications on time, or the failure to act upon shop drawings on time, but this exclusion does not apply if such failures are the result of a negligent act, error, or omission in the drawings, plans, specifications, schedules or shop drawings;

(J)   Express warranties or guarantees, estimates of probable construction cost or cost estimates being exceeded;

(K)   Any loss caused intentionally by or at the direction of the Insured; or any Claim based upon, involving or arising out of any dishonest, fraudulent, criminal, malicious or knowingly wrongful act, error or omission committed by or at the direction of the Insured;

(L)   Arising out of the ownership, copyright, re-use or control of the Insured's plans and specifications, without the written permission of such Insured or infringement of copyright, trademark or patent;

(M)   The specification or recommendation of asbestos in any form, asbestos exposure assessments, appraisal of asbestos containment/removal programs; or any Claim based upon, involving or arising out of the use of or exposure to asbestos or products containing asbestos;

(N)   Any actual, alleged or threatened discharge, dispersal, release or escape of Pollutants or any governmental or regulatory directive or request to test for, monitor, clean up, remove, contain, treat, detoxify or neutralize Pollutants; however, this exclusion shall not apply when such Claim results from the performance of Professional Services by the Insured in the design and construction of treatment systems for:

1.   domestic sewage including those receiving industrial waste but only if such industrial waste is pretreated in accordance with applicable governmental or regulatory standards;

2.   potable water; or

3.   water from rain, hail, snow or sleet.

9.   CONDITIONS:

(A.) INSURED'S DUTIES IN THE EVENT OF CLAIM OR SUIT: It is a condition precedent to the application of all insurance afforded herein that the Insured shall:

1.   Immediately forward to the Company every demand, notice, summons or other process including institution of arbitration proceedings received by him or his representative, if Claim is made, suit is brought or arbitration is instituted against the Insured.

2.   Give written notice containing particulars sufficient to identify the Insured and claimant and full information with respect to the time, place and circumstances of the event complained of, and the names and the addresses of the injured and of available witnesses, to the Company or to any of its authorized representatives as soon as practicable.

Exhibit 6.1   *Continued*

3. In any event, any Claim or suit made or arbitration instituted against the Insured during the Policy Period must be reported to the Company during the Policy Period.

(B.) CANCELLATION:

This Policy may be cancelled by the Named Insured by surrender thereof to the Company or by mailing to the Company written notice stating when thereafter the cancellation shall be effective. This Policy may be cancelled by the Company by mailing to the Named Insured at the Address shown in the Declarations a written notice stating when, not less than thirty (30) days thereafter, such cancellation shall become effective.

Provided, however, if the Named Insured does not pay the premium or deductible when due, the Company may cancel this Policy by mailing to the Named Insured written notice stating when, not less than ten (10) days thereafter, such cancellation shall be effective.

The time of the surrender or the effective date and hour of cancellation stated in the notice shall terminate the Policy Period. The mailing of such notice as aforesaid, whether by ordinary mail or by certified mail, shall be sufficient proof of such notice. Delivery of such written notice, whether by the Named Insured or by the Company, shall be equivalent to mailing. If the Named Insured cancels, Earned Premium shall be computed in accordance with the customary short rate table and procedure. If the Company cancels, Earned Premium shall be computed pro-rata. Premium adjustment may be made either at the time cancellation is effected or as soon as practicable thereafter, but payment or tender of Unearned Premium is not a condition of a cancellation by the Company.

(C) DISCOVERY CLAUSE:

If during the Policy Period the Insured first becomes aware of any negligent act, error or omission which might reasonably be expected to subsequently give rise to a Claim for which insurance is otherwise provided hereunder and, if the Insured gives written notice which is received by the Company during the Policy Period, then any Claim subsequently arising out of such negligent act, error or omission shall be deemed to have been made on the date on which such written notice is received by the Company.
Such written notice shall include:

1. The specific negligent act, error or omission.

2. The injury or damage that has or may reasonably be expected to result from such negligent act, error or omission.

3. The circumstances by which the Insured first became aware of such injury or damage and negligent act, error or omission.

The Insured shall cooperate fully with the Company as provided in Item 7, Defense, Settlement, Cooperation, Supplementary Payments, and any investigation conducted by the Company or it's representatives shall be subject to the terms set forth in this Policy as though an actual Claim had been reported.

(D) SUBROGATION:

In the event of any Claim under this Policy, the Company shall be subrogated to all the Insured's rights of recovery therefore against any person or organization and the Insured shall execute and deliver instruments and papers and do whatever else is necessary to secure such rights. The Insured shall do nothing after loss to prejudice such rights.

Any recovery shall be used to pay costs incurred, in the following order:

1. Subrogation Expenses.

2. Payments by the Insurer.

3. Reimbursement of the Insured's Deductible.

(E) ACTION AGAINST COMPANY:

No action shall be maintained against the Company by the Insured to recover for any loss under this Policy unless, as a condition precedent thereto, the Insured shall have fully complied with all the terms and conditions of the Policy, nor until the amount of such losses has been fixed or rendered certain either by final judgment against the Insured after trial of the issues and the time to appeal therefrom has expired without

5 of 7

Exhibit 6.1 *Continued*

an appeal having been taken or, if an appeal has been taken, then until after the appeal has been determined, or by agreement between the parties with the written consent of the Company. In no event shall any action be maintained against the Company by the Insured or any other persons unless brought within twelve months after the right of action accrues hereon.

Nothing contained in this Policy shall give any person or organization any right to join the Company as a defendant or co-defendant or other party in any action against the Insured to determine the Insured's liability.

(F) ASSIGNMENT:

This policy shall be void if assigned or transferred without the written consent of this Company.

(G) OTHER INSURANCE:

This insurance shall be excess insurance over any other valid and collectible insurance available to the Insured whether such other insurance is stated to be primary, contributing, excess, contingent or otherwise, unless such other insurance specifically applies as excess insurance over the Limits or Liability provided in this Policy.

(H) CHANGES:

Notice to any agent or representative or knowledge possessed by any agent, representative or other person acting on behalf of the Company shall not effect a waiver or a change in any part of this Policy or estop the Company from asserting any right under the terms of the Policy, nor shall the terms of this Policy be waived or changed, except by endorsement issued to form a part of this Policy.

(I) AUDIT:

The Company may examine and audit the Insured's books and records at any time during the Policy Period and extensions thereof and within three years after the final termination of this Policy, as far as they relate to the subject matter of this insurance Policy.

(J) APPLICATION:

By acceptance of this policy, all Insureds agree that the statements in the application and materials submitted therewith are their agreements, representations, and warranties and that they shall be deemed material and part of this Policy. It is agreed by all Insureds that this Policy is issued in reliance upon the truth thereof, and that this Policy embodies all agreements existing between themselves and the Company or any of its representatives relating to this insurance Policy.

Further, it is agreed by all Insureds that misrepresentations on the application and/or on materials submitted therewith, committed intentionally, or which materially affect the acceptance of the risk by the Company under this insurance Policy, shall void the Policy in its entirety.

(K) FALSE OR FRAUDULENT CLAIMS:

If the Insured shall proffer any Claims knowing same to be false or fraudulent, as regards amount or otherwise, this Policy shall become void and all insurance hereunder shall be forfeited.

(L) NOTICE OF CLAIM:

The Insured, upon notice of any Claim or of an incident or circumstance likely to give rise to a Claim hereunder, shall give immediate written advice thereof to the Company, c/o Reliance National Risk Specialists, Inc., 77 Water Street, New York, N.Y. 10005.

(M) SERVICE OF SUIT CLAUSE:

It is agreed that in the event of the failure of the Company to pay any amount claimed to be due hereunder, the Company and Insured, will submit to the jurisdiction of the State of New York, and will comply with all the requirements necessary to give such Court jurisdiction. All matters arising hereunder shall be determined in accordance with the law and practice of the State of New York.

Further, pursuant to any statute of any state, territory or district of the United States which makes provision therefore, the Company hereby designates the Superintendent, Commissioner or Director of Insurance or other officer specified for that purpose in the statute or his successors in office as its true and lawful attorney

Exhibit 6.1 *Continued*

upon whom may be served any lawful process in any action, suit or proceeding instituted by or on behalf of the Insured, or any beneficiary hereunder arising out of this Policy.

The Insured will not exercise any contractual right to either reject or demand the arbitration of any claim made against the Insured, without first obtaining, and abiding by, the Company's written instructions.

10. Nuclear Energy Liability Exclusion

A. It is agreed that this policy does not apply to any injury, sickness, disease, death, destruction or property damage caused by (i) exposure to Radioactivity or to any Nuclear Material, or (ii) the operation of any Nuclear Facility.

B. For purposes of this Section 10 the terms "Radioactivity", "Nuclear Facility" and "Nuclear Material" shall be defined as follows:

1. "Radioactivity" shall mean the spontaneous emission of ionizing radiation, either directly from unstable atomic nuclei or as a consequence of a nuclear reaction, and the radiation so emitted, including but not limited to, alpha particles, nucleons, electrons, and gamma rays;

2. "Nuclear Material" shall mean any material, regardless of its state, that spontaneously emits Radioactivity, irrespective of its use or source, including, but not limited to, (i) materials which are defined as "source material", "special nuclear material" and "byproduct material", as defined in the Atomic Energy Act of 1954, (ii) nuclear fuel, including spent nuclear fuel, and (iii) nuclear waste materials of any kind whatsoever;

3. "Nuclear Facility" shall mean: (i) any nuclear reactor, as defined below; (ii) any equipment or device designed or used for separating radioactive isotopes, processing or utilizing nuclear fuel or in any way handling, processing or packaging any Nuclear Material; (iii) any structure, container, excavation, premises or place, prepared or used for the storage, disposal, processing or use of any Nuclear Material, including the site at which any of the foregoing is located, all operations conducted on such site and all premises used for such operations.

For purposes of this section 10, "Nuclear Reactor" shall mean any apparatus designed or used to sustain nuclear fission in a self-supporting chain reaction or to contain a critical mass of fissionable material.

IN WITNESS WHEREOF, the company has caused this Policy to be executed and attested, but this Policy shall not be valid unless countersigned by a duly authorized representative of the company.

Reliance Insurance Company of Illinois

Secretary

President

SIGNATURE	DATE

SIGNATURE	DATE

Exhibit 6.1 _Continued_

The Insuring Agreement of most Design Professional Liability policies is similar to the following:

> Subject to both the Limits of Liability and Deductible, the Company will pay on behalf of the Insured sums incurred as Claim Expenses and sums which the Insured shall become legally obligated to pay as Damages, both as a result of Claims first made and reported against the Insured during the Policy Period by reason of any act, error, or omission in the Performance of Professional Services of the type described in the Declarations committed or alleged to have been committed by the Insured or by any person or entity for whom the Insured is legally liable.

Regardless of whether it is a structural engineering or an interior design project, there may be a critical issue as to what control the design professional had over construction means and methods at the job site. Depending upon whether the allegations are in the nature of a design defect or supervision of construction activities, there may be a question as to coverage under the professional liability policy that would give rise to the possibility of coverage under a general liability policy.

In such situations, it may indeed be in the best interest of the design professional to seek to have coverage apply under the general liability rather than professional liability policy. If for no other reasons, the general liability policy is usually structured to provide for defense costs coverage without being subject to any deductible amount. Also, and unlike most professional liability policies, amounts expended on defense do not reduce the available limits of liability to satisfy a settlement or judgment amount.

Completing the Application

We have also included a specimen copy of one insurance company's application used for architects and engineers and other design professional risks policy (see Exhibit 6.2). Although application forms used by various insurers vary somewhat, the attached form is fairly typical.

The application should be prepared in a careful and complete manner. Providing false or incomplete information can have very serious consequences in the event of a claim wherein it is discovered that the insurer was provided with false information. Although an experienced broker is an invaluable resource for assistance in completing the application, only the insured professional knows the "facts" necessary to truthfully and completely respond to the questions in the application.

This is particularly true with regard to what are generally referred to as "warranty questions," that is, those questions requiring information as to existing and prior claims and circumstances, acts, or omissions that are known to the insured and which may reasonably give rise to a future claim. These are the questions numbered 27 and 28 in the annexed application form.

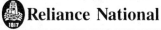

Reliance National

77 WATER STREET, NEW YORK, NEW YORK 10005 PHONE (212) 858-3600

RELIANCE INSURANCE COMPANIES
APPLICATION FOR ARCHITECTS AND
ENGINEERS PROFESSIONAL LIABILITY

a. Please answer all questions completely.

b. If there is insufficient space to complete an answer, please continue on a separate sheet of your firm's letterhead. Indicate number of question.

c. This form must be completed, signed and dated by a Principal or Officer or the firm.

d. Please type or print clearly.

NOTE:
The insurance coverage for which you are applying is written on a CLAIMS-MADE policy; only Claims which are first made and reported against you during the Policy Period are covered subject to the Policy Provisions.

The Limits of Liability stated in the Policy are reduced by the Cost of Defense. Legal Defense Costs also are applied against your Deductible, if applicable to the Claim. If you have any questions about coverage, please discuss them with your insurance agent.

---

1. Name of Firm(s) _____

    _____

    Address of Principal Office _____

    _____

    (List addresses of all branch offices on a separate sheet)
    Date Current Firm(s) Established or Incorporated: _____/_____/_____

    Corporation ☐ Partnership ☐ Professional Corp ☐ Sole Proprietorship ☐

2. Has the name of the firm been changed or has any other business been purchased or any merger or consolidation taken place?
    ☐ Yes ☐ No. If yes, please give full details (including dates):

    _____

3. Indicate Number of Staff Officers

	Full-Time	Part-Time
A. Principals, Partners or Officers	_____	_____
B. Architects, Engineers, Site Representatives, Surveyors, Draftsmen, and all other technical personnel employed by the firm, excluding Principals	_____	_____
C. Office Employees (Clerks, Typists, etc.)	_____	_____
D. Total Staff (A+B+C	_____	_____

4. Name of Owner, Partner or Officer

Name of Owner, Partner or Officer	Educational Qualifications	Date and Place Acquired	Date Licensed	How Long with Firm
_____	_____	_____	_____	_____
_____	_____	_____	_____	_____
_____	_____	_____	_____	_____

5. States in which Professional license is held _____

6. Foreign Work? ☐ Yes ☐ No. If yes, please give full details: _____

    _____

Exhibit 6.2 *Specimen copy of insurance company's application for architects and engineers and other design professional risks policy.*

7. Have any of those listed in item No. 4 ever been the subject of disciplinary action by authorities as a result of their professional activities? ☐ Yes ☐ No. If yes, please give details: _____

_____

_____

8. To what Professional Associations does the Applicant belong? _____

_____

9. Please indicate the approximate percentages of the professions in which your firm is engaged: (This section must equal 100%)

A. _____ % Architecture   I. _____ % Landscape Architecture

B. _____ % Interior Design/Space Planning   J. _____ % Naval/Marine

C. _____ % Civil Engineering   K. _____ % Process Engineering

D. _____ % Electrical Engineering   L. _____ % Structural Engineering

E. _____ % Land Surveying   M. _____ % Testing Lab

F. _____ % Mechanical Engineering   N. _____ % Construction Management

G. _____ % HVAC Engineering   O. _____ % Soil Engineering

H. _____ % Environmental Engineering   P. _____ % Other please specify below

_____

10. Please indicate the approximate percentage of billings, if any, derived from the following categories:

a. Ground Testing _____ %   e. Inspections of homes/commerical properties for prospective buyers _____ %

b. Surveys of subsurface conditions _____ %

c. Foundation design _____ %   f. Projects located outside U.S., its territories or Canada _____ %

d. Continuing service or inspection contracts _____ %

11. Please indicate the approximate percentage of billings derived from each project type: (This section must equal 100%)

____ Apartment	____ Libraries	____ Tunnel
____ Hotels/Motels	____ Jails/Justice	____ Dam
____ One Family Dwelling	____ Convention Center	____ Harbor, Pier, Port
____ Condo/Townhouse	____ Airport	____ Landfill
____ Office Building	____ Water system	____ Mass Transit
____ Shopping Center	____ Sewer system	____ Petro/Chemical
____ Parking Structure	____ Sewage treatment	____ Nuclear/Atomic
____ Warehouse	____ Industrial waste treatment	____ Other (Specify):
____ Manufacturing/Industrial	____ Superfund/Pollution	_____
____ Ecclesiastical	____ Pool/Playground	_____
____ Asbestos Evaluation/Abatement	____ Amusement Ride	_____
____ School/College	____ Site Development	_____
____ Hospital/Healthcare	____ Road/Highway	_____
____ Recreation/Sports	____ Bridge	_____

Exhibit 6.2 Continued

12. Please indicate the approximate percentage of fees derived from each of the following:

Commercial	_____ %	Local Governments	_____ %	Owners Who Act As	
Contractors	_____ %	Real Estate Developers	_____ %	Their Own Builders	_____ %
Other Design Professionals	_____ %	Lending Institutions	_____ %	Industrial	_____ %
Federal Government	_____ %	State Government	_____ %	Other (Specify)	_____ %

13. Does any one contract or client represent more than 50% of annual work? ☐ Yes ☐ No If yes, please give details: _____

_____

14. Does the Applicant foresee any substantial changes in the percentages of Question 9-12 during the next twelve months? ☐ Yes ☐ No. If yes, explain: _____

_____

15. Total fees for professional services for fiscal year (whether or not collected).
Dates of reporting period: From _____ To _____

	Estimate for coming Fiscal Year		Current Fiscal Year		Previous Fiscal Year	
	Fees	CVS	Fees	CVS	Fees	CVS
A. *JOINT VENTURE PROJECTS (YOUR PORTION OF JV FEES):	_____		_____		_____	
B. *PROJECTS INSURED UNDER SEPARATE PROJECT POLICIES:	_____		_____		_____	
C. *PROJECTS WHICH HAVE BEEN PERMANENTLY ABANDONED:	_____		_____		_____	
D. FEES PAID TO CONSULTANTS:	_____		_____		_____	
E. DIRECT REIMBURSABLE (I.E. TRAVEL, PER DIEM, ETC.):	_____		_____		_____	
F. ALL OTHER FEES FOR PROFESSIONAL SERVICES:	_____		_____		_____	
TOTAL FISCAL YEAR (Items D,E & F Only)	_____		_____		_____	

*For A,B and C above, provide the name, location and current status of each project on a separate sheet.

16. Is your firm or any subsidiary, parent or other organization related to your firm engaged in:

A. Actual construction, fabrication or erection: ☐ Yes ☐ No   D. Real Estate development: ☐ Yes ☐ No

B. Design/Build: ☐ Yes ☐ No   E. The manufacture, sale, leasing or distribution of any patented production process: ☐ Yes ☐ No

C. The development of sale of computer software to others: ☐ Yes ☐ No

If answer to any part of question 16 is Yes, please provide full details, including a description of the services performed, construction values involved and fees received: Also enclose sample contract(s). _____

_____

_____

Exhibit 6.2 Continued

17. Are any Principal, Officers, or Employees of your firm engaged in any activities described in question 16? ☐ Yes ☐ No. If yes, please provide full details and relationship of such persons to the firm. _____

_____

18. Has the Applicant, or any of its Principals, Directors or Officers individually or collectively ever maintained a financial interest in any project for which the Applicant has rendered professional services? ☐ Yes ☐ No. BASIC POLICY EXCLUDES COVERAGE FOR EQUITY PROJECTS. If yes, please provide full details of the project, including dates, fees received, coverage provided under current policy (if any) and percentage of the Applicant's, Principals', Director', or Officers' ownership: _____

_____

19. Is the firm or any of its members controlled, owned or associated with any other firm, government entity, Corporation or Company? ☐ Yes ☐ No. If yes, give details: _____

_____

20. Does the Applicant work with other firms in Joint Ventures? ☐ Yes ☐ No. BASIC POLICY EXCLUDES COVERAGE FOR JOINT VENTURES. If coverage is desired, request joint venture supplement form.

21. What percentage of the Applicant's practice involves?

    a. Subletting of work to others _____ %   d. Feasibility Studies _____ %

    b. Type(s) of work sublet _____

    c. Is evidence of insurance from consultants required? ☐ Yes ☐ No.

22. **CONTRACTS**

    A. Do you use written contracts on every project? ☐ Yes ☐ No. If No describe the circumstances when verbal agreements are used: _____

        _____

    B. If non-standard or modified AIA or EJCDC contracts are used, are they reviewed by your legal counsel for liability implications prior to signing? ☐ Yes ☐ No.

    C. Does the firm ever enter into contracts that contain indemnification or "hold harmless" agreements? ☐ Yes ☐ No. If yes, please be aware that the policy provides limited contractual liability coverage only (i.e. limited to negligent acts, errors & omissions of insured).

23. Please specify the approximate percentage of your firm's:

    A. Professional services rendered under AIA or EJCDC standard forms of agreement between Owner and Architect or Engineer:

        _____ %

    B. Projects incorporating specifications based on or derived from the automated master specifications system known as MASTERSPEC: _____ % Do you subscribe to MASTERSPEC? ☐ Yes ☐ No.

    C. Projects ultimately constructed under AIA or EJCDC standard general conditions of the Construction Contract: _____ %

    D. Construction Management services rendered under the unaltered American Institute of Architects B801 Standard form of Agreement: (if any other form is used submit) _____ %

24. **QUALITY CONTROL**

    A. Do you have an in-house quality control procedure? ☐ Yes ☐No.

    B. Is it in written form? ☐ Yes ☐No.

    C. Are all staff members familiar with these procedures? ☐ Yes ☐No.

        Explain if you answered No to any of above: _____

        _____

        _____

    D. Do you have an in-house program of continuing education for employees? ☐ Yes ☐No.

    E. Have members of your firm attended a continuing education seminar in the past 12 months? ☐ Yes ☐No.

Exhibit 6.2 *Continued*

25. **PRIOR INSURANCE**

   A. Has any insurer ever declined, cancelled or refused to renew any similar insurance issued to your firm or any predecessor firm? ☐ Yes ☐No. If yes, give details. _____

_____

_____

_____

_____

   B. Has any similar insurance been issued to any of the firms named in Question 1 or persons named in Question 4 on the application? ☐ Yes ☐No. If yes, complete the following for at least the last five years:

Company	Policy Number	Limits	Deductible	Dates	Premium

   C. Retroactive date in current policy: _____ Please provide a copy of the declarations page or endorsement reflecting above date.

26. Is the Applicant currently insured under a Comprehensive General Liability and/or Umbrella Policy? ☐ Yes ☐No. If yes, give details:

Insurance Company	Type of Coverage	Limits		Effective	
		BI	PD	From	To

27. After inquiry do any of the Principals, Partners, Officers, Employees or Directors have knowledge of any act, error, omission, unresolved job dispute (including owner-contractor disputes), accident or any other circumstance that is or could be a basis for a Claim under the proposed insurance? ☐ Yes ☐No.

     If yes, on a separate sheet give details for each situation, including name of project and claimant, dates, nature of situation and amount of damages.

28. Are there any Claims, suits or demands made in the past ten years (or made earlier and still pending) against your firm, its predecessor(s) or any past or present Principal, Partner, Officer or Director? ☐ Yes ☐No.

     If yes, provide the following information for each claim on a separate sheet:

    A. Date of claim   E. Insurance company reserve (incl. loss & legal expense)

    B. Claimant or plaintiff   F. Defense attorney's evaluation of exposure/potential liability

    C. Allegations   G. If closed, total amount for indemnity and defense costs

    D. Demand or amount of claim   H. Deductible applicable

29. Please attach list of 10 largest jobs in last five years.

     Detail: 1) project name; 2) type of structure; 3) services performed; 4) construction values; and (5) fees.

30. Coverage Requested: Limit _____ Deductible/SIR _____

Please attach any literature, including government forms, which describes the Applicant's capabilities and practice.

Exhibit 6.2 *Continued*

Notice to Applicant: The coverage applied for is SOLELY AS STATED IN THE POLICY, which provides coverage on a "CLAIMS MADE" basis for ONLY THOSE CLAIMS THAT ARE FIRST MADE AND REPORTED AGAINST THE INSURED DURING THE POLICY PERIOD.

I/We hereby declare that the above statements and particulars together witn any attached documents are true and that I/we have not suppressed or mis-stated any material facts. I/We agree that this application, if the insurance coverage applied for is written, shall be the basis of the contract with the insurance company, and be deemed to be a part of the policy to be issued as if physically attached thereto. I/We hereby authorize the release of claims information from any prior insurers to Reliance National Risk Specialists, Inc., Underwriters for the Companies.

NEW YORK APPLICANTS NOTICE: ANY PERSON WHO KNOWINGLY AND WITH INTENT TO DEFRAUD ANY INSURANCE COMPANY OR OTHER PERSON FILES AN APPLICATION FOR INSURANCE CONTAINING ANY FALSE INFORMATION, OR CONCEALS FOR THE PURPOSE OF MISLEADING, INFORMATION CONCERNING ANY FACT MATERIAL THERETO, COMMITS A FRAUDULENT INSURANCE ACT, WHICH IS A CRIME.

It is understood and agreed that the completion of this application does not bind the insurance company to sell nor the applicant to purchase the insurance.

NAME _____

TITLE _____

SIGNATURE _____ DATE _____
            (Principal or Officer)

Note: This application must be reviewed, signed and dated by a principal or officer of the applicant firm.

Exhibit 6.2 *Continued*

While many of the operative terms of the Insuring Agreement require definition, and are usually defined in other sections of the Design Professional Liability Insurance policy, the Insuring Agreement basically sets forth the following:

1. The type of payments the insurer will make on behalf of the insured.

2. The limitation of coverage to only those claims that are first made against the insured *and* reported to the Insurer during the Policy period.

3. The further limitation of coverage to acts, errors, and omissions in the performance of professional services.

4. An enumeration of those entitled to coverage under the policy.

We will now examine the individual elements of the Insuring Agreement and define the operative terms.

A. The first part of the Insuring Agreement states that the insurer will pay damages and claim expenses on behalf of the insured, subject to the policy's limit of liability and deductible. Design Professional Liability Insurance policies generally define *"damages"* as judgments, arbitration awards, and settlements. Significantly however, the definition of damages in most Design Professional Liability Insurance policies does not include punitive or exemplary damages, damages that are a multiple of compensatory damages such as treble damages, fines, penalties, or sanctions.

Claim expenses are generally defined as attorneys' fees and other costs associated with the defense of a claim. Therefore, the first part of the Insuring Agreement essentially provides that the insurer will pay the judgment or settlement of a claim, as well as the attorneys fees and other associated defense costs, subject to the policy's monetary limit of coverage for a claim, and the insured's satisfaction of the deductible obligation.

Unlike general liability policies, professional liability policies are reduced by the payment of claim expenses. Therefore, it is possible that a low policy limit will be entirely or significantly exhausted by claim expenses in the event of a major claim. Items such as pre- and postjudgment interest, court costs, and awards of the prevailing side's attorney fees may be covered as a component of damages or claim expenses, but generally subject to the policy's limit of liability.

B. The second part of the Insuring Agreement limits the policy coverage to those claims that are first made against the insured *and* reported to the insurer during the policy term. Many professional liability insurance policies are now written on this claims made and reported basis, although some policies may provide a more subjective requirement that the claim be reported to the insurance company "as soon as practicable." Others may require reporting by no later than a certain number of days (e.g., 60 or 30 days) after the claim is first made or, in some instances, after the policy expires.

The claims made and reported requirement of the Insuring Agreement renders imperative the insured's immediate action when a claim situation arises. For example, an interior designer has a Design Professional Liability Insurance policy for the term January 1, 1992–January 1, 1993. On July 3, 1990 the Interior Designer was engaged by the owner of an office building to prepare plans and specifications for the addition of an interior stairway between two floors of the office building, and completes performance of the contract on November 3, 1990. On February 1, 1991 an individual is injured on the stairway and commences a lawsuit against the building owner on February 1, 1992, who in turn immediately files suit against and serves process on the interior designer alleging negligent design. Pursuant to the Insuring Agreement, in order for coverage to attach, the interior designer would have to report this claim during the January 1, 1992–January 1, 1993 policy term. However, other conditions of the policy would actually require the interior designer to report such a claim immediately upon receipt of the lawsuit.

The example described above reveals some important aspects of the claims made and reported requirement. Significantly, it is not necessary for the incident, in this example the injury, to occur during the policy term. Also, even if the injury occurs during the policy period, and the claim is asserted against the insured during the policy period, there will be no coverage for the claim unless the insured reports the claim to the insurer during the policy period. This becomes critically important when a claim is asserted against an insured close to the time of policy expiration.

As will be discussed later in this chapter, sometimes a policy may employ a feature known as a retroactive date or prior acts date. In such cases, the insurer will not provide coverage for claims based upon or arising from acts taking place prior to such date. Retroactive dates are commonly employed on policies wherein the insured is purchasing professional liability coverage for the first time or after a lapse in continuous coverage. This is because the insurer will want to protect itself from the possibility that the insured has decided to enter or reenter the market because it knows it has committed an act, error, or omission likely to result in a claim.

C. The third key element of the Insuring Agreement is the limitation of coverage to acts, errors, or omissions by the design professional in the performance of *professional services.* The definition of professional services is based upon the design professional's area(s) of practice as disclosed by the design professional on the application for the policy. Since coverage is limited to only those disciplines that are disclosed on the application, it is very important for the design professional to carefully complete the application, being certain to disclose not only current areas of practice, but also those areas in which the design professional may have previously practiced. Two simple examples will demonstrate the importance of this part of the Insuring Agreement.

In the first example, an interior designer purchases a Design Professional Liability Insurance policy and on the application for the policy identifies interior design as the sole area of practice. Therefore, in the unlikely event a claim is asserted against the interior designer for negligence in the design of a building's landscape, the policy would not respond since landscape architecture was not included by the design professional on the policy application. In the second example, the same interior designer with the same policy of insurance is sued for nonperformance of a contract to perform interior design services. In this case the policy would again not provide coverage even though the contract was for professional services. The reason is that the Insuring Agreement limits coverage to acts, errors, or omissions in the *performance* of professional services, but the policy does not provide coverage for *nonperformance* of professional services.

D. The final key element of the Insuring Agreement is the identification of those for whom coverage under the policy will be afforded. While oftentimes Design Professional Liability Insurance policies are amended for an additional premium to include a schedule of other persons or entities to be covered by the policy, coverage is generally afforded only to the "Named Insured," which is typically defined as the person or entity to whom the policy is issued. If the named insured is a corporation, coverage is generally afforded not only to the corporation itself, but also to the directors and officers of the corporation. Coverage is also generally afforded to present or former owners, partners, directors, officers, and employees of the named insured but only to the extent that such persons' actions were undertaken on behalf of the named insured and relate to Professional Services.

Definition of "Claim"   Design Professional Liability Insurance policies generally define the term *Claim* as a demand made on the insured for money or professional services arising out of an act, error, or omission in the performance of professional services. As previously discussed, professional services are defined as those areas of practice disclosed by the insured on the policy application.

The most familiar forms of claims are lawsuits and demands for arbitration in which monetary awards are sought. However, pursuant to the policy, a claim may simply be the receipt of a letter by the insured from a party for whom the insured performed professional services, in which a demand for money is made against the insured relative to the insured's performance of professional services. As previously discussed, in light of the claims made and reported requirements of the typical Design Professional Liability

Insurance policy, all claims, whether in the form of a lawsuit or otherwise, should immediately be reported by the design professional to the insurance carrier. In addition to the obvious need to secure the available insurance coverage, many times the insurance carrier will be able to assist the insured in resolving a claim before litigation is actually commenced against the insured.

Awareness Provision or Discovery Clause   Many Design Professional Liability policies now offer the insured the opportunity to report not only claims, but also incidents or circumstances which may subsequently give rise to a claim. This policy feature is generally referred to as an *awareness provision or discovery clause*.

Awareness provisions or discovery clauses generally allow the insured to report an act, error, or omission which the insured first becomes aware of during the policy term, and for which coverage would otherwise apply. If such matters are properly reported to the insurer during the policy period, a claim asserted against the insured at a later date, even after policy expiration, arising from such reported acts, errors, or omissions, will be deemed to have been made on the date the insurer received notice of the acts, errors, or omissions, and insurance coverage will be provided for the claim. The design professional may be inclined to report every instance of a client's dissatisfaction on a project under the discovery clause or awareness provision. However, these provisions generally require specificity regarding the design professional's alleged act, error, or omission. Unless the requisite information is provided, the reporting of a matter by the design professional to the Insurer will not serve to secure future coverage for a claim that may later arise. The following example will demonstrate why the inclusion of an awareness provision or discovery clause in the design professional liability Insurance policy is a tremendous benefit to the insured.

Let us reexamine one of the examples addressed earlier in this chapter in which an interior designer has a design Professional Liability Insurance policy for the term January 1, 1992–January 1, 1993 and was engaged on July 3, 1990 by an office building owner to design an interior stairway between two floors of an office building, completing performance on November 3, 1990. On February 1, 1991 an individual suffers an injury on the stairway and sues the building owner on February 1, 1992. In this example, however, the building owner does not immediately join the Interior Designer to the litigation, but instead notifies the Interior Designer for the first time of the injury, and only threatens to join the interior designer to the litigation based upon the owner's belief that the interior designer *may* have been negligent in preparing the plans and specifications for the stairway. If the interior designer properly advises the insurance carrier of this potentially alleged error during the January 1, 1992–January 1, 1993 policy term, that policy will provide coverage in the event the owner ultimately asserts the threatened claim. This is true even if the owner asserts the claim long after the policy has expired, and even if the insured does not renew the January 1, 1992–January 1, 1993 policy or renews with another insurance carrier. The claim, no matter when it is asserted against the insured, will be deemed to have been made on the date the insurance carrier received written notice of the threatened claim. The insured may wish to document the insurance carrier's date of receipt by sending the written notice by certified mail, return receipt requested.

Full Prior Acts Coverage As previously addressed, most professional liability policies issued today are written on a claims made and reported basis. However, the design professional in most instances can negotiate whether the policy will provide coverage for claims arising out of professional services performed many years ago, even dating back to the time the design professional opened its doors for business, or whether the policy will only provide coverage for professional services performed since a certain date, perhaps the inception date of the policy.

If a policy offers *full prior acts coverage*, it means that subject to all of the terms of the policy, claims arising from professional services performed by the insured at any time will be covered. The inclusion of a *retroactive date* in a policy generally means that coverage is limited to claims arising from professional services performed by the insured subsequent to the retroactive date.

Full prior acts coverage is generally provided when the policy contains no retroactive date, or includes as a retroactive date the date the design professional entity came into existence. Let's once again examine the example in which an interior designer has a Design Professional Liability Insurance policy for the term January 1, 1992–January 1, 1993, and completes the performance of a professional services engagement for an office building owner on November 3, 1990. If the policy contains a retroactive date the same as the inception date of the policy, January 1, 1992, there will be no coverage afforded by the policy for the claim arising from an injury on the stairway, or any other claim related to the interior designer's plans and specifications of the stairway since all professional services relative to the stairway were performed prior to the retroactive date of January 1, 1992. However, if the policy contains no retroactive date, the interior designer will have full prior acts coverage, and coverage will be afforded subject to the other policy terms and conditions for the injury claim, and any other claims relative to the insured's professional services on the stairway.

Limit of Liability The extent to which a Design Professional Liability Insurance Policy will cover a claim is generally referred to as the policy *limit of liability*. The limit of liability generally encompasses damages such as judgments or settlements, and claim expenses which are typically the costs associated with the defense of the insured.

Most Design Professional Liability Insurance policies offer a limit of liability for each claim, as well as an aggregate limit of liability for the policy term. For example, a policy may offer limits of liability of $1,000,000 for each claim, and $2,000,000 in the aggregate. If under such a policy, a judgment is entered against the insured for $2,000,000, and there has been no other impairment to the limit of liability, the policy would only provide $1,000,000, less any incurred claim expenses, toward satisfaction of the $2,000,000 judgment. To avoid this deficiency, most policies today are written with the same limit of liability for each claim and the aggregate. Therefore, if a policy carries limits of liability of $2,000,000 for each claim and in the aggregate, in the event of a $2,000,000 judgment, the policy will provide $2,000,000, less any incurred claim expenses toward satisfaction of the $2,000,000 judgment, provided there has not been any impairment to the policy aggregate for other claims.

While having the same limit of liability on a per claim and aggregate basis provides increased coverage for the single claim, it potentially leaves the insured without coverage for future claims during the policy period in the event the single claim exhausts the entire aggregate limit of liability. The selection of the appropriate amount to carry as a Limit of Liability is therefore critically important, and should be discussed thoroughly with a qualified insurance broker.

Some of the factors to be considered by the design professional when selecting the policy limits of liability are:

1. *Contractual Requirements.* Oftentimes contracts between design professionals and owners mandate that a certain minimum limit of liability be maintained.

2. *Construction Values.* While the authors have been involved with relatively modest projects in terms of monetary value that have given rise to extremely significant claims, generally the greater the construction value of the projects in which the design professional is involved, the greater the potential for more costly claims being asserted.

3. *Cost of Obtaining a Greater Limit of Liability.* In many instances the additional premium charged for a higher limit of liability is relatively modest. A design professional considering a $1,000,000 limit of liability may be quite surprised to discover that a $2,000,000 limit of liability is not significantly more money in terms of premium.

Claim Expenses   The policy limit of liability generally includes claim expenses, although as will be discussed below, some states now require that claim expenses, such as attorneys fees incurred in defending an insured, be in addition to the limit of liability. With the ever increasing costs of litigation, the general inclusion of claim expenses within the policy limit of liability is oftentimes a key factor in determining litigation strategy. For example, if a design professional with a $500,000 limit of liability policy is made a party to a complex, multiparty litigation, a decision must be made very early as to whether a vigorous defense of the insured on the merits of the case should be undertaken in light of the costs associated with protracted litigation, or if instead an early settlement should be explored. Since defense costs will erode the $500,000 limit of liability, every effort must be made to preserve as much of the limit of liability as possible for funding a judgment or, if possible, a settlement of the matter. Although usually avoidable, the worst case scenario sometimes occurs where an insured's entire limit of liability is exhausted by the costs of defense, and the insured is left without any coverage to fund a settlement or judgment. This scenario generally occurs only in cases of extraordinary circumstances, or where the insured has an insufficient limit of liability.

Statutory/Regulatory Exceptions to Defense within Limits While the insurer may occasionally be willing to freely negotiate with the insured—for considerable additional premium—a policy that provides defense cost coverage in addition to the limits of liability, a few states now mandate that the defense costs coverage be in addition to the policy limits unless the policy meets certain criteria that would take it outside the scope of the applicable regulation.

An example of such a regulatory scheme would be that imposed by the New York State Insurance Department under what is commonly referenced as Regulation 207. Presently, this regulation only has applicability to policies written with a total limit of liability of less than $500,000. Such low limits would be appropriate only for smaller design firms or sole practitioners, and many insurers have sought to escape the impact of the regulation by only offering policy limits above this threshold.

Although the regulation is somewhat convoluted in its application, an insurer would still be able to offer a policy with defense costs included within the limits, if that policy met the following criteria:

1. The policy had a limit of liability of $500,000 or greater.
2. The insured had the right to select its own defense counsel, subject only to the insurer's reasonable consent.
3. The insurer offered alternative policies at different premiums which provided defense costs in addition to the limits.

Regulations such as these have been enacted or are being considered in other states to protect insureds with low policy limits from having those limits completely eroded by defense expenses, and thus having no effective insurance protection for settlement or judgment amounts. Of course, most states do not offer such regulatory protection to an insured and there the insured must be sure to purchase a policy with sufficient limits to account for anticipated large defense cost exposure.

Deductibles and Self-Insured Retention   Most Design Professional Liability Insurance policies on the market today include a provision which obligates the insured to assume responsibility for a portion of the damages and claim expenses arising from a claim. This provision is generally provided as either a *deductible* or *self-insured retention.*

Deductibles are more commonly found in Design Professional Liability Insurance policies. Under a policy carrying a deductible, coverage for a claim is triggered immediately, subject only to the insured's obligation to satisfy the deductible amount. In contrast, however, under a policy that provides for a self-insured retention, no coverage is triggered for a claim unless and until the Insured satisfies the self-insured retention. Therefore, under policies carrying a self-insured retention, the insurance carrier generally has no duty to appoint defense counsel or take any other action until the self-insured retention is satisfied.

The selection of the appropriate level of a deductible or self-insured retention is another area which should be discussed with a qualified insurance broker. While the premium charged for a policy decreases as the amount of the deductible or self-insured retention increases, the design professional must be realistic in assessing ability to fund the deductible or self-insured retention. Unless a policy is changed by endorsement, the deductible or self-insured retention obligation generally applies to each and every claim. Therefore, one of the key considerations in selecting an amount for a deductible or self-insured retention should be the design professional's loss history, particularly with regard to frequency.

Some insurance carriers now offer a *shared expense deductible* endorsement for an additional premium. Such endorsements require the insurance carrier to assume a portion of the claim expenses within the stated deductible. These endorsements are generally only available to those design professionals that carry a smaller deductible.

Exclusions   All Design Professional Liability Insurance policies contain *exclusions* on the coverage afforded by the policy. Insurance carriers generally exclude coverage for liabilities which are more appropriately covered under other types of insurance policies, and for liabilities that the insurer simply prefers not to undertake because of unfavorable past experience, or a perceived unacceptable level of risk. However, insurance carriers may negotiate the revision of some exclusions, and in some instances delete an exclusion for an additional premium. While most Design Professional

Liability Insurance policies contain several exclusions, the most common are discussed below:

1. Design Professional Liability Insurance policies generally do not provide coverage for claims arising from the insured's agreement to undertake another party's liabilities, unless the insured would have been responsible for those liabilities even in the absence of the agreement. The import of this exclusion is that if the insured enters into a contract that obligates the insured to assume liabilities that the insured would not have had but for the contract, no coverage will be provided for any claims that may arise from such an undertaking. Therefore, an insured would be well advised to have all contracts, particularly those that contain indemnification provisions, reviewed by the insurance carrier and an attorney experienced in this area, prior to execution of the contract.

2. Design Professional Liability Insurance policies generally preclude coverage for liabilities arising from the insured's activities on behalf of an entity other than the one for which the insurance coverage was purchased. For example, firm ABC purchases an Architects and Engineers Professional Liability Insurance policy. Mr. A, a partner in the ABC firm, is also an officer of firm XXX. Pursuant to this exclusion, no coverage will be afforded to Mr. A under the ABC policy for Mr. A's liabilities arising from his activities on behalf of XXX. However, if firm XXX is added by endorsement to the ABC policy (for additional premium), as an additional named insured, Mr. A would be covered for a claim arising from the scope of his activities with XXX. This type of exclusion also precludes coverage for liabilities arising from the insured's participation in a joint venture. Again, the policy may be endorsed to include specific joint venture(s) in which the insured is participating. However, such endorsements typically limit coverage to only the insured's participation in the joint venture, and generally do not provide coverage for all of the joint venture partners.

3. Design Professional Liability Insurance policies typically exclude coverage for claims asserted against the insured by any person or entity having a past or present ownership, operating, or management interest in the insured. The exclusion conversely precludes coverage for claims asserted by the insured against any entity presently or previously owned, operated, or managed by the insured. The intent behind the exclusion is to have the insurer avoid potentially collusive claims brought solely to take advantage of the existence of insurance.

4. Claims arising from an injury or death of an employee of the insured are generally excluded by Design Professional Liability Insurance policies. Liabilities of this nature are more appropriately within the purview of worker's compensation insurance coverage and/or disability benefits law.

5. Claims arising from the insolvency or bankruptcy of the insured are specifically excluded by Design Professional Liability Insurance policies. While a bankruptcy filing will engender many claims against an insured from its creditors and/or clients, such claims do not necessarily relate to acts, errors, or omissions in the performance of professional services. The insurance carrier employs this exclusion to ensure that it does not become a guarantor of such obligations outside the scope of insured professional services.

6. Design Professional Liability Insurance policies generally exclude coverage for claims arising from an insured's rendering (or failing to render) advice with regard to insurance, suretyship, or bonds. The rendering of such advice is generally not within a design professional's area of expertise, and hence the exclusion from coverage for such activities.

7. Design Professional Liability Insurance policies typically exclude coverage for activities that are unrelated to the insured's performance of professional services. Therefore, claims arising from the insured's ownership, rental, leasing, operation, maintenance, use, or repair of any real or personal property are generally excluded. Likewise claims arising from the insured's ownership, maintenance, operation, or use of a motor vehicle are generally excluded. In most instances the insured will have other insurance, such as comprehensive general liability and auto insurance, to respond to these types of claims.

8. Claims arising from the insured's express warranties or guarantees are generally excluded from coverage under Design Professional Liability Insurance policies. The making of an express warranty or guarantee would subject the insured and the insurance carrier to a higher standard of care than that imposed under principles of common law negligence. Insurance carriers do not wish to assume the greater liability associated with an express warranty or guarantee, and therefore specifically exclude coverage in this regard.

9. The intent of the Design Professional Liability Insurance policy is to provide coverage for claims arising out of the insured's negligence in performing professional services. Accordingly, most Design Professional Insurance policies specifically exclude coverage for claims *intentionally* caused by the insured or which arise from the insured's *dishonest, fraudulent, malicious,* or *knowingly wrongful* acts.

10. In light of the significant losses previously incurred by insurance carriers relative to asbestos, Design Professional Liability Insurance policies typically contain a broad exclusion for claims arising from the insured's specification or recommendation of asbestos in any form, asbestos exposure assessments, or appraisal of asbestos containment/removal programs or any claim based upon, involving, or arising out of the use of or exposure to asbestos or products containing asbestos.

11. Because of the proliferation of litigation involving pollution and the significant remediation and clean-up costs associated with the discharge of pollutants, Design Professional Liability insurance policies usually contain various forms of pollution exclusions. These exclusions typically preclude coverage for claims arising from any actual, alleged, or threatened discharge, dispersal, release, or escape of pollutants. The exclusion further precludes coverage for claims arising from a government or regulatory directive or request to test for, monitor, clean up, remove, contain, treat, detoxify, or neutralize pollutants. Design Professional Liability insurance policies typically define *pollutants* as any solid, liquid, gaseous, or thermal irritant or contaminant, including smoke, vapor, soot, fumes, acids, alkalis, chemicals, and waste (including materials to be recycled, reconditioned, or reclaimed).

It is important to note that the typical pollution exclusion does not apply to claims arising from the performance of professional services by the insured in the design and construction of treatment systems for:

1. Domestic sewerage including those receiving industrial waste. The industrial waste must be pretreated in accordance with applicable governmental or regulatory standards.
2. Potable water.
3. Water from rain, hail, snow, or sleet.

Several insurance carriers are now offering less restrictive pollution exclusions on their Design Professional Liability Insurance policies. The availability of such enhanced pollution coverage is often limited to a lower policy limit, and the cost of such coverage can be significant.

WORKING WITH THE INSURER WHEN A CLAIM ARISES

Considerations in Selecting a Carrier and Broker

Although both the insurance carrier and the broker will already be in place at the time the claim arises, both of these parties and their personnel are critical to the effective handling of a claim on behalf of the design professional.

As discussed in the introductory overview to this chapter, it is important to deal with brokers and insurers who are knowledgeable in the area of design professional liability and, since the essential product being purchased under an insurance contract is claims service, one must assess the qualifications of the broker and insurer in this area.

With regard to the broker, some key questions to explore are the following:

1. What percentage of the *individual* broker's total business is design professional related? What percentage is this of the total of his/her *office's* business?

2. Will the broker be able to place your business directly with an insurer or will a wholesale broker be utilized? If a wholesale broker will be involved, ask the same questions of that broker as in No. 1.

3. What continuing education does the broker undergo and what may be available to you as the client in the way of seminars, books, and other material?

The following questions should be asked of the broker about the insurer:

1. How much design professional premium is written on an annual basis?

2. Is there a separate underwriting staff dedicated solely to design professional liability? If so, how large is it and what are the qualifications of the underwriters? Ask for brief biographic sketches of key personnel.

3. What about the claims department? Is there a separate staff dedicated to handling design professional claims? Obtain brief biographic sketches and copies of any writings the staff has done at seminars and conferences or in professional publications. Design professional liability claims can be quite complex and it is usually desirable for an insurer to employ claims staff in this area with legal training and/or an engineering or design background.

4. Does the insurer have an acceptable financial rating from one or more of the recognized agencies that provide such ratings for the industry? Ask your broker to explain the rating system and provide you with copies of the ratings and analyses done on the insurer by all of the rating firms.

Choice of Defense Counsel

More often than not, the insurer will retain the right to select defense counsel under the design professional liability policy. However, as discussed above, sometimes applicable state insurance laws or regulations may not permit the insurer to do so, unless the insured receives other benefits (such as defense costs being paid *in addition to* the limits of liability). Also, where an insured is carrying a rather large deductible or retention, the insurer may endorse the policy to permit the insured to select counsel subject to the insurer's reasonable consent. Thus the insured may select its own defense counsel and the insurance company will pay these expenses after the deductible is satisfied.

Regardless of who selects counsel, it is important to choose counsel that is experienced in both litigation and construction and design-related litigation in particular. As such, counsel who regularly performs transactional work for the design professional, including contract and lease negotiations and other general services, may not necessarily be the best choice for defense counsel despite having familiarity with the general operations of the design practice.

When the insurer selects, it must be careful to employ counsel who are likewise experienced and not arbitrarily resort to a set "panel" of counsel based upon geographic location.

Although competency and qualifications should be the paramount concern, cost is not a factor to be overlooked. Because an insurer is generally a volume purchaser of legal services, it can usually secure the most favorable billing rates. Accordingly, even when the insured may select its own counsel, counsel may have to be negotiable in its rates.

Reservations of Rights and Other Coverage Issues

Upon receipt of notice of a claim from an insured, the insurer must essentially respond in one of three alternative ways after reviewing the substance of the claim in light of the insurance policy.

First, it may determine unconditionally that the claim is covered under the policy. In such a case, the insurer will generally proceed to appoint counsel (if so permitted by the policy and at law) and confirm to the insured the available limits under the policy and the appropriate deductible to be borne.

Second, the insurer may determine that the claim is clearly not covered under the policy. If so, the insurer must promptly communicate that decision to the insured and be explicit as to its reasons for denying coverage. If the insured believes the insurer is misinterpreting certain information or the insured has in its possession information or materials that it believes may cause the insurer to change its decision, it should promptly, clearly, and comprehensively communicate back to the insured. Also, in this situation the insurer must immediately retain counsel to defend the suit against it at its own expense.

The third possibility is that the insurer will reserve its rights to later deny coverage based upon certain facts that it might only develop through future investigation. As with a denial of coverage, a reservation of rights must also be communicated to the insured clearly, comprehensively, and promptly. While the insured should promptly respond with any disagreements it may have, it is important for the insured to appreciate that, unlike a denial of coverage, it is going to be provided with a defense and the insurer may, in certain factual situations, never get to a position to later "convert" the reservations into a denial of coverage. In some situations, particularly where investigation establishes a misrepresentation in the application for insurance, the reservation may evolve into a denial of coverage and the insured would be liable to repay defense expenses paid on its behalf by the insurance company.

Nonetheless, it would be prudent for the insured to consult with independent counsel upon receipt of a reservation of rights. In some jurisdictions, the insurer will not be permitted to appoint defense counsel when it defends under a reservation of rights. In California, under some reservation scenarios, the insurer may appoint defense counsel but must also reimburse the insured for the cost of its own counsel, whom it retains to protect its uninsured or potentially uninsured interests.

Beyond the legal implications, there are some practical considerations to be understood with regard to reservations of rights.

How many times have you felt that your insurance carrier is telling you, "You really didn't expect us to pay anything under this insurance policy, did you?" Too often that is precisely the type of response many insureds and brokers believe they are hearing from the insurer upon submission of a claim. Is the insurance contract nothing more than a few pieces of paper intended solely to give psychological comfort to insureds but no financial benefits whatsoever?

Because an insurance policy is a contract between the insurer and its insured, it must be understood by the latter that the submission of a claim or incident report triggers certain legal rights, duties, and obligations under that contract on the part of both the insured and the insurer.

Unfortunately, these obligations are not always crystal clear at the outset of a given claim situation. Therefore, it is of mutual benefit to both the insurer and the insured for the insurer to reserve rights on a number of issues and promptly communicate those reservations to its insured in writing and with sufficient detail. Hopefully, further development of facts will resolve the reservations or at least bring the insurer to a point where it would be willing to entertain a compromise resolution of the disputed issues.

This is particularly true in the areas of Professional Liability and Errors and Omissions Insurance, including Design Professional Liability, where almost every report of a claim or incident would warrant the insurer's *reservation of rights*.

Here are two reasons why insurers must reserve rights.

1. Almost all of these policies contain a provision that excludes from coverage dishonesty and/or other fraudulent or intentional misconduct. Given the propensity of plaintiffs to assert claims of such intentional wrongs in addition to negligence counts, the insurer has no choice but to reserve the right to deny coverage should such dishonest or intentional conduct be material to any recovery by the plaintiff. Of course, many policies require an *adjudication* before this exclusion can be applied and thus its ultimate application is rare.

2. Many claims involve allegations of wrongful activity which occurred well before the application for and the inception of the policy. While this does not per se suggest misrepresentation on the part of an insured in the

application process, it behooves the insurer to inquire as to when an insured first knew of the claim or the facts or circumstances that gave rise to the claim. Remember, this is only an *inquiry* and not an *accusation.* If an insured discloses the facts fully and promptly and the subsequent investigation supports that response, then the prior knowledge issue is usually resolved.

A reservation of rights or other coverage letter should not create an adversarial relationship between the insurer and the insured. In most claim situations, all the insurer has at the inception of the claim are various unsubstantiated allegations and, at best, a few confirmed facts. In reserving rights, the insurer is merely telling the policyholder of its concerns that the claim may, in whole or in part, not be covered under the policy pending further investigation.

A reservation of rights letter, while obviously sent to protect the interests of the insurer, is also beneficial to the insured. It alerts the insured that some of the elements of the claim may not be covered, thereby allowing the insured to take necessary steps to protect its potentially uninsured interests, such as by retaining an independent counsel or putting aside funds to cover the potentially uninsured exposure. Further, if the insurer and the insured are to have any disputes over coverage or other issues, such matters can be addressed early on and resolved in an amicable manner.

As discussed above, the development of solid factual information facilitates the resolution of many coverage issues. Oftentimes the requisite facts and information are in the possession of the insured and not the insurer. Providing necessary information to the insurer can help resolve many disputed coverage issues and enable both parties to go forward in the common cause of protecting the insured's interest.

Settlement Considerations

Expense, Time, and Risk Factors   Many people who do not regularly deal with litigation and the judicial system are often surprised to learn that somewhat less than 5% of all lawsuits initiated ultimately proceed to trial and have a verdict returned by either a judge or jury. Although some litigation is disposed of before trial, by either summary judgment or dismissal, the vast majority of litigated claims are *settled* in the course of voluntary or judicially assisted discussions among the parties to the dispute.

Why is this so?

First, continuing litigation through a trial on the merits is an expensive proposition. In a complicated matter, costs can easily reach into six figures and even exceed seven figures or more when one considers outside legal costs, expert witnesses, other litigation support services, and the diversion from pursuing other business because the design professional must necessarily assist in the defense of the claims asserted.

Somewhat related to the latter cost element is the burden of time expended by the design professional in the litigation process. The duration of most litigation is measured in terms of years, and not months or some shorter interval. In the case of long-lived litigation, the design professional will be called upon to assist in preparing answers to interrogatories, to prepare for and submit to deposition or other form of pretrial examination, to explain various business and technical issues to counsel and others, and to be available to testify at and perhaps attend a significant portion of a trial. Needless to say, all of this is activity that is not generating any revenue for the designer and is precluding him or her from pursuing more profitable endeavors.

The last element to consider is risk, which is a two-edged sword that dangles over the heads of both plaintiffs and defendants and either overtly or subconsciously pushes the parties into a settlement mode. Under the American system of jurisprudence, determinations as to facts will be made by a jury or by a judge (in a nonjury trial). In any event, both judges and juries are lay persons with regard to the design profession and, despite the best efforts of counsel and expert witnesses, may fail to grasp the facts as well as could another design professional.

Unfortunately for the designer, the exposure in a given claim situation can far exceed the amount of fees the project generated. Our judicial system allows for the possible recovery of varied consequential damages that may far exceed the available insurance policy limits and which may potentially bankrupt the individual designer, the practice, or both. It is difficult, if not impossible, to objectively predict what award will be rendered by a jury or even a judge, who oftentimes will have difficulty comprehending the complex factual issues presented in a claim situation.

Of course, these are risks that the plaintiff must also consider. Especially where evidence of liability is weak, a million dollar damage claim may have an effective settlement value of only a small fraction of that figure. Likewise, damages cannot always be accurately assessed and there may be legitimately wide discrepancies between plaintiff's and defendant's assessments.

Hence in many cases settlement becomes the only reasonable alternative.

Consent to Settle Clause   Design professional liability policies will almost always contain a provision to the following effect:

> The insurer will not settle any claim without the insured's consent. If the insured refuses to consent to a settlement recommended by the insurer, then the insurer's obligation to the insured will be capped at the amount for which the claim could have been settled plus defense expenses through the date the insured refused to consent to settlement.

Somewhat pejoratively this is often referred to as a "hammer clause" because it ensures that the insured does not cavalierly treat the insurer's desire to enter into a reasonable settlement. Of course, at issue here are two sometimes competing interests.

On one hand, the designer has a legitimate interest in seeing that his or her professional reputation is not sullied by the settlement of claims of questionable merit. Also, the designer may have a significant financial stake to the extent the policy has a large deductible.

The insurer, on the other hand, has a right to minimize its own exposure within the policy limits by settling to avoid future defense costs and the risks of a verdict at trial far in excess of the present settlement value of the case.

Regardless of whether the suit is settled or tried to a conclusion, it may have an adverse impact on future premium levels for the policy.

With regard to professional reputation concerns, there are numerous ways to alleviate the adverse impacts of a settlement.

First, the litigation can be settled under the protection of a strict confidentiality order and perhaps even sealing of the litigation records if the court will approve.

If such remedy is not available, appropriate press releases or other documents such as a client newsletter can be issued to indicate that the designer continues to dispute the merits of the claim but is consenting to settle only to accommodate the legitimate business interests of the insurer.

Last, most parties concerned will appreciate that litigation is not always indicative of any problem with the designer's practice or professional competence, regardless of how the litigation is disposed of. Increasingly, sophisticated business people are becoming aware that insurers often "call the shots" as to settlement and that the settlement decision should not necessarily reflect badly upon the professional. Indeed, the releases and other settlement papers filed will undoubtedly contain recitals to the effect that the design professional is not admitting liability in any regard.

7

Interior Design Contracts

As the practice of interior design has evolved into a profession, interior designers have become increasingly concerned about their contracts with clients and with minimizing legal liability. This is one of the most common reasons design clients come to me for legal advice—to review their existing contracts and revise them or draft new ones. They also want to know how they can better manage their practices to avoid problems.

Although the length of contracts may vary, depending on the type of project and the scope of the work, many issues must be addressed in all contracts to avoid misunderstandings and disputes. An attorney who is knowledgeable in this area can help you to draft a succinct contract which covers all the important issues and still protects you or your firm.

There are only a handful of lawyers in the country who concentrate on legal issues involving interior design contracts and litigation. For this reason, many people rely on printed, form contracts published by organizations such as the American Society of Interior Designers and the American Institute of Architects. Clients and designers feel safe using them because major organizations have endorsed them and they form the basis for standards of practice in the industry.

These contracts are very good and cover the important areas, but they do not always meet the parties' special needs for their particular project. Thus the contract may have to be extensively modified with riders and have sections crossed out to tailor it to a given project. This can sometimes make for a messy contract which is very difficult to read and understand. It may also create ambiguities if riders that are added conflict with the printed contract or if changes are not clearly made.

Some designers who do not use these forms draft their own contracts by combining provisions from friends' contracts, books they have read, form contracts, and their own made-up language. These practices can result in poorly drafted contracts which do not provide adequate legal protection or address their interests in the project. Similarly, the designer's clients and their attorneys, who do not always understand the construction industry, also sign contracts without understanding the ramifications of the documents. All this can lead to litigation problems.

As more and more people work with interior designers and spend large sums of money on decorating and renovating their homes and businesses, these contracts become more and more important. They are critical if any litigation should result from the project. Form contracts cannot be blithely signed without understanding their provisions. Designers and clients should understand that often a nonform contract may be more appropriate for the project.

Every designer does different types of work and works differently with their clients. Some mostly handle decorating and purchasing furniture for residential clients. Others are involved in large-scale office renovations and work closely with architects and various consultants. Some designers use sketches and color renderings to show the placement of furniture, while others prepare elaborate architectural-type drawings. Every designer has a different style of working. Therefore, every designer has different contract needs.

Negotiating a contract is not about getting everything you want. The final contract should strike a balance between what both parties want and should reflect a "meeting of the minds." The contract which is ultimately signed should be a document that reflects what both parties have agreed to. Once the contract is signed, it should not be stuck away in a drawer until a dispute arises. Rather, it should be referred to any time the parties are unsure about what was agreed to.

PROPOSALS VERSUS CONTRACTS

Often a client will ask a designer to submit a written proposal to give him an idea of the scope of the work that will be done and the price. These are almost always in a letter format and can sometimes be quite lengthy. When they are too lengthy, they start to look like contracts and consequently some clients tend to treat them as such and proceed with the project without actually ever signing a contract. This is undesirable from the designer's perspective.

A proposal is not a contract and should not be treated as one because many important terms are missing. They are not drafted to be contracts. If an issue arises which has not been addressed in the proposal, it will be unclear what the parties agreed to. The parties then have to negotiate in the middle of the project. If the issue cannot be resolved and litigation results, the proposal may be no more than some evidence of the parties' understanding.

A proposal should be brief and describe in general summary terms what will be done. It should state that if the client agrees to go forward, a contract will then be sent to him for signature. It can also state in summary fashion some of the areas that will be contained in the contract, for example, "Our contract will contain provisions allowing us to own our drawings and for us to agree to use arbitration in the event of a dispute."

Designers often request that the client sign the proposal as a gesture of their intent to proceed, but again, this should not be viewed as the contract.

FORM VERSUS NONFORM CONTRACTS

Many people like to use form contracts because they believe that the provisions reflect industry standards and have been tested in court cases. This is not necessarily true. No matter how many times a form contract is used, should a dispute arise, the facts of the particular case will have to be litigated just like any other contract case. Expert witnesses will be required to explain what the standards are in the industry and in their locale, whether the designer was in compliance with them, and what the contract language means based on the way the industry operates. Unfortunately, using form contracts does not necessarily lessen the likelihood of litigation.

Form contracts are recommended if:

1. They suit the project being undertaken.
2. The parties cannot afford to have a contract drafted or reviewed by an attorney.
3. The parties do not have access in their area to the kind of legal expertise needed to draft such a contract.
4. They are reviewed by an attorney who knows this area of the law.
5. They contain a rider with any special provisions and delete the inapplicable ones.

One of the worst aspects of form contracts is that because they are printed, people often do not bother to read them. People feel that if an organization has had them printed, the terms are etched in stone. Consequently, neither party knows what he is signing until the issue is raised in a dispute or a lawsuit. These documents also tend to be very long, which makes the parties and sometimes their attorney less than enthusiastic about reading them cover to cover. I advise all students of design and practicing professionals to read a form contract word for word at least once as an exercise in understanding contracts.

An interior design contract should be easy to read and understand by lay people and long enough to cover the essential points. It can be in the form of a letter agreement on the interior designer's letterhead, as long as it is clear that it is a contract, contains all the essential terms, and is signed by both parties.

Form contracts should be completely filled in and any riders should be clearly identified as being part of the contract and signed as well. Pages should always be numbered to avoid situations where someone inserts a different page with different provisions.

It also goes without saying that a signed contract is a must. Not having a contract can be an expensive mistake—usually more so for the interior designer than the client. So much testimony is needed to prove the designer's entitlement to fees that it can become economically burdensome, if not impossible, for the designer to pursue such a claim. Invariably the designer will forego many dollars in design fees. Having a signed contract makes your claim for fees that much stronger.

LENGTH OF THE CONTRACT

I am often asked how long the contract should be. There is no magic number of pages. Length is not as important as being thorough. Many interior designers feel that long contracts will scare their clients away. No contract should scare a serious client away. It may scare a client who is having second thoughts about committing to the project because of budget constraints. Such clients will be problematic anyway. Clients should *want* to have a signed contract as much as the designer does. They are spending a lot of money and they should know how it is being spent.

A typical contract for a small- to medium-sized project should be approximately 3–5 pages long. A contract for a larger project may be 8–12 pages long. Certain government contracts can be the length of a small book. The important point to remember is that the content of the contract is what is important, not the length.

An attorney who knows this area of the law can draft such a contract, which can be reused with appropriate modifications by a designer on other projects. This avoids the awkwardness of crossing out provisions in printed contracts which the client can read anyway and having lengthy riders attached. The final contract should only have in it what the parties agree should be in it. Important provisions should not be omitted solely to shorten the contract. There may be more condensed ways to phrase something.

DRAFTING THE CONTRACTS

Usually the designer will present the first draft of the contract for the project to the client. The client or his attorney will have some comments and eventually a final agreement will be reached and the contract signed.

It is rare for the client to insist on drafting the contract. I find that this happens most often with corporate clients.

From the point of view of strategy, the designer will want to present the first contract. It sets the general parameters for the agreement and helps to limit the number of radical changes.

RESIDENTIAL VERSUS COMMERCIAL

Although the scope of the project, fees, and practices may be somewhat different in residential work as opposed to commercial or "contract" work, most of the contract terms and general legal concepts will be the same.

Most residential designers do not go through all the phases one finds in commercial contracts, but all the same principles apply. Residential designers may have more abbreviated agreements with the emphasis on purchasing furniture and furnishings. Commercial contracts may more often include provisions for construction, overseeing the work, and selecting contractors.

Contracts for any type of interior design project can be in a letter format, regardless of the length.

PROJECT DESCRIPTION

The project description should state what work is going to be done by the interior designer. This is different from describing how it will be done. How the project will be done is described under project services. One example of such a provision is the following:

> Interior design of 10,000 square feet located on the 30th floor of the XYZ building, located at _____, as described in Attachment A hereto ("the Project").
> [OR]
> Interior design of master bedroom, dining room, and child's bedroom.

If the space is difficult to describe in words or is part of a larger floor, a drawing can be attached showing the area involved.

Some would-be contract drafters incorrectly combine the project description and the project services. For example,

Working with the client to determine a budget and select fabrics and colors for the conference room.

This omits a description of how the budget will be determined and fabrics and colors selected.

It is also a mistake to describe work which the parties do not plan on having done in the near future. For example, if you were to add to the description given above, ". . . and possibly the 31st floor" or "such other rooms as the client requests," this may create confusion about payment for services. Additional work in different areas can be addressed in a written, signed amendment to the contract or in a separate contract.

The project description should be very detailed. If an interior designer were to give a flat fee for services thinking that he was going to be working on four rooms and said simply "interior design of your house," he would have major problems when the client actually asked for those services on the entire house based on that fee. In this example, the designer contracted for more than he intended. Clearly that contract language does not reflect one party's thoughts and expectations. Such imprecise contract language leads to lawsuits.

A client or a client's attorney should not rejoice in such poor contract drafting and feel that he has gotten a bargain, because the expense of a lawsuit will not be worth it, even if they prevail. The contract should be fair to both sides and correctly state what both parties have agreed to.

DESIGN SERVICES

A thorough description of what services the interior designer will be providing is essential because it is directly tied to his fee. Only the services listed will be included in the designer's fee. Any extra work or services will be billed for as additional services. It is also the language that will be scrutinized if the client feels that the project did not turn out correctly and claims that the designer was in breach of contract.

Interior design work is usually done in six phases:

1. Programming
2. Schematic Design
3. Design Development
4. Contract Documents and Bidding
5. Contract Administration
6. Purchasing and Shopping

Occasionally phases are combined or one or more may be deleted depending on the designer's style of working and the client's needs. In residential work, phases 2–4 may be consolidated. Some clients want the designer to have a very limited role in the Contract Administration Phase or none at all. If so, this phase may be very abbreviated or deleted entirely. Other clients want a great deal of the designer's time in this phase. Some designers just do one set of design plans or layouts after they have met with the client and several revisions, others do architectural-type contract document drawings.

PROGRAMMING PHASE

The programming phase is the period in which the interior designer meets with the client to determine what types of design work they want to have done. For a residential project, do they want to refurbish existing furniture or redo the living room? For a commercial project, do they want to have two conference rooms or one with a sliding door? How many offices do they need to divide the space into? Where will various departments and individuals' offices be located in relation to one another? What sort of seating arrangements are required? This is then written up into a program for the project, which should be approved by the client in writing before proceeding to the next phase.

It is important that the program be agreed upon before moving on lest the designer spend a lot of time doing drawings which may need to be changed because the program is different. If this occurs, the designer can ask that the additional design time be paid for as additional services.

Some projects may require the preparation of stacking and blocking diagrams and diagrams showing the functional relationships between personnel and offices, for example. Clients should also approve these documents and the written program by signing them. This helps assure that the designer and the client are in agreement on the design each step along the way. The agreed-upon program will form the basis for the work done in the next phase.

Typical contract language for this phase is:

1.1   Programming Phase

1.1.1   The Designer shall consult the Owner and other parties designated in this Agreement to ascertain the applicable requirements of the Project and shall review the understanding of such requirements with the Owner.

1.1.2   The Designer shall document the applicable requirements necessary for the various Project functions or operations, such as those for existing and projected personnel, space, furniture, furnishings and equipment, operating procedures, security criteria and communications relationships.

1.1.3   The Designer shall ascertain the feasibility of achieving the Owner's requirements identified under Subparagraphs 1.1.1 and 1.1.2 within the limitations of the building or buildings within which the Project is to be located.

1.1.4   Based on a review, analysis, and evaluation of the functional and organizational relationships, requirements and objectives for the Project, the Designer shall provide a written program of requirements for the Owner's approval.

This language is adequate. There is little cause for negotiation by the client of this language, but it is lengthy.

An example of a simpler and more consolidated way of describing these services would be to say:

The Designer shall consult with the Client to determine the Client's requirements, and shall provide a written program of requirements for the Client's approval.

SCHEMATIC DESIGN PHASE

The schematic design phase is the point in the project when the designer begins to sketch the layout of the project. Rough drawings may be done showing, for example, where offices will be in relation to conference and supply rooms, where the bathroom and kitchen will be in relation to the dining room and living room, or where furniture will be placed. At this point reflected ceiling drawings may also be prepared showing lighting. Other drawings will show the location of telephones. The designer may also become involved during this phase with helping the client to determine what the budget should be or how much renovation can be accomplished for the amount the client has allocated for the project. The designer may also prepare boards showing samples of fabrics, carpets, wallpaper, or molding which will be used.

Not all designers prepare various stages of drawings, such as schematic, design development, and contract document. Particularly in the residential area, it is common to prepare only one or two sets of drawings, one of which is a floor plan. Every designer has his own style of working. Whatever your style is, the contract should clearly state what you will and will not be doing so that the client does not have any false expectations.

Standard contract language for this phase reads as follows:

1.2   Schematic Design Phase

1.2.1   Based on the approved written program, the Designer shall prepare for the Owner's approval preliminary diagrams showing the general functional relationships for both personnel and operations.

1.2.2   The Designer shall review with the Owner alternative approaches to designing and carrying out the Work.

1.2.3   Based on the approved relationship diagrams, the Designer shall prepare space allocation and utilization plans indicating partition and furnishings locations and preliminary furniture and equipment layouts. The Designer shall provide an evaluation of the program and the project budget, if one has been established by the Owner, each in terms of the other.

1.2.4   The Designer shall prepare studies to establish the design concept of the Project indicating the types and quality of finishes and materials and furniture, furnishings and equipment.

1.2.5   The Designer shall submit to the Owner a preliminary Statement of Probable Project Cost, based on the recommended design concept and on current costs for projects of similar scope and quality.

These responsibilities on a commercial project can be condensed into a simpler paragraph stating:

The Designer shall consult with the Client to determine the Client's requirements, and shall provide a written program of requirements for the Client's approval and prepare a schematic design of the Project showing the general relationship between personnel and operations.

Clients will generally want to include language requiring the designer to submit statements of probable cost. This would simply read, "The Designer shall provide sufficient information to the Client to assist in defining the Project budget." Many designers are comfortable taking on such responsibility, but for those who do not have the expertise or desire to calculate costs, this language should not be included in the contract. On very large projects it may even make sense for the client to retain a consultant known as a cost estimator, who specializes in this field.

For residential projects, the designer may be submitting proposals detailing all the items proposed to be purchased for the project. This may or may not be higher than the client's budget and may need to be adjusted.

Budgets and statements of probable cost is an area which often leads to litigation. If the designer and the client are working with and designing for a $200,000 budget for a commercial project with construction and find when bids are taken from contractors that it will actually cost about $300,000, the client will be understandably angry. The client will assume that the bids are high because the designer failed to design for the agreed upon budget. Major changes in the design will be required to bring the project within budget and the designer will not necessarily be paid for his time in revising the design drawings.

If the client shops with the designer on a residential project and finds that everything he wants will cost $100,000 when the designer knew the maximum budget was $70,000, there may be problems.

Often, at such junctures, a rift develops between the designer and client and the designer's contract may be terminated. Therefore, designers should be cautious about taking on this responsibility.

DESIGN DEVELOPMENT PHASE

Before beginning the design development phase, the client should have approved the schematic design drawings. It is best if all such approvals by the client for each phase are done in writing. The client can sign a set of drawings which say "Approved" and are dated.

The schematic design drawings will be further refined during this phase to show details of work being done to floors, walls, and ceilings. For example, custom-built furniture would be shown in detail on these drawings. If the designer has agreed to work on the budget, it too would be refined at this point.

One example of language for this phase might be:

Based on the approved program and schematic design, the Designer shall prepare drawings and other documents to fix and describe the interior construction, and furniture, furnishings and equipment ("FF&E"), colors, materials and finishes of the Project.

CONTRACTS DOCUMENTS AND BIDDING PHASE

During this phase the designer will prepare detailed drawings and specifications showing the contractor exactly how the project will be implemented. These drawings may show the contractor details for nonstructural changes and lights. They may show details for custom cabinetry work. These specifications and designs are incorporated into the documents which will be given to the contractors, subcontractors, and suppliers, such as mill workers, for their bids and will become part of their respective contracts with the client or the designer.

Since other people will be relying on these documents for their work, they are extremely important. The absence of important specifications or details could result in incomplete bids or unsatisfactory work. When these omissions become apparent during construction, the client will be asked by the contractor to pay for correcting them as extras in change orders. This is expensive for the client because he has little negotiating power at this point and will probably pay more than he might otherwise have if the original drawings were properly prepared. The client will no doubt be angry because he thought it was included in his contract with the contractor. Thus, it is crucial that these documents be thorough.

Once again the client will have approved the design development drawings before this phase is started and the budget will have been readjusted. The designer will prepare the package of documents and drawings which will be given to contractors desiring to bid on the project. The designer may recommend one or more contractors to the client or help the client locate some. This service is usually not mentioned in contracts and in fact, designers should avoid recommending contractors, if possible, so that they are not blamed if something goes wrong. Some clients may try to claim that they relied on the designer's recommendation and were damaged. If the client wants such a provision, the designer may agree to "assist the client in selecting a contractor." The designer may offer a few names of contractors and the client will also locate some.

Since the client will be contracting directly with the contractor, the client must perform his own examination of the contractor's background and qualifications. The contractor's business structure should be ascertained (whether it is a corporation, partnership, or sole proprietorship), his length of time in business, the kinds of projects he has worked on and how they turned out, his or his company's financial status, and his ability to obtain the required insurance and bonding.

Some designers contract directly with contractors. They feel this gives them more control over the quality of the work. This is fine as long as the designer realizes the potential risks. Some designers also do contracting as part of their own businesses. If they are hiring an independent contractor, this can be a risky way of doing business because the client will have no choice but to sue the designer if the contractor's work is problematic. The parties should also be aware of some licensing issues involving home improvement contractors. These are discussed in Chapters 8 and 11.

When bidding out the work, a set of bid documents will be prepared by the designer for distribution to interested contractors. This package will include the contract document phase drawings and specifications, any modifications or amendments thereto, a form of a contract to be signed, and any general or special conditions of the work.

The contractors who bid may come from a variety of sources. Some may have been suggested by the client, some may have worked on other projects with the designer, or they may have been suggested by colleagues. Unlike public projects, there is no requirement that the lowest bidder be the one actually selected. If the lowest bidder is selected, the owner should be sure that that contractor is a "responsible" bidder who can actually complete the work satisfactorily for the quoted price.

Of course there is no requirement that any bids be solicited. If the client knows which contractor he wants to work with, the price can be negotiated and a contract signed.

If a designer is working in conjunction with the client's architect, there should be language describing how they will work together and who is responsible for what, since there may be an overlap in services. The client should agree in his contract with the designer to have a provision in his contract with the architect which says that the architect will advise the designer of any changes to the project which may affect the designer's work.

Contractually it is usually the client's or the contractor's responsibility to obtain building permits; however, sometimes the client perceives this as the designer's responsibility. To avoid ambiguity and disputes, the contract should make clear who has this responsibility.

One printed contract's language for this phase reads as follows:

1.4   Contract Documents Phase

1.4.1   Based on the approved Design Development submissions and further adjustments in the scope or quality of the Project or in the Project budget authorized by the Owner, the Designer shall be responsible for the preparation of, for approval by the Owner, Construction Documents consisting of Drawings, Specifications and other documents setting forth in detail the requirements for the interior construction work necessary for the Project. The Work described by such interior construction documents is intended to be performed by the Owner or under one or more Contracts between the Owner and Contractor for construction.

1.4.2   Based on the approved Design Development submissions, the Designer shall prepare for approval by the Owner, Drawings, Schedules, Specifications and other documents, setting forth in detail the requirements for the fabrication, procurement, shipment, delivery and installation of furniture, furnishings and equipment necessary for the Project. Such Work is intended to be performed under one or more Contracts or Purchase Orders between the Owner and Contractor or supplier for furniture, furnishings and equipment.

1.4.3 The Designer shall advise the Owner of any adjustments to previous Statements of Probable Project Cost indicated by changes in requirements or general market conditions.

1.4.4 The Designer shall assist in the preparation of the necessary bidding and procurement information, bidding and procurement forms, the Conditions of the Contracts for Construction and for Furniture, Furnishings and Equipment, Purchase Orders, and the forms of Agreement between the Owner and the Contractors or suppliers.

1.4.5 The Designer shall assist the Owner in connection with the Owner's responsibility for filing documents required for the approval of governmental authorities having jurisdiction over the Project.

1.4.6 The Designer following the Owner's approval of the Contract Documents and of the most recent Statement of Probable Project Cost shall assist the Owner in obtaining bids or negotiated proposals, and assist in awarding and preparing contracts for interior construction and for furniture, furnishings and equipment. All bidding and negotiating activities shall be coordinated by the Designer.

Designers who do not differentiate between bidding, construction documents, and contract administration phases may feel comfortable having language somewhat as follows:

(a) The Designer shall assist the Client in obtaining bids or negotiated proposals and assist in awarding and preparing contracts for interior construction and for FF&E, if requested.

(b) The Designer shall assist the Client in connection with the Client's responsibility for filing documents required for the approval of governmental authorities having jurisdiction over the Project, if required.

(c) The Designer shall assist the Client in coordinating schedules for delivery and installation of the FF&E, and the issuance and pursuance of the punchlist to the completion of the work. However, the Designer shall not be responsible for any malfeasance, neglect, or failure of any manufacturers, contractors, or suppliers of FF&E to meet their schedules for completion or to perform their respective duties and responsibilities, including but not limited to delays or mistakes in delivery and defective or unsatisfactory FF&E.

(d) The Designer shall visit the Project premises on a periodic basis, at intervals appropriate to the stage of construction, to become generally familiar with the progress and quality of the work to determine in general if the work is proceeding in accordance with the contract documents, but shall not be required to make exhaustive and continuous inspections of the Project. The Designer shall review all contractor submittals such as shop drawings, product data, and samples, but only for conformance with the design concept of the work.

If the designer will not have any responsibility for assisting the client in filing with governmental authorities, because, for example, the contractor will be taking care of it, then that language should be deleted from the contract.

Another very important issue can arise at this time. Let us assume that the client has given all the necessary approvals up to this phase and during the preparation of the construction documents decides to change the design. Does the designer have to do this work or can he bill for this as additional services? Some form contracts do not address this issue and therefore imply that this service would be part of the designer's regular fee. This would obviously benefit the client, but is unfair to the designer. The contract should allow the client to make a certain number of changes in the design in the early phases of the project, but once that limit is met, additional changes should be paid for as additional services.

The designer who wants to be paid extra for this might want language in this phase saying:

> The designer will make up to two major changes in the Contract Documents as part of the Fee. Any changes requested by the Client thereafter shall be billed as Additional Services.

ARCHITECTURAL SERVICES

While the practice of interior design has expanded tremendously, it is still a distinct and separate profession from that of architecture in state statutes. An interior designer still cannot file drawings with local building departments for substantial structural renovations, although in some areas of the country they can file drawings for certain types of nonstructural work.

For projects requiring an architect, contracts should make it clear that the client will separately retain a licensed architect or engineer to provide whatever services of that nature may be required. The designer will then coordinate his services with that of the architect or engineer.

In most states the interior designer cannot contract with the client to provide architectural services and then subcontract them out to an architect. It may be construed as practicing architecture without a license, even though the designer will not actually be providing the architectural services. In some states, this would be allowed as long as it was clear that the designer would not actually be doing architectural work.

Of course the interior designer may coordinate his services with those of the architect and an architect may subcontract out interior design services to a designer. Since the laws vary from state to state, the designer should be aware of this issue and consult with local legal counsel to find out what is allowable in his state.

CONTRACT ADMINISTRATION PHASE

The Contract Administration Phase is the phase in which the renovation or construction work and installation is actually done. The walls and doors are put up, the paint and wallpaper is applied, and the furniture and carpets are delivered and installed. The extent of the designer's involvement in this phase is often the subject of intense negotiations between the client and the designer.

Some clients would like the designer to visit the project every day, stay all day, and oversee the construction, deliveries, and installation from start to finish. Other clients view this as a needless expense and prefer to ask the designer to stop by occasionally as needed or requested and just pay for that time. For the designer's part, he would like to only be required to periodically visit to make sure that the work is progressing and looks like what he designed. The resolution of this issue and how it is described in the contract will have a major impact on any litigation which might occur. The parties should not have different expectations about what the designer will do in this phase, otherwise a dispute is sure to arise.

The language for this phase in typical form contracts is usually very lengthy. The portion pertaining to site visits may read:

1.5.6   The Designer shall visit the Project premises as deemed necessary by the Designer, or as otherwise agreed by the Designer in writing, to become generally familiar with the progress and quality of the Work and to determine in general if the Work is proceeding in accordance with the Contract Documents. However, the Designer shall not be required to make exhaustive or continuous inspections at the Project premises to check the quality or quantity of the Work. On the basis of such on-site observations, the Designer shall keep the Owner informed of the progress and quality of the Work, and shall endeavor to guard the Owner against defects and deficiencies in the Work of the Contractors.

The important point is that there be a clear understanding of what you will and will not be doing and what you will and will not be responsible for.

Clients may want the designer to have a high degree of contractual responsibility and oversight. They may want the designer to agree to "provide daily supervision of the contractor" or "to inspect the work being performed by the contractor." The words "supervision" and "inspection" connote a higher degree of involvement by the designer and greater potential legal liability than agreeing to visit and observe the work. Designers should be careful about signing an agreement with such language.

A balance must be struck between each party's interests because the designer is not really being paid enough in most instances to be there every day and should not be taking on the role of a construction supervisor, foreman, or manager. The contractor should have his own supervisor and construction management involves different responsibilities and skills than those of a designer.

Some designers unwittingly sign contracts with this type of language in them and are therefore more likely to be involved in litigation if something goes wrong with the construction. The client believes that if anything goes wrong with the project, it must be because the designer failed to "supervise" the work. This is another reason why all contracts in this area should only be drafted by attorneys who know this area of the law and reviewed by an attorney before they are signed.

Most contracts require the designer to "endeavor to guard the Owner against defects and deficiencies in the Work of the Contractors." This is fine from the designer's perspective. Clients sometimes want to add some extra language such as "the designer shall use his best efforts to guard the Owner against defects and deficiencies in the Work of the Contractors."

Some form contracts make the designer the interpreter of the Contract Documents and the "impartial judge of performance" by the Owner and the Contractors. In other words, if a question arises as to whether some work is part of the contractor's contract or should be billed as an extra, the designer's decision will be final. The designer is also required to "endeavor to secure faithful performance by both the Owner and the Contractors . . ."

This language may place more of a legal burden on the designer than he really wants or should want. Some might argue that the designer has met his contractual responsibility if he merely brings problems to the attention of the client and helps the client decide how to handle it, rather than being the final arbiter. Such language may be more favorable to the client than the designer, and some designers might want to delete such language from contracts given to them by clients.

In a similar vein, some clients might want the designer to be involved in preparing Change Orders. The contractor should do this. The designer, however, may review them to determine whether the sum being requisitioned is fair relative to the amount of work done.

The designer should suggest that the client put language in his contract with the contractor stating that no change orders will be valid and paid unless they are in writing and are signed by the client and the contractor. The contractor will not be able to claim fees for this work in *quantum meruit* (the fair value) either. If the contractor does extra work without change orders, there may be a claim that it was done with the designer's verbal approval. If the designer feels he wants written authority from the client to order minor changes, there can be a provision in the contract allowing this and possibly also a dollar limit on the authority.

This helps the designer because contractors often ask the designer for permission to do work. If the designer says "Yes" and the contractor takes this as an oral change order, the client may later feel that the designer exceeded his authority. If written change orders are required and this practice is observed, the designer will not get caught in the middle.

PURCHASING OF FURNITURE

In this phase, the designer with the Client's assistance, specifies which furniture will be redone and which new furniture, furnishings, and equipment (sometimes called "FF&E") will be purchased. The designer will also prepare drawings and specifications for any custom work, such as cabinets, bookcases, and tables. Drawings will be prepared showing the location of these items in the space.

Large companies often order their own FF&E using the designer's specifications. If this is done, the designer usually agrees to coordinate the preparation of these requisitions and any bidding which may take place.

The designer will also help by coordinating the installation of the furniture and any move from the client's former offices or home. Although the designer will not usually take responsibility for accepting and rejecting FF&E, he will prepare a "punchlist" for the client and help coordinate getting these items taken care of. This is a list of all the fine points that must be attended to in order for the project to be complete, such as fixing scratches and loose screws.

Of course if a designer orders FF&E directly and in his own name, he may be fully responsible for taking care of and correcting any problems with it. This can become quite complex when FF&E is delivered from another state and it must be determined whether the problem arose from manufacturing or the delivery process.

Designers also need to protect themselves against the possibility that clients will purchase items they have helped them select and then not pay the designer his fee. The contract with the client is the place to address this issue. The client may purchase items on his own, but should still pay the designer a fee.

SHOP DRAWINGS

When a designer designs custom furniture, shop drawings are crucial. Usually these drawings are the responsibility of the contractor to prepare and the designer just reviews them. Problems arise when the contracts with the designer and the contractor do not make it clear who is responsible for preparing and checking the accuracy of these drawings. In those cases, there is a lot of finger pointing when a problem comes to light.

Some designers assume that the contractor will do field measurements to verify the accuracy of the dimensions. Never assume anything. Always put it in writing. I have seen custom wine cabinets that do not fit and custom wall units in which the television does not fit. If verification of dimensions is the contractor's job, it should be stated in his contract. The designer's contract should say it is not his responsibility.

Shop drawings are so important that they are considered to supersede the project drawings and specifications. So if there are ambiguities in the various project drawings, the shop drawings govern.

ADDITIONAL SERVICES

If the description of the project services is thorough, only a brief statement should be required concerning additional services. Additional services include anything that was not mentioned in the statement of services. It does not have to be an extensive list of every possible additional service either party can think of.

One way to address this issue would be to state:

> If the Client requests services not included within the scope of services provided in this Agreement ("Additional Services"), they shall be paid for by the Client as provided in this Agreement, in addition to the compensation for Services, at the following rates: (describe rates).

With certain clients it may be useful to list a few representative examples of the anticipated additional services to avoid any claims of surprise. This might include meeting with the landlord of an office building to explain the work or doing extensive revised drawings after the initial design has been approved.

There are many circumstances under which a designer may be required to provide services in addition to those originally set forth in the scope of services. Examples include:

1. The client may decide to have the master bedroom decorated when only the kitchen and child's room were originally contemplated.
2. The contract may call for the designer to visit the project to observe the progress of the work once a week and the client decides he would like the designer to visit three times a week.
3. The client is thinking about decorating other parts of the house and wants to see preliminary sketches of design and decorating ideas.

These are only a few of the ways in which additional services may be required. Obviously if you are spending time and providing different services than were originally contemplated, you should be paid. If you anticipate the possibility of such work before the contract is even signed, you can include it in the contract. These services are usually provided at an hourly rate. However, if the additional work is so extensive that it is tantamount to a whole new project, the parties might consider negotiating and signing a new contract.

The other aspect of this issue is to see to it that you not only have such a provision, but you enforce it. If you do extra work for the client and do not mention getting paid for it, most clients will be more than happy to accept those services and will not offer to pay for them. When you see that additional services will need to be provided, discuss it with the client and then confirm it in a letter.

The subject of additional fees should be raised *before* the work is done. It is not businesslike to do the work and surprise the client with a bill at the end. This can lead to disputes. It is always best to be up front with the client and to discuss these issues fully so that both parties understand what is expected.

REIMBURSABLE EXPENSES

As with additional services, many people like to make exhaustive lists of all the types of reimbursable expenses there may be on the project. Generally it is not necessary. If the list says ". . . including, but not limited to . . ." with some representative examples, that should be sufficient. Special items might be listed, such as the cost per page of local and international facsimile (fax) transmissions, blueprints, models, trucking, storage, and insurance. Some designers also mark up the cost of these items to reimburse themselves for administrative time in preparing invoices and providing back-up information. If that is the case, the markup should be specifically stated. Of course, the designer should be prepared to furnish the client with very detailed breakdowns of these expenses and backup upon request.

Designers frequently use taxis and rent cars for local work on behalf of the client. Clients do not usually consider this a reimbursable item. If there is any possible question about this being reimbursable, it should be specifically discussed and listed.

Some clients want the right to give their approval before certain expenses are incurred or after a dollar limit has been reached. This should also be stated in the contract.

THE OWNER'S RESPONSIBILITIES

Although most of the work on any project is performed or coordinated by the interior designer, the client also has certain responsibilities. For example, if the premises to be designed have friable (crumbly) asbestos in them, it is the client's responsibility to have it removed by appropriately licensed contractors so that the design and construction work can be done.

Having someone in the owner's camp who has authority to make decisions can sometimes mean the difference between a successful, on-time project and a failed and delayed one. It is the owner's responsibility to see that such a chain of authority is set up. On a commercial project this is essential since the designer will be dealing with many different people from the company. Only one or two of these people will have authority to issue orders and make decisions. In a residential project, a designer may get in the middle of a husband and wife who do not always agree. He needs to know who to turn to for the final say. It is not enough to only require the owner to designate a representative "when necessary."

Commercial projects can be difficult because there are usually a number of people who contribute ideas toward what the client wants and it is difficult to achieve a consensus. The designer has to pull all of these ideas together. A restaurant may have a managing partner and several investors. A corporation will have several executives and a lot of personnel who have to work in the space being designed and have their own ideas. The main decision maker may often be out of town. The only way to assure that the proper authorizations are given is to provide for it in the contract.

The designer should make that an affirmative obligation. An executive officer in a corporation who knows he will be out of town a lot or busy at meetings should also want such a provision. Nothing can delay a project more than a situation in which the client's approval is needed in a hurry and he is unavailable.

If the renovation work is being done in an office building, approval may be needed from the landlord. If the work is being done in a building designated as a landmark, approval from the Landmark's Commission may be required. If the work is in a cooperative apartment building, the Board of Directors' approval may be required. Getting the requisite permission should be the client's responsibility, although the designer may be contractually obligated to assist the client in providing necessary information and drawings.

Sometimes it is important for the designer to have access to the "existing condition" drawings for the house, floor, or building. It should be the client's responsibility to provide these.

The client may have to make arrangements to ensure that the designer has easy access to the apartment, house, or office being renovated.

CONSULTANTS

In the course of the project, various consultants may be required for special issues such as lighting, acoustics, and audio equipment. From a legal standpoint, it is best for the client to hire and pay them directly. If there are any problems, they can deal directly with each other. If the designer hires them and a problem arises, the designer will definitely be caught up in the dispute, because he was the one who retained the consultant. He has the contract with the consultant. If the client feels he was somehow damaged, he will have no choice but to sue the designer and the designer will, in turn, sue the consultant.

Many designers choose to hire consultants directly because they feel it gives them more control over the project. This should not be the case, but if you choose to proceed this way, you should be aware of the risks. Also, if for some reason the client does not pay you, you may not be able to pay the consultant and this may result in a dispute.

COMPENSATION

Types of Fees

There are three main ways in which the designer can be compensated:

1. Hourly
2. A flat fee
3. A percentage of the cost of construction and/or furniture, furnishings, and equipment

Most firms use a combination of these methods.

Billing for employees based on a multiple of the designer's direct personnel expense is just a variation on hourly billing, but some designers prefer it to plain hourly because it is easier to get the client's approval. Billing based on square footage is another variation of a flat fee which is used sometimes on commercial projects.

Designers may charge differently for each phase and in a typical contract, more than one type of compensation will be used. For example, some designers look at all the design work as a group and bill for that on a flat fee or hourly basis and then bill for visiting the project, administering the work, and ordering FF&E on an hourly or percentage basis. In my experience, no two designers bill their clients in exactly the same way. Designers can be innovative in structuring their fees, as long as they are fairly compensated.

Clients want predictability and certainty when it comes to expenses on a project. For many, this means negotiating the entire project on a flat fee basis or hourly with a "not to exceed" amount. A certain number of revisions to drawings would be factored in and a certain number of site visits for that fee. This should be clearly stated in the contract. This eliminates the possibility of having to pay the designer more money if bids are high or if there are a lot of revisions to the designs. Conversely, if the client requests more changes to the drawings than what has been agreed to, that work will be paid for as additional services. Such a contract might read:

> For Services in phases 1 through 5, the designer shall be paid a fixed fee of $_____. This Fee shall include two revisions to the Design Development Drawings and one site visit a week for six weeks. Any additional services shall be billed by the Designer as Additional Services.

A slightly different contract might read:

> For services on phases 1 through 4, the designer shall be paid at the following hourly rates:
>
> | | |
> |---|---|
> | Designers | $_____ |
> | Draftsman | $_____ |
>
> For Services in Phase 5, compensation shall be computed as follows:
>
> _____% of Construction Cost as defined herein.

A client might agree to this language but want to add a "not to exceed cap" on the hourly billing. This puts a little more control on how much the designer can bill.

FACTORS DETERMINING FEES

When a designer thinks about what fee to charge, a number of factors should be considered to determine whether the fee is adequate:

1. *Profit and Overhead.* When setting a fee, you must have a clear understanding of what your office expenses are so that you can determine the minimum amount you need to be paid in order to break even. This involves taking into account your rent, salaries of employees, costs of producing the work, and how much time it will take to design, shop, and complete the project. Once you do this exercise you will know how much you need to be paid to make the project worthwhile.

2. *How Much the Market will Bear.* If you have done your calculations and find that your fee would be much higher than would be typical for such work in the locale in which you are working or because of the economy, then an adjustment must be made.

3. *Reputation in the Industry.* To some extent, designers who are well known and published may charge more for their services than lesser known colleagues. However, the ability to obtain such fees will depend upon going after the appropriate market. Thus an average homeowner may not care so much about a designer being famous and will not want to pay the extra fees, whereas a businessman who wants a project which may receive publicity in magazines would want to pay more.

4. *What Colleagues are Charging.* Obviously you must be aware to some extent of how much your fellow designers are charging for similar work. If your fee is much higher than a colleague with similar experience, it may be difficult to explain why you should get the job.

5. *Experience with Similar Projects.* This is a big factor in landing any project. If a client is opening a new restaurant and you have done a lot of restaurants, the client may be willing to pay a little more to have the benefit of your expertise. By the same token, if you have never designed a restaurant, but would like to have one to add to your portfolio, you may charge a lower fee than you normally would to try to attract the client.

6. *Desperation.* Depending on how business is going, this may well be a major factor in determining your fee. However, you must be careful in determining how big a factor it will be, because no sooner will you sign a contract with a low fee than a great new long-term job will come along. You may go from having time to kill to being so busy that you need extra staff. In such situations you must remember that you still must honor the contract for the low fee. So be very careful before signing agreements out of desperation.

HOURLY AND FLAT FEE

Hourly rates can vary tremendously from one designer to another. These differences are due to the designer's general level of experience, reputation, and experience with the particular type of project. The fact that one designer offers to do the project at $90 per hour and another at $45 per hour does not mean that the more expensive designer is overcharging. The client should meet with several designers before signing a contract.

Flat fees or hourly fees with a guaranteed maximum are popular with clients because there is more certainty in the final cost. However, since most designers cannot predict accurately how much time a project will take, because things always take more time than anyone expected, for a variety of reasons, the designer may greatly exceed the predicted number of hours and be left working essentially for free. This is not a desirable result and both parties should carefully think about the fairness of the amount before agreeing to a flat fee. A client may agree to pay hourly up to a flat fee ceiling. A client may agree to a fixed fee based on a certain budget and agree to pay more if the budget increases and the scope of work is greater.

COST OF CONSTRUCTION

Being paid on a percentage of the cost of construction can sometimes be tricky. In a classic situation, a general contractor is retained to do construction work based on his bid and the interior designer is paid a percentage for all materials and labor the contractor provides, plus change orders. It should be very straightforward and the interior designer only needs to see copies of the contractor's bills to verify payment of the designer's fee.

However, occasionally the client is able to obtain construction services at less than fair market rates through a friend or he decides to save money by acting as his own general contractor. If this occurs, the designer's fee may be far less than what was originally anticipated when the designer signed his contract.

To avoid such problems, the interior designer's contract should make it clear that the cost of construction should be based on fair market rates by general contractors who possess the requisite licenses (for residential work only in certain jurisdictions). Thus the client can get the benefit of the contractor's discount, but the designer will still get his fee.

FEES FOR PURCHASING FURNITURE

Most designers charge a percentage of the cost of furniture, furnishings, and equipment (FF&E) as their fee for shopping and specifying these items. This percentage may vary from 20 to 35%. It can be based on either the retail price with the designer's discount factored in or the wholesale price. This covers everything they design, order, or specify. What this means is that if the designer shops with the client and specifies a certain type of marble, and the client agrees but later changes his mind, the designer is still entitled to a percentage of the anticipated cost of marble for the time spent. Sometimes designers just get a percentage of what is actually ordered.

Some corporate clients do their own ordering of FF&E and this should be stated in the contract. The designer may still receive a percentage of the total amount for their services in selecting, specifying, and coordinating or be paid on an hourly or flat fee basis.

If the designer does the ordering, the contract should require the client to give at least a 50% deposit upon ordering and 50% upon delivery. A client might want to try to negotiate a lower deposit if the manufacturer only requires a 30% deposit, but this should be discouraged. The deposit protects the designer if the client changes his mind. Orders should be noncancelable if possible.

RETAINER

The designer should obtain an initial retainer before starting any work. This should be roughly 10–15% of the total anticipated fee. The areas of controversy come into play when negotiating how the retainer should be credited to the client. The designer will want the retainer to be credited to final payment, so there will be some security for the last payment. The client will want the retainer credited to the first or second payment so he has to pay less money out of pocket early on. However, a retainer makes no sense if it is credited to the first payment due from the client. In that case, it is not security at all for final payment and defeats the purpose of having one.

Retainers should be nonrefundable if the project terminates prematurely. The client may want to negotiate a sliding scale for refunding the retainer, depending upon the size of the retainer, and which phase the project is in when the termination occurs. This also assumes that neither party is in breach of contract.

PAYMENT

Payment for design services is usually done on at least a monthly basis. If fees are based on a percentage of cost of construction, the designer will be entitled to different percentages of the total fee for each phase. The designer then bills each month until he reaches the allocated percentage for that phase.

A flat fee will be paid in specified amounts for each phase except for the last payment. Hourly fees are very straightforward and can be billed monthly. Furnishings are paid for as the designer receives the deposit and final payment for the items.

Various penalties can be inserted in the event that the client does not pay on time. This can vary from interest on late payments, to stopping work, to being able to collect attorney's fees if the designer has to bring legal action to collect fees.

INTEREST ON LATE PAYMENTS

It is common in contracts for services to have a clause allowing the designer to charge interest monthly on late payments. On a practical level, if it reaches the point at which this provision needs to be invoked, there are probably other problems on the project. However, it is a useful clause to have in your contract, even if you decide not to invoke it.

LEGAL FEES FOR COLLECTION

Some designers include a clause in their contracts stating that if they have to take legal action to collect their unpaid fees and are successful in winning a judgment or an arbitration award, they may also be entitled to reimbursement of their reasonable attorneys fees.

This can be a very important provision, since legal fees are not usually recoverable in most states in the absence of an explicit contractual provision. Not all clients will sign contracts with such clauses. Some will agree to such clauses if they too can recover their legal fees if they have to sue the designer and are successful.

BUDGETS

Most clients have a certain sum of money in mind that they are willing to spend. Once they have discussed what they want with the designer, they may ask the designer to prepare a budget for them. This budget will have to be periodically updated as the project progresses and changes.

Problems can arise when the client looks upon this budget as being etched in stone, yet approves orders that exceed it. At the end of the project the client may claim that the designer negligently exceeded the budget. This is an area that frequently leads to litigation.

The designer should carefully review contract provisions on this subject and be sure that he understands his responsibility in this area. If changes are made in the budget, the client should sign them to evidence his approval.

SALES TAX

Effective June 1, 1990 there is an 8¼% sales tax in New York City on interior design services. It is less outside of New York City. Other states have similar sales taxes on interior design services. This type of tax can be difficult to enforce, as well as comply with, because of the lack of a precise definition of what constitutes interior design services as opposed to architectural services. Compliance with such tax laws is more difficult for architects who provide both architectural and interior design services, since they will have to somehow divide up their services for sales tax purposes. For interior designers, all services are taxable in New York City.

Under New York's tax law, interior decorating and design services include, but are not limited to the preparation of layout drawings; furniture arranging; design and planning of furniture, fixtures, and other furnishings that are not permanently attached to a building or structure; selection, purchase, and arrangement of surface coverings, draperies, furniture, furnishings, and other decorations or any similar service. When an architect specifies finishes, it is a taxable service.

Many designers mistakenly look only at whether or not a capital improvement is involved to determine taxability. A better rule of thumb is whether the work needs to be filed by a licensed architect with the building department. If it does, that portion of the work is nontaxable. Furthermore, if you mix taxable and nontaxable services, they will most likely be construed as taxable. Thus it is important to contractually divide the services if you are also providing architectural services.

There are many fine points in such laws which should be discussed with an attorney or an accountant who specializes in this area. For example, under the New York City law, if design plans are delivered to a client in Connecticut, but they relate to property in New York City, they are taxable in New York City. Although generally tax is due when the sale is completed, tax may also have to be paid on partial completion.

Although the design professionals collect the tax, ultimately it is the client who pays it. If it is not collected, the client can be personally liable. In addition, the design professional can be *personally* liable, even if his firm is incorporated. The design firm can be enjoined or stopped by the state from continuing to conduct business. I know of one case in which an interior designer collected the tax from the client, but did not realize it had to be paid to the state and just held onto it. Obviously, even such innocent mistakes can have serious legal repercussions. Advice should be sought from both an accountant and an attorney.

Since these laws are new in many locations, there has not been much opportunity yet for audits and rules and regulations. However, there is a lot that design professionals can do by way of planning to lessen the likelihood of an audit or to be prepared if one occurs. Some of my architectural clients have divided their services and now have separate contracts for architectural and interior design services; others have one contract that spells out which services are interior design services and how they will be paid for.

HOME IMPROVEMENT CONTRACTORS LICENSES

Some states and localities require those contractors who do construction or renovation work in houses which have no more than a certain number of units or in cooperative and condominium apartments, to have home improvement contractors licenses. This is a consumer protection requirement.

Designers who also act as general contractors or who subcontract out work may be required to comply with these laws. Clients entering into contracts with designers providing such services may want to insert a provision in their contract in which the designer represents that he has such a license. In this situation, the designer is wearing two hats: one as a designer and one as a contractor.

Within a given state there may be different home improvement contracting license requirements in the various counties. If the designer works in different counties, he may need to be licensed in each county.

Home improvement laws have some strict requirements for the legal provisions which must be in such contracts. In New York, for example, they must be in writing and in plain English. Among other things, the contractor's address, telephone number, and license number must appear on the contract. It must specify the date on which work will begin and describe the work to be done, the materials and equipment to be used, and the agreed upon price for the work.

Homeowners usually have the right to cancel within a few days of signing the contract. This protects the homeowner who changes his mind or feels he was pressured into signing. Most important, payments must be deposited in an escrow account prior to completion of the job or else a performance bond must be deposited with the owner.

Licensed home improvement contractors can file valid mechanic's liens if they are not paid; unlicensed contractors cannot. If such a lien is accepted for filing by the county clerk, lack of this license may be legal grounds for vacating the lien. Thus it behooves you to have the requisite license.

While it is not difficult to obtain such licenses, not having one can have serious consequences. These statutes are strict and anyone who does such work without a license may not only be prohibited from suing for the balance of his fee, but may be required to *refund* the entire fee to the client. This is true even if the client knew the contractor did not have the license.

In some of these statutes, if a homeowner's suit against the contractor is without merit, the court may award reasonable attorney's fees to the contractor.

In New York City, for example, the administrative code defines "home improvement" as follows:

> The construction, repair, replacement, remodeling, alteration, conversion, rehabilitation, renovation, modernization, improvement, or addition to any land or building, or that portion thereof which is used or designed to be used as a residence or dwelling place and shall include but not be limited to the construction, erection, replacement, or improvement of driveways, swimming pools, terraces, patios, landscaping, fences, porches, garages, fallout shelters, basements, and other improvements to structures or upon land which is adjacent to a dwelling house. "Home Improvement" shall not include (1) the construction of a new home building or work done by a contractor in compliance with a guarantee of completion of a new building project, or (2) the sale of goods or materials by a seller who neither arranges to perform nor performs directly or indirectly any work or labor in connection with the installation of or application of the goods or materials, or (3) residences owned by or controlled by the state or any municipal subdivision thereof, (4) painting or decorating of a building, residence, home or apartment, when not incidental or related to home improvement work as herein defined. Without regard to the extent of affixation, "home improvement" shall also include the installation of central heating or air conditioning systems, central vacuum cleaning systems, storm windows, awnings or fire or burglar alarms or communication systems.

There are forms to be filed and fees to be paid in order to be licensed. It is not usually a complicated process and is well worth the trouble if the designer also does this type of work.

PUBLICITY AND PHOTOGRAPHIC RIGHTS

Publicity is very important to the designer. When projects are published in magazines, it helps generate new projects. Therefore, a provision should be inserted in the contract in which the client agrees that if the project is published, the designer will get credit as "the designer." The designer should also be allowed to seek publicity for the project. This might read:

> In the event the Client publishes or causes to be published photographs or other representations of the Project after completion of the Services under this Agreement, the Client agrees to include reference to the Designer as the designer for the Project in any such publication.

The designer should also get the client to agree to allow him to have the right to take photographs for his own purposes. Occasionally the client may have certain confidentiality requirements and these should be set forth in the contract. For example, the client may want there to be no reference to his identity or the location of his home. He may want prior notice of any possible publications. You do not want to have to negotiate this issue after the project is complete.

ARBITRATION

This provision appears in most printed, form contracts published in the industry. It is recommended that this provision be left in the contract as the method of resolving disputes. Clients often request that it be deleted.

Litigation in the courts in this area can be very time consuming and expensive. The fees paid to the designer on most projects are usually not enough to justify or pay for the expense of a protracted lawsuit. For this reason, many designers avoid litigating for their fees. Also, when a designer sues for fees, there is invariably a counterclaim for negligence and breach of contract.

Arbitration, on the other hand, provides a less expensive, relatively fast method of resolving disputes. A client might not want this provision if he wishes to exert economic pressure on the designer if a dispute arises.

Of course, there are also those who do not like arbitration. They feel arbitration awards tend to be split down the middle. All things considered, arbitration works well for resolving design disputes because the construction arbitration panel is comprised of people who know the industry. This is discussed in more detail in Chapter 11. The point to remember here is that in order to invoke arbitration, there must be an arbitration clause in the contract and the contract must be signed by both parties.

TERMINATION

Design industry contracts usually provide for the right of mutual termination only in the event of a breach of contract. One party must give the defaulting party seven days written notice. However, both parties may want to have the right to terminate for any reason after giving the required notice. The client may also want to be able to terminate the contract if the project is abandoned (e.g., if he changes his mind about buying a house).

There is also usually a provision in industry form contracts for termination expenses to be paid to the designer if the termination is not the designer's fault. Termination expenses compensate the designer in part for the profit he would have made if the project had been completed. The client will usually argue in favor of deleting the provision for termination expenses. The basis for this belief is the notion that if the designer is paid to the date of termination, that is adequate compensation for his services. This should be discussed in detail before a contract is signed, since many projects are terminated before completion.

SIGNING A CONTRACT

The formal mechanics of signing a contract can sometimes be crucial. All contracts should be dated on the day they are actually signed. Sometimes a contract will be drafted in April and sit unsigned on a client's desk for two or three months. When it is finally signed, the date no longer applies. If the designer had told the client the project would be completed in four months, having a correct date would be crucial to establish that the project was completed in a timely fashion.

If any additions are made to the contract, they should be clearly written in and readable. Any deletions should be carefully crossed out. You never want a situation where one party can claim an important word does not look like it was crossed out and the other party claims it was.

All changes should be made on all copies of the contract. The client, the designer and their respective attorneys may each want an original of the contract. No one should be able to say, "But my version says . . ." All copies should be identical.

Every change should be initialed by both parties next to the change. Once again, this ensures that both parties have agreed on the change and there are not different versions of the contract or different pages inserted.

Both parties should sign the contract in order for it to be binding. In other words, if the designer signs the contract, sends it to the client, starts work and does not receive back a signed contract, then there may be some question as to the nature and extent of their agreement. The designer cannot just assume that the contract he mailed out is binding on both of them.

If you are signing as an officer of a company, your official capacity should be clearly indicated next to your signature. If it is not, it can open the door to a claim that you signed in your individual capacity, not in your capacity as an officer of the corporation.

SIGNATURE

The client should be sent at least two originals of the contract for signature and asked to return one to the designer with a retainer check.

If the contract is in the form of a letter, the signature section should look something like this:

Very truly yours,

XYZ Design, Inc.

Dated:_____   By:_____

Name, President

AGREED AND ACCEPTED:

ABC Corporation, Inc.

By:_____

President

[OR]

_____   _____

Michael Smith   Doris Smith

This avoids situations where the client claims that he entered into a contract with you as an individual rather than with the corporation.

The client should give you a retainer check simultaneously with signing the contract. Work should not begin on the project until these formalities have been completed, otherwise you may find yourself well into the project without a signed contract.

CONCLUSION

No one should ever sign a contract just to get a project started. Parties sign printed contracts in which they agree to provide services they never intend to provide, but do so because they are part of the form. When this happens and a dispute arises, everyone is always surprised when they go back and finally read the contract. Invariably one party says in shock, "I agreed to that?" A lot of money is involved in interior design projects and a little time spent in the beginning negotiating the terms and having a carefully drafted contract can mean less money spent in litigation later on.

8

Contracts with Contractors

There are several different reasons why designers should be concerned about contracts with contractors. First, many of their clients will want the designer's assistance in selecting a contractor and possibly in reviewing their contract. Some of the provisions in the contractor's project relate to the designer's services. Second, some designers provide construction services themselves, in addition to design work, and need to present contracts to clients for this work. Third, the same concerns apply to contracts with sub-contractors, as well as to general contractors.

However, while the designer can be helpful to the client in giving advice concerning the role of the contractor on the project, designers should avoid being placed in the position of doing legal work and drafting or substantively reviewing the contract with the contractor. The client should retain an attorney to do that. The designer should also not be asked to make the actual selection of a contractor. This should always be up to the client.

SELECTING A CONTRACTOR

On most projects the client will want to obtain bids from various contractors. It is always best to have contractors from a variety of sources, such as others who have done similar projects, recommendations from property managers or friends who have worked with the contractor, and some that the designer is aware of from his other projects. The designer should avoid urging the retention of a particular contractor unless he is prepared to share part of the blame if it does not work out. Sometimes designers feel strongly about working with a particular "team" of contractors and tradespeople and tell the client that this is how they work. This is fine, as long as the designer understands that if something goes wrong, the client will try to hold him responsible.

It is best if the designer suggests several firms or individuals and encourages the client to seek out other applicants on their own.

The client should independently check the references of each applicant carefully. They should try to speak with recent clients of the contractor and visit some of the projects. I know of one instance where a contractor tried to get hired as a general contractor to renovate an apartment. Although he gave a reference as having worked on a substantial project, it turned out that he actually worked as a drywall subcontractor on only a small part of the project. So the client should try to find out all that he can about the contractor's capabilities.

The contractor's financial stability should also be examined. Some contractors overextend themselves financially and then cannot complete jobs. Occasionally, financial problems cause them to disappear during a project or even file for bankruptcy. Sometimes contractors have had other companies which went out of business because of litigation, bad debts, or tax problems. If possible, the client should try to inquire about such subjects or get reassurance that these are not problems at present.

BIDDING

When most people think of selecting among bids, they tend to think only of the lowest bidder. They want to find the contractor who can do the job for the least amount of money. However, the criteria should really be whichever firm is the lowest "responsible" bidder. A contractor may bid very low to get a job and find that they cannot possibly do the job for so little money. This may result in numerous requests for change orders, inability to complete the job, or long delays in completion because they cannot adequately man the job.

Any time there is a big discrepancy between one bidder and all the others, it should cause you to question whether the bid is a *bona fide* one. In other words, has the bidder taken into account what it would realistically cost to do the job or did he just come in with a low bid to get the job? Did he leave some aspect of the job out of his bid? Also, if the designer's fee is based on a percentage of construction, a bid which is too low for the amount of work being done can result in the designer losing fees. Of course, bidding is not required. The client can simply work out a negotiated fee with a particular contractor.

FORM OF CONTRACT

The American Institute of Architects (A.I.A.) contracts are probably the most widely used form of contract for construction, together with the General Conditions.

However, you will also frequently see nonform contracts drafted either by attorneys or the contractors themselves. These are acceptable so long as all the necessary provisions have been included.

Sometimes people insist on using only A.I.A. form contracts, but this is not necessary. What is important, regardless of which contract you use, is that the contract be tailored to suit the project. Using a printed form contract with provisions that do not apply to the job serves no purpose and can lead to misunderstandings and litigation.

Make sure that every aspect of the agreement is included in the final, signed agreement. Sometimes the parties have verbal agreements which are not incorporated and disputes develop as to whether they should have been and what to do since they were not.

LENGTH OF CONTRACTS

Construction contracts tend to be much longer than design contracts. They are usually comprised of the main contract, riders, general and special conditions, and of course the drawings and specifications. Change orders become part of the contract.

Contractors tend to present their contracts (usually nonform ones) to the client. As a general rule, unless the contractor has an attorney who will prepare a thorough contract, they tend not to be very comprehensive. Often the ones I see have a few pages describing the work, then a description of the amount and terms of payment, and that is it. There is no mention of insurance, warranties, retainage, termination, and other important terms.

Thus clients may be more involved in having their attorneys redraft such agreements.

VISITING THE PROJECT

The contractor should be encouraged to visit the project before work begins to ensure that he is familiar with the office, house, or apartment and any special conditions that need to be taken into account. If the contractor was not aware of some special aspect of the building or house when he bid the job, he may wind up asking for a change order shortly after the project begins. For example, complicated arrangements may need to be made to gain access to the building each day. This may take up a lot of the contractor's time, which was not anticipated. There may be some unusual existing conditions which require special attention. The contractor should be responsible for checking these conditions before signing a contract so that they are taken into account in his price. The contract should make it clear that these items are part of the contract price and are not an extra.

PERMITS

Usually the custom and practice in the construction industry is that the contractor is required to obtain and pay for building permits. However, I have seen projects where each party points his finger at the other and says "I thought you were going to do it." For example, this can result in there being no building permit and the building department stopping the job. The contract should make it clear who is responsible for obtaining permits, who will pay the fees, and who will make the necessary arrangements for inspections once the work is done.

SCOPE OF WORK

This is one of the most important considerations in the contract and the one which most often leads to litigation if it is not well defined. When a contractor agrees to do some construction work for a fixed sum of money, you need to nail down exactly what you can expect to receive for that amount. If the scope is unclear, the contractor will request increases in his fee for change orders before he undertakes certain work. This can result in the cost of the project doubling in some cases from what was originally anticipated. This can also occur if the designs are not detailed enough.

Hence specifications and drawings should be as detailed as possible. The contractor's scope of work should also be as detailed as possible. For example, if a contractor specifies that he will furnish a "toilet" as part of his fee, that does not make it clear what quality or brand he will be furnishing. He will have met his contractual obligation if he furnishes a toilet, but the client may want or be expecting a higher quality item. Before supplying a higher quality toilet, the contractor may insist that the client agree to a change order. You will need to know what dollar amount the contractor has allowed for a toilet, so you know how much more you will need to pay if you want one of a higher quality, or you will have to agree that a toilet of the calibre you want will be provided as part of the contract price.

All drawings and specifications should be clearly identified and dated so that they are part of the contract and can be easily listed in the contract. This can become especially important when and if there are many revisions or amendments. There also may be a number of versions of the design drawings and you should be sure that the contractor is basing his prices on the correct set.

PROJECT REPRESENTATIVES

The contractor must know from whom he can accept orders and directions. On residential projects, he may be getting orders to do things from both husbands and wives, as well as the designer and the building manager. On commercial projects, he will be getting orders from various executives, staff, building managers, and landlords. Many times the instructions will conflict and the contractor needs to know who has the final say.

I know of many instances in which the contractor thought he was being given valid oral authorizations for extra work by partners and their designer and found at the end of the job, when he presented his bill, that they did not agree on having given such authorization. The contractor will have incurred additional expenses which he will want to pass on to the client. The client may blame the designer for having authorized this work. This forms a classic scenario for a potential lawsuit.

Thus a specific individual should be identified in writing in the contract as the person from whom orders can be taken. Also, to avoid disagreements, make sure that any oral authorization is confirmed in writing.

PAYMENT

Contractors should generally be paid in relation to the amount or percentage of work completed. Often it is the designer who observes their work and confirms to the client that the amount of work the contractor is claiming in his application for payment is correct. On small projects of limited duration, the contractor may be paid one third of his fee upon execution of his contract, one third in the middle, and one third upon completion.

Problems can arise when the designer approves payment to the contractor for having done a percentage of work which is greater than the amount actually completed. Clients tend to rely on the designer's assessment of the status of the project. Applications for payment should be carefully reviewed and reduced, if necessary. This can be another area in which litigation is likely to arise, so the contractor's requisitions should be carefully reviewed by the designer or the designer's contract should say he has no responsibility for such a review.

Occasionally very busy clients will give the designer total control over payments to the contractor. In rare instances, clients who travel a great deal even transfer the funds to the designer and authorize them to write checks to the contractor. This is a major responsibility and careful records should be kept to document all payments made.

RETAINAGE

It is common in the industry for a portion of each payment due the contractor to be held back as security for satisfactory completion. This is known as "retainage." It is usually between 10 and 15% of the amount due the contractor. Once the project is successfully completed, this money is paid to the contractor, subject to his signing various documents (which are discussed later in this chapter) and to final completion of all punchlists and inspections.

Although this is commonly done, most contractors will not suggest the inclusion of such a clause in their contracts. If their attorney has not done so, you may want to remind your client of this option.

TIME FOR COMPLETION

There are several critical time periods on any project. The first is the date of commencement. The second is the date of substantial completion. The third is the date of final completion.

Date of Commencement

Usually projects begin on the date the contract is signed. However, contractors have to order materials and supplies and so sometimes the project is not actually started until weeks after the contract is signed. Sometimes projects begin within a period of days after receipt of a notice to proceed.

Clients should be aware of whether the contractor is agreeing to complete the project "within six months of signing the contract" or "within six months of receipt of materials."

Substantial Completion

This is the date on which the project is basically complete and ready for occupancy. Some additional work still needs to be done, but people can safely occupy the space. Usually only the punchlist is left—those odds and ends that need to be completed or adjusted.

Sometimes after the substantial completion date, the words "time is of the essence" will appear. This means that the contractor is being put on notice that the completion date is critical and that there may be serious financial repercussions or consequential damages if it is not met.

For example, when a couple has sold their house and is waiting to move into their new house, if it is not ready on time, they may have nowhere to live and be forced to stay in a hotel. They may have two mortgages to pay. If an office is not ready on time, the client may lose business. If a retail store is not ready on time, profits will be lost. These damages will all be demanded in a lawsuit, should the project not be completed on time.

Final Completion

This is the date on which the project is complete. All necessary inspections by governmental agencies have occurred and have been satisfactorily completed. The Certificate of Occupancy, if one is required, has been obtained or amended. All punchlists have been satisfactorily completed.

The contractor will have to furnish a Waiver of Lien, evidencing that he has been paid in full and has no reason to be filing a mechanic's lien. He should also furnish these waivers from his subcontractors and suppliers since they have an independent right to file liens. Occasionally there have been instances in which the general contractor has been paid but has not paid his subcontractors. This avoids such problems. Actually, partial waivers of lien may be required each time the contractor receives a payment. This assures the client that everyone who needs to be paid has been paid along the way.

The contractor may be required to sign a General Release of the client of all liability in connection with his fee. In other words, he is acknowledging that he has been paid in full and has no reason to sue the client for unpaid fees.

The fact that final payment has occurred does not mean the client cannot still call the contractor to come back to repair things. The contractor must comply with any warranties and guarantees in effect.

CHANGE ORDERS

These are amendments to the contract which either increase or decrease the amount of the fee paid to the contractor. If a portion of the work is deleted, the client will receive a credit. If new or unanticipated work needs to be done, a change order may be issued increasing the contract amount.

Ideally, change orders should always be in writing and be signed by both parties *before* the work is done. It should state the nature of the work and how much will be paid to the contractor.

Unfortunately, many times the demands of the job cause the parties to be lax and work is often done without change orders being signed in advance.

This means that the work has been done, but the parties have not agreed on a price for it in advance. You can immediately see the potential for a dispute. The client has less power to negotiate a good price and litigation is often the result.

If work is done based on an oral authorization, there should be some type of letter confirming the terms of payment, at a minimum. If there are many change orders, it may indicate that the designer's drawings were not detailed enough. Of course it can also mean that the client changed his mind a lot. Generally speaking, there should not be a lot.

SUPERVISION OF WORK

This is one of the most important issues to clients in their agreements with designers. Who will make sure that the contractor does his job properly?

The actual workmen should be supervised daily by a foreman or supervisor from the contractor's firm. The designer's role usually is only to see that the design is being implemented. The designer is not on the job on a daily basis and even if he or she is, it is only for a part of the day. It is simply not a designer's job to supervise the contractor, nor is he necessarily trained to do so. The client must be made to understand this. Again, if the designer does agree contractually to supervise the contractor, he should understand the legal responsibility he is taking on. In addition, the designer's fee does not usually justify this level of involvement.

On larger projects, a construction manager may be hired to act as the owner's representative and to supervise the work on the client's behalf.

INSURANCE

Most contracts require the contractor to obtain various types of insurance in various amounts relative to the value of the job.

General liability insurance is necessary in case anyone is injured on the job or any property is damaged. A visitor may trip over a hammer and be injured. The contractor may do demolition work which causes property damage, such as cracks, in a neighbor's apartment.

This insurance also protects the owner against lawsuits, since the owner is named as an "additional" insured on the policy. The designer may also request to be named as an additional insured.

Most contracts require such insurance, but not everyone is as careful as they should be to see that the contractor actually purchases such insurance and names the correct parties as insureds and additional insureds and in appropriate amounts. More than one client has been surprised to find that the project was not covered by insurance when the contract called for it. The client should make sure that the contract provisions are complied with.

LIQUIDATED DAMAGES

When a contract must be completed by a certain date, it is common to provide for liquidated damages. This is a sum of money the contractor is liable to pay for each day he is late. The damages the client will suffer from each day the project is delayed have been liquidated or reduced to a *per diem* amount.

The key to this concept is that the sum must bear a reasonable relationship to the amount of actual damages. It is not supposed to be punitive and if it is, it may be declared invalid by the courts. In other words, it may be several hundred dollars a day, not one million dollars per day.

This sum might include the *per diem* charges for a mortgage or rent when a store cannot open on time.

Often when there is a provision for damages arising from late completion, there will also be a bonus provision for early completion to balance things out.

TERMINATION

If the contractor fails to complete the work on schedule or to comply with the terms of the contract, he may be terminated. Usually advance notice must be given in writing so that the contractor has an opportunity to correct the problem. The typical time period is seven days notice. If the work has not improved, the contractor will be terminated and the client will take over the job and hire another contractor to complete the job. If the project costs more money to complete than the original contractor's contract, he can be held liable for damages.

PAYMENT AND PERFORMANCE BONDS

Bonds are another type of insurance. Payment bonds ensure that all subcontractors and suppliers on a project will be paid. Performance bonds ensure that the contractor will complete the project.

Not all contractors can obtain bonding because of the size of their business or the number of years they have been in business. Bonds are routinely required on commercial projects and only occasionally required on residential projects. In those states that require home improvement contractors licenses, bonding may be part of the licensing process. It is also common for the cost of such bonding to be passed on to the client.

In New York City some cooperative apartments won't allow a contractor into the building unless he is bonded. Should the contractor default on the job, the bonding company will step in to see that the project is finished.

ARBITRATION

As with the designer, if the client wants to have the right to arbitrate, there must be a specific provision in the contract and the contract must be signed by both parties.

Sometimes the client will want the designer to agree that if the client has a dispute with both the contractor and the designer, it can be argued at one combined arbitration. This is not done automatically. The parties must agree to it in their contracts. If they do not agree, separate hearings would be held. From the client's perspective, it saves time and money. However, the designer and contractor may be concerned that the claim against them will be tainted by the inclusion of the other party. This should be discussed with an attorney before the contract is signed.

HOME IMPROVEMENT CONTRACTORS LICENSES

These licenses are required in many jurisdictions for contractors who do renovation and construction work in homes. This is described in detail in Chapter 11.

Although it is not very difficult to obtain such a license, not having one can be devastating to the contractor, and may mean that the contractor's contract with the client may be void. Thus a contractor suing a client for the balance of his fee may not only be precluded from obtaining that fee, but he may be required to refund what he has already been paid. It may also be a basis for petitioning the court to vacate any mechanic's lien filed by the contractor for the project.

When a designer hires various trades and subcontractors, he can become a home improvement contractor and be subject to those laws. Thus a designer who wears two hats must be sure to be in full compliance with licensing laws for both interior designers and home improvement contractors in his state and county.

WORK STANDARDS

There are a variety of concerns clients may have for their work. For example, the contractor may only be allowed to work during certain hours. If they need to work at night or on weekends, they may need permission. There may be requirements for leaving the project "broom clean" and disposing of debris. Arrangements will have to be made for storing certain materials. Sometimes special security requirements must be met. There may need to be new locks installed or security guards hired.

The contractor may be required to have a certain number of workmen on the job. There should be a supervisor or foreman on the job at all times. Clients often want the contractor to agree to standards such as "the best" work and the "highest quality." These provisions should be reviewed with an attorney so that the contractor understands his legal obligations and the risk of agreeing to such terms.

9

Licensing of Products

Many designers design products in the course of their careers which are mass produced or sold in quantity, but on a limited distribution basis. The product can be anything from a chair to bed linen to dishes. Usually this work is done for a large company that has the ability to mass produce and market such items. Large companies will then sign an agreement with the designer for the company to license the right to sell these products. Sometimes a one-time flat fee is paid. Other times a royalty is paid for each item sold. The contract discussing these arrangements is called a "Licensing Agreement." This agreement gives the manufacturer the right to use your design for specific purposes, subject to specific terms and conditions, and you still own the design.

Large companies that have these types of arrangements with designers on a regular basis are apt to have fairly standard form agreements which are given to the designer for signature after the blanks concerning royalties and term of the agreement are filled in. At first glance it may seem as though the designer has little ability to negotiate; however, I would advise the designer that this is not the case. Also, you will not know what can be negotiated unless you try. So whatever agreement you are given, it should be reviewed by an attorney. Then either you or your attorney can contact the company to discuss whatever areas you are concerned about.

Unfortunately, often the designer is so thrilled and flattered to have been invited to do this work that they feel "I'll just do the work, take my chances, and if anything comes of it, so much the better." However, if the item is a surprise hit, you cannot then go back and try to renegotiate the deal. You must go into the arrangement thinking, "If this is a fabulous success, what would I think is fair for me to be paid?"

Sometimes items are designed on a much smaller scale for sale to a small group of the designer's clients and contacts. A furniture maker may do a prototype of an item and then if certain individuals want to order it, they can have it made for them. In such cases, the designer will either have an agreement to share profits with the furniture maker or will have a completely different type of agreement in which the furniture maker agrees that he is being given these designs solely for reproduction as requested by the designer and cannot use them for his own purposes. The designer would just pay the furniture maker the agreed upon price for each item ordered.

THE PRODUCT

One of the first things that must be defined in the agreement is what product is being licensed, since there may be related or spin-off products that are not covered by the agreement. You might design something to be used and marketed as a fabric design, but would not want it made into dishes without a further agreement. If you do not have such a provision, the manufacturer may be able to use the design for other products, without paying you any additional compensation or giving you credit as the designer.

EXPENSES

If the product must be developed and worked on, the designer should be paid or reimbursed for any expenses incurred in this process. If the licensing company will be providing any services to help develop the product, this should be discussed and clarified in the agreement. For example, if prototypes of a chair need to be made, the licensing company may do that for the designer at its facilities, rather than having the designer make his own arrangements. The designer should be reimbursed for travel, but may not be for art supplies.

ROYALTIES

The actual royalty amount can be very complex. Usually it will be 3–5% of the net sales. Sometimes it will be on a sliding scale, such as 5% of the first $100,000 of net sales, 4% of the next $100,000, and so on. The point is, it is negotiable.

What constitutes "net sales" can also be the subject of much negotiation. After a company deducts startup costs, advertising, and other expenses, there may not be much money left from which to take a percentage. This all needs to be documented.

Royalties are usually paid on a quarterly basis. A statement is issued periodically—monthly, quarterly, or semiannually. There should be some agreement to allow the designer or his accountant to audit books and records in case there is a disagreement as to what is owed or just to confirm that what has been paid is correct.

OWNERSHIP OF THE DESIGN

Often the company will copyright the design in its name. If the company decides to discontinue the item, it may agree that ownership will revert back to the designer. Sometimes the company will allow the designer to copyright the item or there may be a joint copyright. You should pay particular attention to this issue in the contract. It should also be kept in mind that separate agreements must be made for marketing in countries other than the United States.

WARRANTIES

The company will require that the designer warrant that the designs are original. After all, it does not want to sell products which may legally belong to someone else. It will also ask the designer to indemnify the company against any claims against it for copyright infringement. This means that the designer agrees to pay any damages if someone successfully sues for infringement.

The manufacturer must also protect the designer from any claims due to damages for a defective product or to theft of the design by another designer or manufacturer.

FINAL APPROVAL

As with any artistic creation, the designer will want to try to retain control over the design and quality of production. The extent to which this is allowed should be discussed in the agreement. If the designer wants veto power over decisions on quality, colors, or the final prototype or sample, it must be specifically stated in the contract. Otherwise the company has no particular obligation to discuss this with the designer.

DURATION

The agreement may last for one or more years and be renewed or it can be for a fixed period of time. The length of the agreement will depend on which company you are dealing with, the type of product, the usefulness of the product in the future, and a variety of other factors. Be careful not to lock yourself in for too long in an agreement.

ORAL NEGOTIATIONS

It is important to understand that once you sign an agreement, all prior negotiations and agreements are superseded by it. The signed agreement is the final agreement. The designer cannot later claim that there was some separate oral agreement that was not included in the signed agreement. The only time oral agreements may be a factor is if they are made subsequent to the contract and then only subject to certain conditions. Even then, they will not be of legal effect since most written contracts have a clause in them stating that they can only be modified or amended by another signed, written agreement.

ARBITRATION

I highly recommend arbitration as a method of resolving disputes in this area. Litigation can be extremely expensive and the designer will have financial difficulty in litigating for many years against a large corporation. Arbitration is discussed in detail in Chapter 11.

SHOWING YOUR DESIGNS

To attract the attention of a company, a designer will often send or take samples of his work to a company. Designs should be copyrighted to protect against their being stolen or copied. All drawings should bear the copyright symbol, the date, and the owner's name on them. A detailed cover letter should accompany them so that there is a record of what was sent to the company.

PUBLICITY

In most instances, the manufacturer will want to promote its name, rather than the designer's. If having your name on the product label or in advertisements is important to you, the terms must be negotiated with the manufacturer. The designer may want the right to approve advertisements and other publicity using his name. Of course, all of this is subject to the designer's requests being reasonable.

EXCLUSIVITY

Designers should be careful about agreeing to design exclusively for one manufacturer. If the designer intentionally or unintentionally breaches such an agreement and it is valid, he may be enjoined by the court from doing design work for another company for a period of time.

MARKETING

There should be a clear understanding as to the manufacturer's obligation to market the product. This may involve placement of the product in a show-room, preparation of catalogues, and trade shows. Once again, the designer may want the right to approve the marketing program.

SUMMARY

This is just an overview of some of the issues the designer must be aware of before signing a licensing agreement. It also underlines the importance of consulting with legal counsel before entering into such an agreement.

10

Purchasing Furniture and Selecting Products

PURCHASING

The selection of furniture, carpets, fabrics, and wallpaper is the meat and potatoes of a design professional's business. This is the area in which most of their income is made. It is also the area in which most of their problems with clients can occur.

Problems can range from having a long-awaited sofa that arrives in the wrong fabric to a scratched custom-made piano or a carpet with water stains. As a general matter the design professional should not be legally responsible for such problems; as professionals, they have a moral obligation to assist their clients in remedying such problems. It is also part of being a good businessperson.

Occasionally, because of the wording of their contract or their course of dealing with the client, they may be legally as well as morally responsible. This occurs when the designer places orders in his own name. There are also rare instances in which clients have given their designers funds for deposits on furniture orders that were never placed. This creates a whole different set of problems.

When a designer selects furniture for a client, he will usually visit a number of showrooms with the client. On commercial projects, catalogues may be relied on or even purchasing agents. The designer may not actually place any orders.

Once the merchandise has been selected, the designer will then prepare a Purchase Order. The designer should get a deposit from the client, then obtain a written confirmation of the order.

The amount of the deposit will vary. The manufacturer may have certain minimum deposit requirements and the designer may, in his contract, either demand the same amount as required by the manufacturer or a higher deposit.

The Purchase Order is usually a printed form on the designer's letterhead. It contains details about what item is being purchased, the price, and where it will be shipped. The actual form of the Purchase Order should be reviewed by an attorney before it is printed or typed for the client. The designer will receive back an Acknowledgement of the order from the manufacturer.

If the Purchase Order and the Acknowledgement have different or conflicting terms, reference will have to be made to the Uniform Commercial Code. This is a statute which sets forth the laws concerning sales of goods, among other things. It will then depend on whether the provision is a material alteration to the agreement. Then other facts must be examined, such as whether the Purchase Order expressly limited acceptance to the terms of the offer or the term was objected to. Courts examining these issues will also look at trade practices in the industry and the course of dealings between the parties to determine whether the particular clause should be part of the agreement.

CONFIRMATIONS OF PURCHASES

A Confirmation of Purchase is a written agreement with the client in which he consents to the proposed purchase and its cost. The designer prepares this and the client signs it and sends it back to evidence his approval. This helps eliminate the possibility that the client will change his mind or claim that the wrong thing was ordered or even that no authorization was given to order at all.

When the client returns these signed, he also sends along the requisite deposit as provided for in the contract. As we discussed in the chapter on contracts, a 50% deposit should generally be required. This shows that the client is serious in wanting to purchase the item. It also shields the designer from major losses if the client does not complete his obligation because the designer is buying the item at a substantially lower cost than the list price and the order may be noncancelable.

The designer should always keep a copy of the Purchase Order as it is sent to the client. The client will sign two copies—he will keep one and return the other to the designer. A designer is well advised to never order furniture from a vendor until he receives the *signed* confirmation and the deposit from the client.

Since the confirmations are contracts, it is common to have the terms and conditions of the order on the back. I also recommend to clients that these same terms appear in the main contract with the client. These should include the following:

1. Nothing will be ordered until the signed confirmation is returned with a deposit.
2. Orders are noncancelable. (If the company does allow cancellation, the designer can always discuss that with the client at a later date.)
3. Prices may be subject to change. Sometimes confirmations give estimated yardage if the fabric is a print, so the exact price may vary.
4. Shipping, freight, trucking, insurance, storage, and sales tax are all additional expenses to be paid by the client.
5. The order is being placed on the client's credit solely.
6. The designer is not responsible for delays and defects in the merchandise and does not guarantee or warrantee it against wearing or fading.
7. Patterned fabrics may be ordered based on estimated yardage.

FURNITURE LOSS AND DAMAGE

It is not uncommon for a piece of furniture to occasionally arrive damaged. Correcting this situation is sometimes complex, but need not be if you understand the general legal principles.

On a practical level, the manufacturer should immediately be notified of any damages. Sometimes the delivery men will arrange to take the item back immediately. Other times arrangements will have to be made to return it, depending on who is or may be responsible for the damage.

Your contract with your client should make it clear who is responsible for inspecting furniture when it arrives. Often the designer will be there for the delivery, but this may not always be the case. Sometimes furniture will be delivered, left in boxes, or put into storage without being examined. By the time it is opened, if there is damage, it can be impossible to determine when the damage occurred and who is responsible. For example, if a rug is delivered and put into storage in a room or a basement without having been opened, and is opened later and found to have water damage, each party who came into contact with the rug will claim that it was someone else's fault. The designer will say it arrived that way. The manufacturer will say it must have been damaged in storage. The client will not care when the damage occurred, he will just want an undamaged rug.

From a legal point of view, resolution of these transactions is governed by the Uniform Commercial Code. The key to determining who bears the risk of loss is whether the contract for the sale of goods is F.O.B. (free on board) the place of shipment or the place of destination.

When a delivery is "F.O.B. Place of Shipment," (usually the seller's address), then the seller is obligated at that place or location to ship the goods in the manner stated in the contract and to bear the risk and expense of putting the goods into the carrier's possession at the seller's address.

If the shipment is "F.O.B. Place of Destination," (usually the buyer's address), then the seller's obligation is to deliver the goods, at its risk and expense, to the place of destination and tender the goods to the buyer at the buyer's address. The manufacturer will be responsible for insurance. These laws apply when the parties so indicate in the purchase order and sales confirmation or when the parties do not indicate otherwise.

If there has been a loss and no indication of F.O.B. terms, the statutory section on "Risk of Loss" applies. The general concept is that the risk should be placed upon the party having control over the goods and the loss should fall upon the party most likely to insure the goods. However, there are no easy answers. It all depends on the particular facts. While designers may not be legally responsible for defective goods, some may choose to take on responsibility for helping the client to replace defective merchandise. This should be done with caution lest the client assume that you are accepting liability.

SPECIFYING PRODUCTS

Designers are always being approached by vendors with new products, which they then specify for use in projects. If anyone claims injury from such products, the designer who specified it will certainly become a party to such a lawsuit. This is a prime area of concern in "sick building syndrome" cases.

Obviously the client feels that he is relying on the designer's expertise in specifying these products. The contractor will no doubt claim that he was just following the designer's specifications. The manufacturer will claim that the product was not intended to be used in the manner specified by the designer or that it was not applied as specified. Paint or wallpaper might be a good example of this. I have had cases in which wallpapers came off the walls because the wrong glue was used.

When claims are filed, the client will argue two things: (1) that the designer negligently selected or specified the product and (2) that he negligently "supervised" the contractor's application or installation of the new product. "Negligence" is usually defined as the failure to use the care ordinarily exercised in like cases by reputable members of his profession and to use reasonable diligence and his best judgment in the exercise of his skill and the application of his learning, in an effort to accomplish the purpose for which he is employed. This standard is always viewed in terms of the designer's locale.

When selecting products for a project, you should keep a record of how that selection was made. For example, you may have written to the company and asked them to send you information about the product. Depending on what the product is, the manufacturer may give you a list of projects where the product was used and those users can be contacted for references.

Sometimes the manufacturer's representative may be contacted concerning any problems regarding the product. It is always helpful if the manufacturer is well known and has a good reputation for timely delivery, stands behind its products, offers warranties, has other products in the same line, and has reliable field representatives.

If possible, the designer should try to obtain information about the manufacturer's financial condition. From time to time manufacturers file for bankruptcy in the course of the project. This can make it impossible to resolve the problem.

Sometimes the risk of a product may be presented to a client and they decide to use the product anyway. This decision should be clearly documented and the designer may even request to be indemnified.

Depending on the product, it may be appropriate for you to send the manufacturer information about what you plan to do so that they can advise you about the best product to use and how to use it.

The manufacturer may send a field representative to observe the installation and to certify, upon completion, that the product was installed according to the manufacturer's recommendations.

ACCOUNTING FOR ORDERS

Unfortunately, on occasion a client will pay the designer for ordering furniture and the designer will not place the orders. Obviously this is rare, but a client does have the right to an accounting as to how his money has been spent. Even if all orders have been properly placed, a client has a right to see some reasonable amount of documentation to satisfy any concerns he may have. This does not necessarily mean that he has the right to see all your paperwork and to know your percentage of profits on items you order and charge at retail prices.

11

Legal Disputes

The idea of litigation is a frightening prospect for anyone in business. Unfortunately, for this reason some designers only seek legal advice when they have actually been sued. However, the seeds of litigation are planted long before a lawsuit is actually started and sometimes can be avoided if planning is done before there are any problems or if they are caught in time. A good lawyer can sometimes work in the background to help bring about the resolution of a problem before a lawsuit is started. If you know what to look for, the beginnings of a lawsuit can be detected in the early stages and you will know what to do to avoid it.

HOW TO SPOT A LAWSUIT IN THE MAKING

Long before a summons and complaint or demand for arbitration is served, a knowledgeable observer can spot the signs of a lawsuit in the making. It may start with the client not paying the designer on time, telephone calls that are not returned, or meetings that are canceled. The client may be very critical of the designer.

Usually it can be traced back to an event. Maybe some furniture arrived damaged and the client has unilaterally decided to hold the designer's fee until it is resolved. Perhaps the contractor's work was poorly executed and the client feels that the designer should have been there to avert the problem.

If you look back on any project, you can probably see when the problems first started. How you handle those problems will determine whether or not there will be an actual lawsuit. Avoiding the client, canceling appointments, and delaying furniture deliveries only add fuel to the fire. When these things occur you must get legal advice so that you do not overreact and you respond appropriately. An attorney who knows this area of the law can explain what you can expect and recommend what you should say or how to conduct yourself. In cases where the issues cannot be resolved, this interplay helps you to position yourself better for any litigation when and if it does arise. The client does not even have to know that you have gone to an attorney. The attorney may just be advising you in the background. Sometimes a meeting with the client and both sets of attorneys can be helpful in getting things back on track. If not, litigation will result.

There are several methods for resolving disputes. Going to court is the best known. Other methods of dispute resolution include arbitration and mediation.

THE COURT SYSTEM

In every state there are different levels of courts, with different names. The courts differ with regard to the amount in controversy which can be tried there.

Every state has a court that hears only small claims matters. The ceiling or dollar limit for these claims varies. In New York City the limit is $2000. In Florida it is $2500.

The next higher level of courts has different names. In New York it is called Civil Court and cases can be filed for up to $25,000. In other states it may be called County Court or District Court. There are usually many of these courts throughout the state.

The next higher court in New York is the Supreme Court. In other states it may be called the Circuit Court.

There will be variations within these courts. In some civil courts there is an arbitration section within the court for smaller cases, usually up to $6000. Unlike the arbitration process discussed elsewhere in this book, this arbitration is *not* binding. It can be appealed. So even when the courts require that the parties participate in this process, they can overlook the decision and proceed within the court system.

When parties represent themselves, it is called being *pro se* (a Latin term meaning "for himself"). Technically, no one is required to have an attorney to appear in court. However, it is somewhat like being a fish out of water if you do not. In the other courts, the procedural framework is so complex that only attorneys trained in litigation can navigate through its twists and turns. Even attorneys who do not regularly go to court find themselves not knowing what to do. Small Claims Court, on the other hand, is intended to be a people's court. Almost everyone there is without an attorney.

HOW DOES A LAWSUIT WORK

A lawsuit is started with a summons and complaint. These papers are usually served personally by a process server on the individual or corporation being sued. They can also be served by "substitute service," such as leaving a copy in a conspicuous place and mailing a copy by certified mail. A corporation can be served by serving a copy on the Secretary of State. The rules on service of complaints vary from state to state. The person who starts the lawsuit is called the "Plaintiff." The person being sued is called the "Defendant."

Once the papers have been served, they must be responded to. Generally this is done with an Answer. If there is some objection to the adequacy of the service of the papers, a Motion may be filed before the Answer.

Assuming an Answer is filed, the case will then proceed through "Discovery." This is the period during which both sides "discover" what the strengths and weaknesses of each other's case are and the facts of the case so that they can prepare for trial.

This can be done through requests to see various written documents, such as contracts, time records, correspondence, drawings, and purchase orders. There may also be written questions called "Interrogatories" or oral questions called "Depositions."

Depositions are much like being in court without a judge present. The person being asked questions, the deponent, is given an oath in which he swears to tell the truth. Whatever he testifies to is recorded by a court reporter. Not only can these depositions be used for preparing for trial, but they can actually be used at trial if the person gives different testimony and needs to be reminded of what he said (impeachment) or if the person is unable to be at the trial due to illness or death. Any objections to questions are recorded in the transcript and the judge makes rulings on them prior to trial. Depositions can last anywhere from an hour to several days, depending on the complexity of the case. This is one of the reasons lawsuits can take so long before they go to trial.

If the discovery process goes smoothly, it may take only a matter of months to complete. However, often the parties have disputes over which documents they should be required to produce and which questions they should answer. This requires the filing of motions to the court to have a judge decide what should be done. This process can take a few months from the time the motion is made until a decision is rendered. And finally, the courts are just so backlogged with cases that judges are not necessarily available to hear a case when you are ready to try it.

For this reason, many cases are settled out of court. Since no one can predict exactly when or if a settlement will occur, the cases must be litigated vigorously in anticipation of an actual trial. This work can also mean the difference in how favorable the settlement is.

The individual or corporation which has been sued may also have a basis for bringing a lawsuit. This is called a "Counterclaim." There may also be multiple defendants and they may have bases to sue one another. All of these factors can combine to make a lawsuit very complex.

When the case is ready for trial, it will be tried by a judge or a jury. If the decision requires one party to pay the other some money, they will either do so voluntarily or the attorney will have to use various techniques to collect on the judgment. Most states allow judgments to be collected on for a long period of time, such as 20 years. So even if you cannot immediately locate the defendant's funds to collect on the judgment, you have plenty of time to try.

ARBITRATION

Arbitration is an alternative method of resolving disputes. It is particularly useful in resolving construction-related disputes because there is a special construction panel of the American Arbitration Association to hear such claims.

The American Arbitration Association (AAA) is a nonprofit organization which acts as a kind of clearinghouse to arrange such hearings. They provide lists of arbitrators and hearing rooms at their offices, and schedule the hearing dates. They have offices in all major cities.

A "Claimant" begins the process by filing a Demand for Arbitration, a copy of the signed Contract with the arbitration clause and the appropriate filing fee. An elaborate complaint is not necessary. The AAA sends the demand to the "Respondent" who must then appear in the case either personally or through an attorney. "Appear" in this instance means file a response.

Once this occurs, both parties receive a list of potential arbitrators, their biographies, and a calendar of potential hearing dates. If the parties know one of the arbitrators or feel they would not be appropriate to hear the case, the name can be stricken from the list. After the list is returned to AAA, only the names not crossed out by either party will be considered. An arbitrator is then selected by AAA based on these lists, and dates for hearings are scheduled.

It is an excellent tool for resolving construction-related disputes because it takes much less time than a court case. This is because the lengthy period of "discovery" has been eliminated. As we discussed, this is the period in which the parties "discover" or find out about their adversary's claim. This is done mainly by written interrogatories, requests for documents, and depositions. In a court case, this can take years. In an arbitration, it is either eliminated entirely or done on a very abbreviated basis. There may be only one meeting with the Arbitrator to discuss the exchange of documents. There are no depositions.

Another unusual aspect of arbitration is that the rules of evidence do not apply; much more information is allowed at the hearing than in a court case. Some view this as advantageous, others dislike arbitration for this reason alone. The idea is that the parties should be able to come before the arbitrator and just tell their story.

Most design-related cases should take only a few days of hearings at the most. Some may take only a day. A decision or award is issued in writing by the arbitrator usually within 30 days thereafter. This award can be confirmed by the court into a judgment, just as in a court case, if it is not paid promptly.

Arbitration is binding on the parties and is virtually nonappealable. The courts feel that if this is the mechanism chosen by the parties for resolving disputes, then they should abide by the decision. Thus, it can be appealed only in very limited circumstances, such as fraud or abuse. An example might be if the arbitrator turned out to have a business interest in one of the party's companies.

MEDIATION

This is yet another method of dispute resolution. It resembles arbitration in the way it is conducted, but unlike arbitration, it is non-binding.

The idea behind this method is for the parties to have an opportunity to get together around a table and be able to talk about their dispute without fear of an adverse verdict. The mediator hears both sides and gives his recommendation as to which side he would rule in favor of and for how much. The parties can abide by his decision or ignore it and go further with the litigation process by way of arbitration or the court. It is a very flexible process with few rules as to conduct.

Because of the backlog in many courts throughout the country, some entrepreneurs have started their own profit-making mediation businesses to set up such hearings. They provide the parties with a forum for hearing these disputes and help them to find a mediator in exchange for a fee. The AAA also arranges such mediations.

Arbitration and mediation can be done on a voluntary basis with individuals selected in advance by the parties themselves. In one contract I negotiated for a designer, the client was reluctant to agree to arbitration. I proposed selecting a neutral party to decide any disputes and then they and my client agreed on a well-known architect in the community whom they both trusted to act as the arbitrator if they ever needed one. Of course, they never needed to use him.

The parties are not required to use attorneys to present their case. Actually, the parties are not required to be represented by attorneys in court either. However, without an attorney, the designer will find himself at a disadvantage in effectively presenting his case. This is particularly true when your adversary is represented by counsel. Thus, the parties should seriously consider being represented by legal counsel.

WHAT DO DESIGNERS GET SUED FOR?

No lawsuit is ever about just one issue. Lawsuits in the design and construction industry usually contain a laundry list of allegations. The following are a representative sampling of some typical claims or allegations in lawsuits against interior designers:

1. The project cost exceeded the designer's budget estimate.
2. There were defects in furniture, furnishings or equipment which the client feels were the responsibility of the designer to repair or have repaired or replaced by the manufacturer.
3. The client may feel the designer should have inspected furniture upon delivery to avoid the problem of discovering defects later and having the manufacturer potentially claim it was not his responsibility.
4. The designer promised that the project would be completed by a certain date and it was not.
5. The designer failed to properly "supervise" or "observe" the contractor and the work was defective.
6. The designer misrepresented himself to be an architect.
7. In certain states which have home improvement contractor's licenses, if a designer also acts as the general contractor and does not have such a license, it can be the basis of a claim by the client for a refund.
8. The prepared drawings do not reflect what the client believes he wanted or contain defects.
9. Perceived overcharging.
10. Disagreements over the amount of fees owed to the designer when a project has been terminated or abandoned before implementation.
11. Actual errors in the designs, such as mismeasurement, the specification of unsuitable items, or the failure to specify things.
12. Increased construction costs due to alleged errors by the designer.

13. The designer has agreed to indemnify the client against work done by others.

14. Damages caused to the premises.

15. The designer has verbally authorized the contractor to do work which was not approved in writing by the client.

16. The client does not like the design and feels he did not receive value for his money and should receive a refund.

17. The client decides after four months of shopping not to buy anything and wants a refund of the retainer.

18. Stains on countertops and carpets that the client claims were caused directly or indirectly by the designer.

19. The designer was given funds by the client to order furniture and furnishings and the items were never ordered.

20. The client asks for the designer's advice before purchasing or renting real estate and later has problems and claims he relied, to his detriment, on the designer's opinion.

21. The designer contracted for the services of subcontractors and did not have a home improvement contractor's license.

22. The client felt the designer bought too many rolls of wallpaper or overestimated yardage for fabrics.

23. The contractor put in the wrong tile and the designer failed to notice and bring it to the client's attention.

Usually several of these items will be alleged in a complaint. Although there are several different theories of recovery, the plaintiff can only recover once. Of course, merely because these things are alleged does not mean they are true. They must still be proven in court or at an arbitration hearing.

WHAT TO DO IF YOU ARE ABOUT TO BE SUED

If you are sued or think that a lawsuit may be brewing, the first step is to locate an attorney who knows this area of the law and make an appointment. Be prepared to bring your contract, key correspondence, and any applicable insurance policies.

If no lawsuit has been started, the attorney can help you to formulate a strategy and direct your conversations or correspondence with your client so that one may be avoided.

If you have not been paid, you can determine whether you should start a lawsuit or wait for the client to start one. If the lawsuit has started, it may be possible to negotiate an early settlement before the litigation becomes too expensive.

One of the things I enjoy about my design clients is that some of them are so well organized. I have had new clients come to my office with looseleaf binders with section dividers containing all the pertinent information on the case. It makes my job that much easier. I will discuss later in this chapter what you should bring along when you consult with an attorney.

WHAT TO DO IF YOU ARE ACTUALLY SUED

If you have in fact been served with court papers, usually a summons and complaint, either personally or by mail, or with a demand for arbitration, you must immediately seek legal counsel.

There are very definite time periods the defendant to a lawsuit has in which to file an answer or responsive papers. If the time passes and you have not filed such papers or obtained an extension of time, the plaintiff may try to obtain a judgment by default. Depending upon how much time passes and the reason why you did not respond, the court may or may not allow the default to be vacated and there may be a large money judgment against you or your firm. So service of a lawsuit should be taken very seriously.

If you have professional insurance which may cover the claim, you may advise your broker of the claim, contact the insurance company directly to advise them of the claim, or have your attorney contact the insurance company. The company has the right to receive timely notice of the claim so they can protect your interest and theirs.

WHY DESIGNERS BRING LAWSUITS

The main reason a designer ever has occasion to bring a lawsuit is to collect unpaid fees from a client. In the majority of cases, when the designer does this, the client will bring a countersuit or counterclaim against the designer for various things they claim went wrong on the project which justifies their nonpayment.

There are other reasons designers may also bring lawsuits. They may feel their designs for a project or for furniture or decorative objects have been copied or stolen. These suits may be with fellow designers, retail stores, or manufacturers.

There are any number of other types of lawsuits they may become involved in, such as litigation with fellow partners or shareholders over profits or how to run the business.

They may have disputes with consultants they have retained to do work on projects. They may have suits against manufacturers for defective furniture. If they hire subcontractors, such as painters, wallpaperers, and plumbers, they may have suits with the client or with them over the quality of their work.

MISCELLANEOUS LITIGATION ISSUES

As with any person or company in business, a designer can become embroiled in all types of litigation. Some may be unrelated to their design work. Suits may range from disputes with a landlord to copyright infringement of designs. There may be lawsuits with landlords over rent or damages to the premises from things such as water leakage. One designer may agree to share fees with another designer and this may result in a dispute. Litigation may arise when a partnership or corporation breaks up.

Designers should always be wary of crossing the line allowed by law and being accused of practicing architecture without a license. What constitutes crossing the line will vary from state to state. Not only can there be repercussions from state agencies, but the clients may initiate litigation claiming fraud and misrepresentation.

The designer and the design firm may take out bank loans and default in repayment. If the loan is for the design firm, the principal shareholder may have also personally guaranteed repayment of the loan. There are usually few, if any, defenses to such lawsuits, but an attorney may be able to work out a payment plan so that you are reinstated.

SETTLING A DISPUTE

This is always a difficult concept to explain to clients, because often the decision to do so has nothing to do with who is right and who is wrong. Litigation is an expensive, time-consuming, and emotionally draining process. Thus it is not at all unusual for a party to a lawsuit to decide to settle just because they do not want to incur legal expenses, time out of the office, and emotional stress.

However, settlement cannot always be achieved at the moment when the designer wants to settle. The parties may be far apart in the dollar amount of the settlement proposed. Thus a settlement can occur at any point in the case—even on the day of trial. Sometimes the parties are not ready to settle early on in the lawsuit, but after discovery they may feel more incentive to settle because of facts that have come out during that process.

Of course, settlement is always optional and the parties may simply wish to have their day in court and have a judge or jury decide the matter. However, it should be kept in mind as an option.

COLLECTING UNPAID FEES

Not all fee disputes have to wind up in litigation. Sometimes litigation results from a fee dispute just because both sides are being very stubborn.

Anytime a fee dispute develops, you must expect that if it is resolved, you will be paid less than whatever you are claiming. Clients rarely refuse to pay just because they feel like it. So you must factor in that there is at least *some* truth to their reason for not paying.

Once you balance this against the cost of litigation, you can soon see that it makes sense to try to work out a compromise and settlement.

Thus, any time there is a dispute with a client over fees, an attempt should be made to try to resolve it. This may mean having a meeting with the client and/or sending a letter describing what you are owed.

If these measures do not yield any results, of course you must then consider seeking legal advice. Even then, your attorney can still try to work out a settlement before commencing a lawsuit. Sometimes it is easier for a client to work out a settlement with an attorney acting as an intermediary.

In my experience, on the average, most disputes of this type settle for between 50 and 75% of what is being claimed. Not everyone immediately sees the wisdom of settling for less and getting whatever money is agreed upon right away versus litigating, paying legal fees, and either getting less money two or three years down the road or risking getting nothing, if a judge or jury finds against you. The decision to settle is often just a pragmatic business decision.

ARBITRATING A FEE COLLECTION CASE

Arbitration can be an excellent vehicle for collecting unpaid fees from a client for design services. It can resolve disputes much faster than a court case and therefore is much less expensive. However, design professionals should be aware of certain pitfalls when selecting this method.

It is important to remember that arbitration must be the agreed upon method of dispute resolution in your signed contract with your client. It is contained in many form contracts. If you use a customized contract, be sure that you have such a clause. If there is no signed contract or no arbitration provision in the contract, it is very likely that your adversary will not agree to arbitration when a dispute arises. I have only seen two cases in which the parties voluntarily agreed to arbitrate after a dispute arose.

After your client responds to the demand, both parties get to select arbitrators from a list of individuals who all work in construction-related fields. They can be attorneys, contractors, architects, interior designers, or property managers. Usually there is only one arbitrator. For large cases, usually involving more than $250,000, there may be three. Mutually agreeable hearing dates are also selected. You are not required to be represented by an attorney, but it is recommended that you have one so that your case is well presented.

When the design professional initiates such an action, it is not covered by errors and omissions insurance. However, if the client responds by filing a counterclaim alleging negligence or errors and omissions in the design, the defense of that counterclaim may be covered by your insurance carrier. Thus you could wind up having two sets of attorneys representing you. If your attorney specializes in construction law, some insurance companies may allow that person to handle the entire claim and they will pay the defense costs after the deductible is paid.

Some criticize arbitration because they feel that arbitrators tend to render split decisions. I do not find this to be the case. Also, in a worst case scenario, receiving half of what you are suing for in six months may be better than receiving half after three years of litigation and the attendant expense. Decisions by judges and juries can sometimes seem just as incomprehensible. Usually, unless the contract or a statute provides otherwise, legal fees are generally not reimbursable.

Hearings are held in conference room type surroundings. They tend to be conducted much like court cases, but do not have to be. The rules of evidence do not apply and it can be a more relaxed atmosphere. The scope of examination is up to the arbitrator. Despite that, however, it is just as serious in consequence as a court case and should be taken seriously. I have heard of instances in which parties ignored arbitration demands thinking they were of no consequence. They found awards were issued against them since they were in default. Such demands are very serious, since they are virtually nonappealable.

Arbitrators issue written awards which are received in the mail. They do not discuss their decisions or the reason for their decisions at the hearing. If the client is required to pay, he usually has 30 days to do so after the award has been issued. If he does not, the award can be turned into a judgment by the court and collected as would any other judgment. The party who has received the judgment has many years to collect on it. In some states it may be as much as 20 years.

The process of arbitration brings parties to the table and often settlements are reached before the hearings begin. In one case in which I was the arbitrator, the parties had to wait in my reception area while I finished a telephone call. When I came out, the case had been settled.

Arbitration can be an excellent tool for collecting unpaid fees, but since there is a high probability of a counterclaim by the client, it should not be started lightly. Before I start such suits, I always have a long meeting with my client to discuss any possible bases they can think of for their client to file a counterclaim. This way we know whether we are opening up a can of worms by starting an action to collect fees.

MECHANICS LIENS

These liens are a method of recording in the public records for real property that money is owed to certain categories of individuals for improvements they made to real estate which have not been paid for in full. It is a creature of statute in each state and very specific requirements must be met in order for the lien to be validly filed.

Basically the lien states (1) who is filing the lien, (2) who it is filed against, (3) what type of work it was filed for, (4) the property it is being filed against, (5) the amount of the contract, and (6) the amount owed. Contractors, materialmen, suppliers, architects, and engineers may file such liens in all states. Generally interior designers cannot because they are making cosmetic rather than structural and physical changes to improve the real property itself.

However, this option is available to interior designers in a few locales (e.g., the state of Florida). Of course, if the designer is also working as a contractor, liens are available to them for the contracting work they have done.

While liens are a very important tool in the construction industry for obtaining payment, they do not guarantee it. If a lien is filed before a transfer of the property is about to occur, it may well precipitate payment or settlement. However, if the owner is not planning to move and does not have a co-op board pressuring them to have the lien removed, it may just sit unresolved. They do not last indefinitely and need to be renewed. The thinking is that if you are really owed this money, you will probably file a lawsuit to collect it, rather than renewing your mechanic's lien year after year.

The type of lawsuit used to pursue collection of a lien is called "foreclosure of a lien." If you are successful, the property will be foreclosed on and sold to satisfy the amount owed. Obviously, this rarely occurs. A settlement is usually reached somewhere along the way.

Liens should be prepared and filed by legal counsel, since they can be vacated or removed if they have defects. If they are inflated and a property owner can establish that they were "willfully exaggerated," you can be subject to damages of as much as three times the amount of the lien. You may not assume that your lien is valid and will stand up to legal scrutiny just because the clerk accepts it for filing.

OTHER TYPES OF LITIGATION

Designers may have other kinds of legal disputes besides those they have with clients. They may have disputes with their partners in business or fellow shareholders.

LEGAL DISPUTES ENCOUNTERED BY PARTNERS

There are two general categories of lawsuits partners face. One category involves lawsuits between partners over issues involving the partnership. The other category involves lawsuits between the partners, the partnership, and third parties, such as clients.

LAWSUITS BETWEEN PARTNERS

When partners have disputes between one another, it is usually in the context of a breakup of the partnership or the withdrawal of a partner. One partner may be leaving of his own free will or may have been forced out.

In some cases this may cause the entire partnership to fall apart. In others it will continue and the one partner will leave. The main issue in such situations is generally money. More specifically, the partners often disagree about the distribution of profits and the projects. For example, in larger firms not all partners have access to the firm's books and records. An outgoing partner may be told that there are no profits to distribute, when he knows the firm had a good year. This can make for a major dispute.

In some rare situations partners may even disagree about whether monies paid to a partner were drawn against partnership profits or loans to be repaid to the partnership. The partnership may dispute whether monies paid by the partner were contributions to the partnership or loans. This sort of confusion can occur when there is no formal written partnership agreement.

Other controversial issues which may be raised when a partnership breaks up or one partner leaves are: (1) who keeps which projects and how the fees will be divided; (2) who gets to keep the office space and how the lease will be paid for; (3) how office files and equipment will be divided; (4) how outstanding invoices and taxes will be paid; and (5) whether the partners can seek new business from the firm's existing clients. Courts do not like to get involved in such issues, but do if legal actions are started to divide up the assets. These subjects may be more easily decided in an arbitration hearing. As was discussed earlier in Chapter 7, an arbitration clause can be placed in the partnership agreement if you wish to have disputes resolved through arbitration.

Many of the subjects of such lawsuits could and should have been addressed and resolved in the partnership agreement. If they are not in the partnership agreement or there is a dispute over the interpretation of a provision, litigation is likely. Arbitration is a widely used dispute resolution vehicle for partnerships. It can only be used to resolve partnership disputes, however, if an arbitration provision is in the written partnership agreement. Otherwise, disputes between partners must be resolved in court. If partners seek legal counsel promptly, there is also the possibility that some of these issues can be resolved and a settlement reached without resorting to a lawsuit.

If there is a dispute, generally the partners will want what is called an "accounting." This is commonly done when one partner leaves, voluntarily or involuntarily, and feels that the other partners have converted partnership property to their own use or wrongfully excluded him from the partnership business or possession of its property. It may also occur if the partnership agreement calls for it or if it is reasonable to do so under the circumstances. Sometimes it is a prerequisite for a lawsuit.

If, for example, a partner advances money for his interest in a partnership and wants to recover that money, he cannot sue for it like a loan, but must bring an action for an accounting instead. Unfortunately, many partners leave partnerships without any accounting. They have a feeling that they are entitled to some money, but do not want to take steps to determine if any is truly owed, for fear of litigation resulting and the attendant expense.

An accounting involves having someone review all the partnership's books and records. Sometimes this can be done by agreement of the parties. If not, it will be done in the context of a court case and the court will appoint someone to handle this.

In my experience, the partners do a great deal of fighting over very little money and wind up not having much money to divide. After all the dust from the litigation settles, it is best if the partners can work out a settlement through their attorneys.

LAWSUITS BETWEEN SHAREHOLDERS

As with partnerships, corporations can also have internal disputes. One shareholder may want to sell his shares or be forced out or the entire corporation may be in disarray and the shareholders may want to close the business.

PIERCING THE CORPORATE VEIL

As was discussed in Chapter 1, the most fundamental principle of corporate law is that a corporation is a separate entity from its shareholders. As such, the corporation's shareholders are insulated from the liabilities of the corporation. Courts are reluctant to pierce the corporate veil unless there has been fraud, some great injustice has been committed, or the corporation is being used as a means of carrying on business for personal rather than corporate ends.

Some of the criteria looked at by courts in determining a corporation's "corporateness" are:

1. Whether the business is conducted on a corporate rather than a personal basis, with corporate formalities being observed, such as keeping corporate minutes of meetings of the Board of Directors and the shareholders.
2. The corporation must be established on an adequate financial basis.
3. Separate bank accounts and records must be maintained and there must not be commingling of funds.
4. Corporate loans and financial transactions must be separate from personal ones.

Many designers find that when lawsuits are started both the main designer and the corporation are sued. This is because they have been careless and intermingled their individual identity with that of the corporation. For example, they may not have the corporation's name on their letterhead and business cards and clients may give them checks payable to the designer as an individual. Thus, even though there is a corporation and the check may have been deposited in the corporation's bank account, the designer has given his adversary a loophole for claiming the right to sue both the corporation and the individual. Both may not ultimately be found liable at trial, but both will have to defend themselves and go through the trial process.

If a designer goes through the trouble of incorporating, he should adhere to the corporate formalities in all aspects of his business to eliminate this type of claim.

DOCUMENTS TO BRING TO YOUR ATTORNEY

When you have a dispute with a client or are involved in an actual lawsuit, you will need to gather relevant documents to bring to your attorney. At the top on the list is your contract with your client. If it has not been signed, it may be helpful to bring any other drafts of the agreement.

Correspondence between the parties can be helpful in explaining how the disagreement developed and what the main issues are. This should all be in chronological order.

All of your invoices to your client should also be in chronological order along with information detailing what you have been paid to date. It may be helpful to know which items are on order and have yet to be delivered.

If you have any applicable insurance policies, they should be part of the package.

If there is a set of plans or drawings for the project, this can be useful in explaining to your attorney what happened. Photographs of the project can be extremely useful but should show a date either on the print itself or with a newspaper in the background.

If there is a dispute as to whether the right color fabric or marble was ordered, having the approved sample can be important for winning the case.

All of this information should come from the various folders the designer keeps for each project. The information should not be scattered around the office.

LAWSUITS WITH OTHERS

In lawsuits between partners and third parties, each partner is legally responsible for the acts of his copartners in the course of partnership business. In other words, the partner must be engaged in some partnership business which results in a lawsuit, not personal business, in order for him to be held liable.

Partners are generally liable "jointly and severally" for everything chargeable to a partnership because of a partner's breach of trust or wrongful act or omission. Thus each partner in a partnership will usually be a named party in any such a lawsuit and will be separately served with legal papers. If the partnership assets are not sufficient to satisfy an obligation, the obligation may be satisfied out of the partners' separate property.

This can be an eye-opening experience in a partnership where there are many partners and they each handle their projects separately. Usually such partnerships do not have written partnership agreements and function more like an expense sharing arrangement, rather than a cohesive business. Nevertheless, they hold themselves out as partners and legally are a partnership.

If there is a lawsuit arising from any partner's project and it alleges negligence, all of the partners can and will be named as parties. Of course, the alleged negligence must have been committed in the course of the partnership business. This is also true, by the way, even if the wrong was committed by an employee.

This is why partners have to keep abreast of the progress of projects being handled by other partners in the firm. They should meet regularly and discuss the status of projects and any problems they have encountered. Maintaining professional liability insurance can also help alleviate anxiety over the individual liability aspects of being in a partnership. Finally they should seek legal advice if there are any budding disputes, either between each other or with third parties. This will help lessen the likelihood of litigation.

12

New Areas of Concern for Interior Designers

AMERICANS WITH DISABILITIES ACT

The American with Disabilities Act (ADA) is a federal civil rights law designed to improve access to jobs, work places, and commercial space for people with a wide range of disabilities. The relevant areas of application are stores, offices, and private residences, if they are used for business. Existing buildings, new construction, and alterations all fall within the Act. These buildings must be accessible to and usable by individuals with disabilities. The businesses not covered by the Act include private clubs, religious institutions, residential facilities covered by fair-housing laws, and certain owner-occupied inns.

Architectural barriers must be removed, except when it is not "readily achievable" or too difficult and expensive. The regulations identify factors which may be deemed to cause a hardship, such as (1) the cost and nature of the action; (2) the financial resources of the parties involved; (3) the financial resources of related entities and the extent of the affiliation; (4) the impact of the action on the site; and (5) the effect of the action on profitability. These factors are flexible, to allow a case-by-case approach. However, a business can still be liable even if it attempts in good faith to comply.

The final rules define discrimination under the Act as a failure to design and construct facilities for first occupancy after January 26, 1993, that are "readily accessible and usable by individuals with disabilities." If a new facility cannot be made entirely accessible, it must comply to the fullest extent possible.

Modifications to existing facilities that are "readily achievable" must be made immediately. Alterations to a place of public accommodation or a commercial facility made after January 26, 1993 must "ensure, to the maximum extent feasible, the altered portions of the facility are readily accessible to and usable by individuals with disabilities, including individuals who use wheelchairs." Any construction that involves a change that could affect the usability of the building requires that the Title III standards of the Act be met.

The Act is not limited to the removal of barriers that affect mobility. It also requires removal of barriers in connection with other disabilities, such as visual, hearing, mental, tactile, and reading impairments.

Measures taken to remove architectural barriers are to comply, if possible, with the technical design guidelines applicable to alterations. However, when strict compliance with these standards is not readily achievable, minor deviations are permitted if they do not pose a safety risk to disabled or able-bodied individuals.

Violations of Title III of the Act are enforced in the same manner as the violations of other civil rights acts. Actions may be brought by aggrieved parties.

Remedies for noncompliance may include injunctions to require modification of the facilities, money damages, civil penalties up to $100,000, and attorney fees.

The Attorney General may also bring "pattern and practice" cases against owners or tenants. When considering the imposition of a civil penalty under the Act, the courts may consider a covered entity's good-faith efforts to comply.

In order to facilitate consistency between local and state laws and the federal standard, a state or locality may request the Attorney General to certify that its building code's accessibility requirements comply with the provisions of the Act. Where state and local requirements are less stringent, the Act will supersede local and state codes and accessibility requirements.

Although the standards are tantamount to a national building code, there is no federal, state, or local agency obligated under the ADA to review or approve drawings and specifications for compliance, even if the local codes are certified to be in compliance with the standards. Thus an entity has no way of knowing for sure if it has properly discharged its obligations under Title III unless a complaint is filed.

The Act should not expand legal liability for design professionals, since they are already legally bound to design in compliance with applicable codes, regulations, and standards whether or not such a provision is specifically included in a contract. Failure to design in compliance with applicable codes may be negligence. However, design professionals should be careful about agreeing to express warranties of compliance and indemnifications of their clients without regard to negligence, since this may not be covered by insurance and would increase their potential liability.

Ultimately, it is the building owner or tenant who decides on the method and money to be invested in compliance. Also, the Act will be interpreted by the courts. Thus design professionals should avoid guaranteeing or certifying compliance with the Act and should seek legal counsel knowledgeable in this area before signing any contracts.

INDOOR AIR POLLUTION

Indoor air pollution can occur as a result of the presence of statutorily defined "hazardous substances" or from the accumulation of unacceptable levels of various pollutants such as gases, vapors, radon, and bacteria due to inadequate fresh air ventilation. Such pollution can also be generated by asbestos, formaldehyde foam insulation used in building materials, fiberglass duct lining, radon from granite building materials, pentachlorophenol from logs, polychlorinated biphenyls (PCBs) from electrical transformers, diisocyanate insulation, wall fabrics and pressed wood furniture, plasticizers in rugs, paint, tobacco smoke, and microbes in the ventilation system. Copy machines generate ozone. Furnishings such as carpet, drapes, chairs, and sofas may "act as a wick, absorbing toxics" from the indoor air that came from other sources.

These pollutants accumulate because buildings are designed with sealed windows and insulated walls to be "tight" so as not to allow heat to escape. Consequently, not enough fresh air may come in. Their heating, ventilating, and air conditioning systems may be inadequate to clean out these pollutants and recycle in sufficient quantities of outdoor air. There may also be building maintenance problems which prevent the building equipment from functioning properly. When the building occupants become sick with illnesses such as eye irritation, nausea, headaches, heart problems, and cancer, it is called "sick building syndrome" and may provide a basis for litigation against building owners, managers, contractors, architects, interior designers, HVAC installers, manufacturers, and others who have worked on the building.

Certain substances are clearly toxic and have been acknowledged as such in federal, state, and local legislation. Others, such as tobacco smoke, are arguably so and have been regulated only at the local level in some areas. Asbestos, in particular, is a hazardous substance which has and will continue to receive a tremendous amount of attention.

Case Law

It is surprising that only one classic sick building case has come to a jury trial so far; most cases seem to settle. However, it may have tremendous implications for the architectural and engineering communities. This occurred in Southern California. The case was settled one month into the trial with the dollar amount kept secret by a confidentiality agreement. Such agreements seem to be increasing in popularity and make dissemination of information about such cases very difficult.

The most interesting aspect of the case is the suggestion that strict liability law could prevail in similar cases. The judge ruled that if the jury were to find the heating, ventilation, and air conditioning (HVAC) system in the building to be defective, then the designer and contractor of the building could be subject to liability under a strict liability theory of law. Using this approach, the building would be like a sold product. Presumably anyone in the chain of people who designed, manufactured, and installed the HVAC system or its components (architects, engineers, designers, retailers, manufacturers, distributors, contractors, installers, and subcontractors) could conceivably be potentially liable.

In this particular lawsuit, the general contractor is likely to pay the settlement because he constructed the shell and core of the office building and agreed in his contract to indemnify the owner, even though this occurred years after the building was constructed. As would be expected in such cases, everyone in the chain will be sued eventually, either directly or for indemnification—subcontractors, architects, designers, and engineers.

The case arose in 1985 when contractors were renovating the interior of one of the suites in this office building. The plaintiffs were two firms and their employees who occupied one half of the floor and shared the HVAC system. After work began, employees experienced dizziness, nausea, nosebleeds, headaches, disorientation, and respiratory problems allegedly due to toxic fumes drifting to their side of the floor from new carpets, furniture, and paint on the other side. The problem was allegedly intensified by leaks in the ducts in the HVAC system. The corporations alleged business interruption losses and lack of productivity.

One solution might have been to pump fresh air in to flush out the contaminants, but the building's outside dampers were not big enough to circulate 100% fresh air. The HVAC system was capped so that only 10% outside air could be brought in.

As with many such cases, the problems may have been caused by a combination of elements: tight construction of the building shell; inadequate HVAC system; untrained building managers; extensive interior renovations by tenants; and the use of synthetic materials and furnishings containing volatile organic compounds such as formaldehyde, toluene, and methyl ethyl ketone. This is the type of case we will see more of in the near future.

The sick building cases are of considerable concern to the construction and design industries, because everyone involved with the building can become a party to the lawsuit and it may occur years after the building was constructed. Indemnification clauses in contracts and insurance coverage in this area should all be carefully reviewed before starting on a new project since they can be invoked years after the work is done.

Most sick building cases have their origin in HVAC problems—either bad design or maintenance. Since so many people contribute to the work done on HVAC systems, there are many possible defendants in such lawsuits. Building owners can be sued by tenants. Tenants can be sued by employees. Building managers may be liable for maintenance problems. Designers and consultants may be liable for HVAC designs. Interior designers conceivably may be sued for floor plans which do not take into account the combination of air supply and smoking areas.

Proposed Legislation

Despite all the controversy about indoor air pollution, it still remains a very unregulated area. There are no real governmental standards for conduct. However, it should be noted that certain problems may be violations of current building codes and can be handled through the appropriate agency.

The American Society of Heating, Refrigerating, and Air-Conditioning Engineers (ASHRAE) has issued a new Standard 62-1989 in which it recommends that HVAC (heating, ventilating and air conditioning) systems be designed to deliver at least 15 cubic feet per minute per person (cfm/p) of outdoor air in mechanically ventilated buildings. The standard applies to hotel lobbies and certain retail shops. Higher minimum rates are recommended for most buildings, such as 20 cfm/p for office buildings. This standard is not a legal requirement. However, if it is ever adopted by national model and local building codes, it will be. However, it is widely adhered to at the present time and is the standard looked at in most court cases.

There are currently two indoor air quality bills which have been proposed and both are called the "Indoor Air Quality Act of 1991." As they are amended and reintroduced each year, the name changes to reflect the year.

One Indoor Air Quality Act of 1991 was introduced by Rep. Joseph P. Kennedy (D-Mass.). Briefly, it proposes that any public or commercial building which receives a permit for construction or for significant renovation must have an HVAC system designed to provide a minimum of 20 cfm of outdoor air per occupant to all occupied space and a minimum of 60 cfm of outdoor air per smoking occupant where smoking is permitted. Exhaust air from a room where smoking is permitted shall not be returned to the general ventilation system.

There is a similar bill in the Senate introduced by Senate Majority Leader George Mitchell (D-Maine). Each of these bills has been reintroduced annually and it is likely that there will be further versions of these proposed bills.

COPYRIGHT

Designers can become involved with copyright issues for a variety of reasons ranging from product design to the conceptual (not architectural) design of a building to artwork.

Under recent amendments to the U.S. copyright laws, buildings can be subject to copyright protection. In addition, a building owner can face liability if he alters or destroys works of art placed in buildings even if the owner has purchased all right, title, and interest, including the copyright, to the artwork from the artist.

Prior to this amendment, copyright protection extended to architectural drawings and blueprints, but not to the buildings themselves. Now there is a new category of copyright protection for "architectural works." This covers architectural designs in building exteriors and interiors. It also protects designs embodied in blueprints and other two-dimensional works. This protection is in addition to the prior law, which basically protected blueprints as works of art.

Unauthorized copying of a copyrighted work is one type of copyright infringement. Under the old law, a building was not considered a copy of a blueprint, with the consequence that the unauthorized construction of a building from blueprints did not constitute infringement. Under the new law, a building is considered a copy of a design embodied in a building. As a result, four types of copying are now prohibited:

1. Copying blueprints by making blueprints.
2. Copying blueprints by erecting a building.
3. Copying a building by making blueprints of the design embodied in the building.
4. Copying a building by erecting a building (without making blueprints as an intermediate step).

The law applies to structures such as houses, offices, factories, and warehouses but not to bridges and dams.

The law applies to buildings erected after December 1, 1990. Designs of buildings which were not erected as of that date but which are embodied in unpublished plans are also covered, but these designs will lose copyright protection if the building is not constructed by December 31, 2002. Copyright protection arises automatically as soon as the work is created. Unlike patent or federal trademark protection, copyright protection does not require an application to the government or the issuance of a certificate by the government.

The designer owns the copyright unless: (1) he has assigned it to the owner or (2) the designer was an employee of the owner and created the design within the scope of his employment. This is known as a "work for hire." In such a case, the firm owns the copyright. This is why it is important for design professionals to have an attorney knowledgeable in this area draft or review the contract language on ownership of drawings. It is also important to have contracts with consultants who may do design work for your firm.

The owner of the copyright in a building can prohibit others from making copies of the work (i.e., a "look-alike" building) and from making what the Copyright Act refers to as "derivative works," which in this context are buildings designed after the original building was designed and which are derived from or are modifications of the original building design. For example, a building owner who does not own the copyright may face a lawsuit for copyright infringement if he or she erects a second building similar to the first one—even though the owner commissioned and paid for the original building. Similarly, if the designer does not own the copyright, he or she may face liability if a building designed for a second client is similar to the one designed for the first client.

Infringement is also protected in foreign countries which are members of the Berne Convention.

It is worthy to note that the owner of a copyright cannot prevent others from taking or distributing photographs of the building. Hence developers can use photographs of the building in sales brochures without the designer's permission, but cannot make models of the building. Of course, this can be modified if the parties provide for it in their contract.

Thus there are now two required copyrights. One is for "architectural works" and the other is for blueprints and drawings protected under the category for "pictorial, graphic and sculptural works."

Copyright protection extends for the life of the author plus 50 years unless the work was made for hire, in which case it extends for the earlier of 75 years from the date of publication or 100 years from creation (i.e., the moment the design is drawn on paper), if the work remains unpublished.

While copyright notices are not required, they can prevent an infringer from having a damage award reduced and provide an inexpensive way to make it clear that a copyright is claimed and thus deter infringement.

To institute a copyright infringement suit, the work must first be registered with the Copyright Office. There are various formalities in filing which must be met and it is recommended that an attorney familiar with this area of the law be consulted.

For those designers who also produce fine art, such as murals, sculptures, drawings, prints, and photographs, there are now new "moral rights" under the Visual Artists Rights Act. The "right of integrity" provides an artist with (1) the right to prevent intentional distortions, mutilations, or other modifications of his work which are "prejudicial" to his "honor or reputation" and (2) the right to prevent destruction of works of "recognized stature." The "right of attribution" allows the artist to (1) claim authorship of the work; (2) prevent the use of his name in connection with a work he or she did not create; and (3) prevent the use of his name in connection with a work which has been mutilated or distorted in a way "prejudicial" to his "honor or reputation."

The Act applies to qualifying works created on or after June 1, 1991, with retroactive application for works created before that date if the artist had not transferred title by then. For works created on or after that date, the Act's rights are limited to the life of the artist. Somewhat anomalously, for works created but not transferred before June 1, 1991, the term of the Act's rights is the same as the term of traditional copyrighted protection, which is longer—the life of the artist plus 50 years.

The remedies for infringement of the Act's rights are basically the same as those for infringement of traditional copyrights, as discussed above. The Act's rights do not prohibit the reproduction of qualifying works of fine art in other works of art. Thus a building owner can rent the building interior to a film producer and allow sculptures in the lobby to be shown in the movie without violating the artist's rights.

The Act provides one set of rules that apply to art work that is physically separable from the building and a second set for work that is not separable. The second set is important when the building owner wants to renovate or tear down the building.

A building owner's rights to make changes in art that is physically separable from the building are subject to the Act's requirements of integrity and attribution which apply to all owners of art work. For example, the Act's rights would prevent a building owner from reducing the height of a sculpture or making other changes to the art work, even if the owner bought the art and all the traditional copyrights therein from the artist. These limitations can be avoided, however, if the work is created as a "work for hire" by an employee-artist or if the artist executes a written waiver of the Act's rights. To be effective, the waiver must meet the specific statutory requirements. It is unclear, however, whether a waiver of the Act's rights is transferable to a subsequent purchaser of the art. The legislative history indicates that waivers are not transferable, but the statute itself contains no such limitation.

Special rules apply to art "incorporated in or made part of a building" (such as a mural or a sculpture which is an integral part of a wall) which do not apply to other art, and the Copyright Office has adopted filing requirements which apply only to building owners and artists of works incorporated in buildings. The treatment of art incorporated in buildings depends on whether the work can be removed with or without harm.

If a work cannot be removed without destruction or harm to its integrity, a potential exception is provided with respect to (1) the integrity rights and (2) the artist's right to disassociate his name from works that have been modified in a way which violates the right of integrity (which is one part of the right of attribution). Works installed after June 1, 1991 can be removed by the building owner without violating those rights if the artist has signed a written instrument acknowledging that removal might result in the destruction, distortion, or modification of the work. This prevents building renovation from being held hostage to the art. The artist's acknowledgement extends to a subsequent purchaser of the building, making it a valuable asset of the original building owner and an item that should be added to the developer's checklist of "rights" to be acquired. Works installed before June 1, 1991 are deemed covered by such an acknowledgement.

If it is physically possible to remove a work from a building without destruction or harm to its integrity, then a different rule applies. In this case, a building owner must make a diligent, good faith attempt to notify the artist of the owner's intent to remove the work and provide a 90-day period for the artist to remove the work (which is to be done at the artist's expense). If the artist does not remove the work, the owner can alter or destroy the work free of the Act's liability.

To facilitate notification, artists can record their names and addresses with the Copyright Office, and an owner who sends notice by registered mail to the recorded address is deemed to have provided the required notice.

State law is also a source of moral rights and one that must be considered along with the new federal legislation in evaluating artists' rights. New York and 10 other states have enacted statutes that provide some form of moral rights for artists. State artists' laws are not preempted to the extent that (1) they protect types of art work that are not protected under the Act; (2) they provide that the attribution right is violated in the absence of injury to honor or reputation, which the federal law requires; (3) they provide a cause of action for misattribution of a reproduction of a work of visual art, because reproductions are not covered by the Act; or (4) they provide rights and remedies that extend beyond the life of the author. Accordingly, building owners should consider broadening a waiver of moral rights to include state rights. In short, both state and federal law must be analyzed in connection with building renovations and alterations to art work. Artists should consult with legal counsel to be sure that their rights are protected.

Appendix A

Education for Interior Design

Kerwin Kettler

With the increase in the number of states requiring licenses for interior designers, even experienced designers must be concerned with education programs to help them pass licensing exams and continuing education in order to stay licensed and meet requirements for various professional organizations. This material will help you to understand what is available whether you are just starting out in the profession or are increasing your skills.

THE CRITICAL NEED FOR INTERIOR DESIGN EDUCATION IN THE LATE TWENTIETH CENTURY

The Case for Education in Interior Design Today

Just about everyone we know does interior design. We live in interior spaces, have furniture, lamps, and other possessions which all make up the interior

---

Kerwin Kettler has taught design at Drexel University and Cornell University and served as Dean of the New York School of Interior Design from 1977–1990. He was founding Chairperson of the Positions Committee for the American Society of Interior Designers, has been involved in licensing issues at both the national and the New York State level, and currently represents the design educators in the United States on the National Legislative Coalition for Interior Design (NLCID). He is on the Board of the National Symposium for Healthcare Design.

environment. We make decisions on basic planning, where to locate that sofa, what table to buy, what color to paint. In a sense, we are always involved in interior designing.

Although this very personal process of interior designing appears to be universal, the layman does not normally say "I am an interior designer." However, the process of shaping the interior space, fitting it to our physical, artistic, and symbolic needs reaches back to the beginnings of man, witnessed through cave paintings and early forms of human habitat, and even to the animal world. The need for shelter, fulfilled through the process of inhabitation, is fundamental to us all.

Consistent with other occupations in the late twentieth century, interior design is now called a profession. It has become legally recognized as a profession in one-third of the United States, employs hundreds of thousands of people in daily practice, and represents between 1 and 2% of the United States gross national product. The process of design is fastened to complex social, economic, and legal ramifications. But what is the great divide between the personal act of "feathering the nest" and the professional act of "interior designing"?

Essentially, the difference involves education and economics. Interior design has evolved as a professional activity throughout the past two centuries along with other forms of work such as medicine, architecture, engineering, and accounting. In this century, a number of sociologists have been dedicated to studying what has been termed "the process of professionalization." What they have discovered is a transformation of work into a highly ordered process which involves formal education, definitions of practice (such as the specific tasks involved in performing the professional work), an organized body of knowledge which is required to perform the work, a formal point of entry into the profession,* and the payment of fees by clients which are generally based on knowledge and expertise (not products for sale)—the diagnosis of an illness, the prescribing of medicine, the design of a building, the handling of a divorce. This last feature seems to be the great divide which separates our twentieth century professional from the layman, and from many other forms of labor in history.

These forms of work, which we now call professions, have been reorganized around the concept of expertise and grounded in knowledge. Knowledge and expertise have become the salable commodities of today's professional. Knowledge and expertise have been converted into a form of

---

*This may be a college degree in the field, the passage of a professional examination, such as the Bar Exam for lawyers or the NCIDQ examination for interior designers, receiving a state license to practice or use a specific professional title, or performing a supervised internship for a specific period of time. Some professions, such as medicine, may require all of the above.

property, offered for sale in the open market.* It is hardly possible to separate knowledge from the modern concept of profession—thus the critical focus on education.

That this great divide between professional and nonprofessional interior design is closely bound to the possession of knowledge and expertise is often evident beyond reasonable challenge. A tour through a typical interior design office reveals that design work today is more complex than the finished product reveals. Hidden beneath the wonderful spaces, containing beautiful furniture, lit by the most advanced lighting systems, which highlight the array of wonderful colors and materials, is a process that would astonish the layman.

Designing is more than a visual art. Beneath this immediate, visual surface lies a vast number of important decisions which can affect the health, welfare, and safety of the public and the financial health of both client and designer, not to mention the designer's right to continue practicing interior design.

Laws Governing Design Work   Essential to undertaking design work as a professional activity is an understanding of the laws that govern practice. Because the work of interior design is closely related to that of architecture and engineering, one must recognize that architecture and engineering are defined as professions under state licensing laws. Most important to this fact is the nature of those laws and definitions: they are "practice" laws, similar to medicine. If you are not licensed under those titles, you are not legally permitted to perform—or even promise to perform—any activity listed in their definitions.

*Abbott, Andrew, *The System of Professions: An Essay on the Division of Expert Labor*, Chicago: University of Chicago Press, 1988.

Barber, Bernard, "Some Problems in the Sociology of the Professions." *Daedalus*, No. 92 (1963):669–688.

Bledstein, Burton, *The Culture of Professionalism: The Middle Class and the Development of Higher Education in America*. New York: W. W. Norton & Co., 1978.

Bucher, Rue and Joan G. Stelling, *Becoming Professional*.

Carr-Saunders, A. M. and P. A. Wilson, *The Professions*. London: Frank Cass & Company, Ltd., 1933.

Derber, Charles, *Professionals as Workers: Mental Labor in Advanced Capitalism*. Boston: G. K. Hall & Company, 1982.

Freidson, Eliot, *Professional Powers: A Study of the Institutionalization of Formal Knowledge*. Chicago: University of Chicago Press, 1986.

Haskell, Thomas L., Ed, *The Authority of Experts: Studies in History and Theory*. Bloomington: Indiana University Press, 1984.

Holzner, Burkart and John H. Marx, *Knowledge Application: The Knowledge System in Society*. Boston: Allyn & Bacon, 1979.

Larson, Magali Sarfatti, *The Rise of Professionalism: A Sociological Analysis*. Berkeley: University of California Press, 1979.

It is therefore important that you understand these definitions under your own state law and take care to avoid overlapping your work as an interior designer with that of architecture and engineering. The dividing line between what is illegal or legal can be subtle, depending on your state laws and the manner in which they are interpreted. Local legal advice on the scope of your practice as a designer is advised.

Interior Design Licensing—The National Movement   Of all these forces affecting interior design practice and moving it toward education as a fundamental necessity, the national movement to certify or license interior designers may be the most potent.

Gaining momentum throughout the past decade, nearly one-third of all states in the United States and all provinces of Canada have statutes governing interior design as a profession. In the United States, only Washington, D.C. has a practice law, similar to those in architecture and engineering. In other states with interior design laws, the statutes are milder—what we term *title laws*. These laws may or may not outline a strict definition of practice; however, they will not permit you to use the title—usually, but not always, "interior designer" or "certified interior designer"—without having followed the education, experience, and examination path outlined in the law. Therefore, you must have completed these requirements.

While the details of these laws differ, in general each covers certain essential material:

1. *Education.* Is it required? How much? What type? If not required, what alternatives, such as work experience, are permitted?

2. *Examination.* Is it required? Which one? How can you qualify to take that examination? What are the alternatives if you have never taken it?

3. *Experience.* How much? How is the quality judged?

4. *Grandparenting.* Is there a provision in your state law which allows for the waiver of any of the requirements listed above? These vary. Some may allow you to become licensed or certified without the stipulated education or examination, if you have practiced interior design for, say, 12 years. Some statutes may waive only the education, but require you to pass an examination regardless of your vast experience.

5. *Reciprocity.* If you live in a state, such as New Jersey, which might not have a law governing interior design practitioners, can you practice in the neighboring State of New York, which does have a governing law? The states can vary widely on reciprocity; however, the national design and legislative organizations have been working toward national unity of the basic standards.

The national professional organizations which make up the National Legislative Coalition for Interior Design* (NLCID), in conjunction with state and local legislative coalitions, have been working toward the acceptance of national standards. Such coordinated national standards would make it easier for a licensed designer to move from one state to another, while having his/her license accepted on reciprocal terms if the standards for education, examination, and experience are similar.

A comparative table, listing all legislation now in effect regarding the interior design profession, demonstrates that these four basic issues are "nearly" consistent across these states, but not identical. Most have adopted some form of education, but have not specified the type of degree program accreditation, such as the specialized accreditation through FIDER† for interior design programs. In addition, all have adopted the NCIDQ examination as the standard.‡ Most have similar levels of practice requirements.**

What is Design? What Must You Know to Practice?

Is Formal Design Education Required or Even Necessary? While we cannot fairly say that an organized, formal education is required to practice interior design today—it was definitely not the case 50 years ago—it is more likely that today's practitioners, and more true of those tomorrow, will have the benefit of some formal design schooling. Interior design, or even fine arts, architecture, or possibly industrial design, may provide the needed background for design practice. Alternatively, and more rarely, it may be an unusually fine internship under a well-seasoned interior designer, or work experience in a setting conducive to learning the theory, craft, and business which, in this field, have recently become so rich with complexity.

On the other hand, we must note that the traditional process of learning by doing may be prolonged beyond your tolerance. And the learn-by-doing

---

*American Society of Interior Designers (ASID), Council of Federal Interior Designers (CFID), Institute of Business Designers (IBD), Interior Design Educators Council (IDEC), International Society of Interior Designers (ISID), and the advisory members, the Foundation for Interior Design Education Research (FIDER) and the National Council for Interior Design Qualification (NCIDQ).

†The Foundation for Interior Design Education Research—the nationally accepted organization empowered to set educational curricula standards and accredit college level programs in the United States and Canada.

‡The National Council for Interior Design Qualification.

**Despite these apparent similarities, your personal planning will require that you seek local/state advice. Contact your local chapter of one of the interior design organizations which make up NLCID membership regarding specific requirements that apply to you.

exercise may become dangerously chronic, because it has no formal and clearly defined point of passage from student to professional status. Education, it has always been said, is the shortcut to experience.

Consider also that on-the-job training can be risky and undependable. After all, to the uninitiated, innocent, and unknowing apprentice, poor experience can be the more likely consequence of this approach.

Following that well-worn path of formal education, with its highly developed and constantly monitored system of degree program accreditation, provides some measure of assurance that knowledge, skills, and experience will be acquired in a reasonable time frame.

Yes, there are successful, well-known designers who have never had formal design schooling. Most fields present great, inspiring examples along the margins of the mainstream. In considering your options, do not be misled by those "outliers" in the system. Statistical mavericks, these are those rare, and usually very well-known, designers who have never incurred the advantage of formal study. Before you conclude it's that easy, scratch the surface here a bit. Exactly what was their background? A special early education; an artistic family orientation; a very special, prolonged working relationship with a great master; unbelievably hard work over many, many years; or a rare talent. Consider also the difficult issues: How do you know they are that good? What do their peers think? Are they especially good at promotion and little else? Do they have extraordinary assistants which they manage well, and garner the credit to themselves?

Your main question remains: "Is formal education necessary to practice interior design today?" The answer may be irregular, and possibly inconvenient. There is no universal answer which is good for all; however, a few points should help define the best answer for you:

1. Formal education is *not* legally mandatory for interior designers in all 50 states.

Technically you can practice interior design freely, using any title you wish, in more than 30 states as of this publication. But, there's a catch here! Do you know what that phrase "practicing interior design" means?

Interior design may not be regulated in your state, but the design process today is very complex, and the need for comprehensive, intelligent interior design forces overlaps with several other professions, particularly architecture and engineering. And these two, in particular, are legally regulated with very strict practice laws. This means that it is not legal for you to perform certain tasks that are covered in their practice laws. Again, these are regulated under your state law, and these laws differ throughout the United States.

Are you permitted to move a wall? Can you even "suggest" that wall be moved or removed, if your design requires it? Are you allowed to make detailed construction drawings specifying the removal of that wall? Do these drawings need to be filed with a local buildings department? Does your design work need a permit to commence the interior construction? Are you legally permitted as a nonlicensed person to file your drawings to receive that permit?

And we're only considering a simple wall here! Each question may be answered differently depending on legal definitions for architects and engineers, and other related state and local regulations.

There is another issue worth noting if you are somewhere midstream: those of you with some education, or no education, but with some experience. Most laws currently in effect have grandparenting provisions which are worth checking into. In effect, these special regulations could permit some of the education and examination requirements to be waived if you have fulfilled professional work experience requirements.*

2. If you have completed a college degree in a design field, but not one dedicated to interior design, check your state regulations.

You may have some catching up to do in an apprenticeship. The laws may stipulate the specific education necessary for interior design practice in your state. There could be many variations on this. Some may stipulate a formal interior design degree from a state or regionally accredited college; some may be more expansive in allowing alternatives such as a degree in architecture; some may avoid using the terminology of degrees and program titles, choosing to outline a curriculum or subject matter which must have been covered for the education to qualify. It is possible for some states to require that your degree be from a program accredited by the national organization FIDER. This is the only nationally recognized organization to grant interior design program accreditation.†

3. The complexity of interior design projects requires a greater commitment from the designer today.

The expansion of legal requirements—such as barrier-free design legislation, fire and other life safety codes, gender equity in design (such as the recently enacted Virginia law), changes to laws defining the practice of closely aligned fields such as architecture and engineering, as well as complex business, financial, accounting, and project management issues all

---

*You can get in touch with one of your state professional interior design organizations that monitor these regulations closely by contacting NLCID—The National Legislativve Coalition for Interior Design, 608 Massachusetts Avenue N.E., Washington, D.C. 20002-6006, (202) 675-2370.

†You can contact FIDER for a list of the programs currently accredited by them: 60 Monroe Center, N.W., Grand Rapids, MI 49503, (616) 458-0400.

suggest that you acquire some education and apprenticeship prior to tackling that first project or opening your own firm. In good conscience, the head-first approach, consisting of *no education and no apprenticeship experience* can be dangerous: *think twice, get good advice.*

4. Change is eternal.

It is indeed a simple cliche we recall when commenting that nothing in our social system remains static. Simple or not, the cliche is clearly applicable to interior design education. As time passes, changes are delivered to us that must be acknowledged in order to understand the scope and scale of this particular educational process.

No one can predict the future in detail; you must keep up with the changes to set successful career plans. While the need for design education and the nature of that education are *today* clearly defined through a variety of institutional systems, such as testing requirements, program accreditation, and state certification/licensing laws, it is as important to understand the general trends, as well as the specific details. This way you will at least have the capability of understanding the directions that changes are likely to take and plan accordingly.

Consider the history of professionalization in our culture, the expansion of design requirements to address social needs and problems, and the advance of legal regulations to certify/license interior designers across the United States. It is likely that the necessity for education, internship, and examination will expand.

THE NATURE AND CONTENT OF INTERIOR DESIGN EDUCATION

Shifting from the *need* for education, there is much that can be said of the *nature and content* of interior design education today. What is this education about? How did it reach its present form? Who decides on its content?

Logic and history suggest that the needs and requirements of professional practice dictate the nature and content of a professional education system. To a large extent, social need dictates the professionals' area of responsibility. The rise of our medical care system has stimulated enormous demand for designers of health care facilities. Increasing longevity and an expansion of our elderly population has fostered a need for housing to suit both well and frail elderly (air travel, thus the terminal). The women's movement, combined with the economic necessity that sent women into the work force, spawned the growing need for child care facilities, even adult day care facilities for the elderly who live with their adult children. The increase in white collar, information, and service workers in society, combined with the vast technological developments in communications, delineates the highly sophisticated—and fast changing—office environment. We could go on and on detailing social change and the interior design responses.

If you can grasp the essential force at work here—social need as a driving force—you have come a long way toward understanding how design practice and its foundation—education—evolves.

Social institutions have emerged to integrate these social changes and needs, and place them within a workable framework.

Any interest in the nature and content of interior design education today conjures up several basic questions.

Definitions and Definition Makers: Who Decides What Interior Designers Do and Therefore Need to Learn?

This question has a two-pronged answer. On one hand, professions in our society—interior design functioning much like the others—often develop and promote new services for clients to buy. This can be seen most dramatically in sophisticated developments in office design methods since World War II: techniques for large scale space planning—many now computerized—and programming procedures for researching and analyzing office functions. Many design firms have developed new techniques for handling specialized problems in the health care field. In more general areas, designers have expanded their function to include lighting design, furniture systems development, and interior detailing regarding specialized partitions and built-in cabinetry. For cost efficiency, many firms specializing in large-scale planning projects have incorporated CADD—computer aided drafting and design—into their general office procedures.

On the other hand, society and the client have placed demands on interior designers to provide more services. If designers have created and marketed new techniques for office planning and design since World War II, it may have been due to the enormous social need for workplaces for the tremendous increase in white collar office workers. We are in a service-based, information-oriented economy. Post World War II expansion of business, and more sophisticated office worker needs, usually involving communications and computer technology, has demanded change in interior design services.

No small matter is that of health care in our world today. A hot social topic, health care is prominent in our homes in (1) the concern we have for caring for the increasingly elderly population; (2) the increase in personal medical expenses; (3) the burden to government, insurers, and businesses for rising costs; (4) and the demands and expectations we have come to place on the medical care system. It is prominent as a political and economic issue as our society and government debate the prospects and needs for some type of national health insurance.

Our society has come a long way in health care. We now have specialties in geriatric care, cancer care, AIDS, hospice programs, outpatient services, and health maintenance and lifestyle programs and the necessary developments in equipment, technology, and facilities to support them. These social trends have design consequences in the form of complex medical facilities, AIDS and hospice facilities, new forms of outpatient, community-focused service clinics, and drug treatment centers, to mention only a few new forms unseen 50 years ago.

Glance over the shoulder of any designer engaged in one of these new projects, and you will see much more than traditional furniture arrangement and color and material selection. Even these more traditional, mainline design functions have been transformed by the new knowledge required to satisfy the needs inherent in these new facilities.

Furniture can now be a therapeutic piece of hardware with different requirements for the child cancer patient as for the geriatric patient. Selection, comfort, placement, and moveability go beyond the traditional concerns of style, design, and esthetic appeal. Color, texture, and lighting may add that special edge to the healing atmosphere of a long-term hospital facility, or much needed comfort and solace to those many patients with only months or days remaining. Patient-centered care forces designers to consider the effects on patient health and well-being of lying in a bed, staring at a ceiling flooded with cold, blue—even warm white—fluorescent lighting. You might try it when you are feeling well; imagine it when ill. These factors only suggest one area in which social needs have fostered changes in design practice.

Whether initiated by design professionals themselves, or demanded by the changing needs of society, each of these developments have expanded the nature of interior design practice. As practice expanded, so too did the skills required of the designers. New areas of knowledge and new skills appear on the horizon almost daily. No wonder educational trends shift toward expansion. In general interior design education has been intensified and extended in the past 25 years. The future, no doubt, will yield more.

But who decides what should be included in your education? These decisions are generally collective, not individual. It has fallen to a number of social institutions to monitor contemporary interior design practice and respond with appropriate educational standards.

Education Related Institutions

Each interior design organization, from its own vantage point, plays a role in contributing to interior design education. The essential one, of course, is the Interior Design Educators Council. With nearly 500 members—college educators—throughout North America, IDEC has played a fundamental, immediate role in shaping interior design education since its founding in 1962. Through its various committees, annual national conferences, regional meetings, and primary publication *JID—the Journal of Interior De-*

sign—IDEC is concerned with the nature and quality of interior design education.

An interlocking component of this vast and multifaceted national program of interior design preparation is NCIDQ—the National Council for Interior Design Qualification. The role of NCIDQ is testing. It serves the public and the profession by identifying those designers who have met minimum standards for professional practice. The interlocking nature of the interior design community is revealed in reviewing the membership of NCIDQ. The governing force behind this organization is constructed of the primary interior design organizations in North America. Currently these include the following groups: American Society of Interior Designers (ASID), Council of Federal Interior Designers (CFID), Institute of Business Designers (IBD), Institute of Store Planners (ISP), Interior Design Educators Council (IDEC), Interior Designers of Canada (IDC), and International Society of Interior Designers (ISID). These constituent members of NCIDQ require their full professional members to pass the examination. In addition, those states in the United States, and provinces of Canada, with statutes governing the practice of interior design, or use of the title "interior designer," have generally accepted the NCIDQ as the primary examination for licensure or certification.

The NCIDQ studies current interior design practice through what they term *a job analysis* and develops the national qualifying examination. Incorporated in 1974, NCIDQ has worked with Educational Testing Services, the nationally recognized leader in testing, in developing several examinations throughout the past two decades. In the job analysis research, which reaches out in broad surveys to design practitioners and educators, the shape of examination requirements takes on specific form. It is here that the areas of knowledge and skill are formally and systematically outlined. It is here that the daily demands of professional practice feed into the system of education via this ultimate qualifying test. This outline becomes the foundation for the national examination.

The most recent job analysis, undertaken in 1987, confirmed specific categories of knowledge required in professional design practice, and, more important, their respective weight in the examination.

Theory: 9%

Programming, planning, and predesign: 16%

Contract documents: 16%

Furniture, fixtures, equipment, and finishes: 4%

Building and interior systems: 21%

Communication methods: 4%

Codes/standards knowledge: 13%

Business and professional practices: 7%

Project coordination: 7%

History: 3%

The current examination is constructed of six separate parts, all of which must be passed within a five-year period to receive an NDICQ Certificate.

The Consensus Definition of Interior Design Practice Growing from years of national research and discussion across professional organizations, a consensus definition of interior design practice has emerged—one more piece of evidence suggesting the scope and content of education for professional practice:

The interior design profession provides services encompassing research, development, and implementation of plans and designs of interior environments to improve the quality of life, increase productivity, and protect the health, safety, and welfare of the public. The interior design process follows a systematic and coordinated methodology. Research, analysis, and integration of information into the creative process result in an appropriate interior environment. Practitioners may perform any of all of the following services:

Programming. Identify and analyze the client's needs and goals. Evaluate existing documentation and conditions. Assess project resources and limitations. Identify life, safety, and code requirements. Develop project schedules, work plans, and budgets. Analyze design objectives and spatial requirements. Integrate findings with their experience and knowledge of interior design. Determine the need, make recommendations, and coordinate with consultants and other specialists when required by professional practice or regulatory approval.

Conceptual Design. Formulate for client discussion and approval preliminary plans and design concepts that are appropriate and describe the character, function, and aesthetic of a project.

Design Development. Develop and present for client review and approval final design recommendations for space planning and furnishings arrangements; wall, window, floor, and ceiling treatments; furnishings, fixtures, and mill work; color, finishes, and hardware; and lighting, electrical, and communications requirements. Develop art, accessory, and graphic/signage programs. Develop budgets. Presentation media can include drawings, sketches, perspectives, renderings, color and material boards, photographs, and models.

Contract Documents. Prepare working drawings and specifications for non-load bearing interior construction, materials, finishes, furnishings, fixtures, and equipment for client's approval. Collaborate with professional services of specialty consultants and licensed practitioners in the technical areas of mechanical electrical, and load-bearing design as required by professional practice or regulatory approval. Identify qualified vendors. Prepare bid documentation. Collect and review bids. Assist clients in awarding contracts.

Contract Administration. Administer contract documents as the client's agent. Confirm required permits are obtained. Review and approve shop drawings and samples to ensure they are consistent with design concepts. Conduct on-site visits and field inspections. Monitor contractors' and suppliers' progress. Oversee on their clients' behalf the installation of furnishings, fixtures, and equipment. Prepare lists of deficiencies for client's use.

Evaluation. Review and evaluate the implementation of projects while in progress and upon completion as representative of and on behalf of the client.

Eligibility to Take the NDICQ Examination

- Four- or five-year degree in interior design (or allied field) or equivalent educational credits, plus two years of practical professional experience.
- Three-year certificate in interior design (or allied field) or equivalent educational credits, plus three years practical professional experience.
- Two-year certificate in interior design (or allied field) or equivalent educational credits, plus four years practical professional experience.

FIDER—Curriculum and Program Accreditation

The creation and coordination of national standards regarding the length of educational programs and curriculum content rests with FIDER, the Foundation for Interior Design Education Research.

Founded in 1971, FIDER is a nonprofit organization that accredits postsecondary interior design education programs in the United States and Canada. "Its primary purpose is to ensure a high level of quality in interior design education to meet the needs of students, the interior design profession, and society."

This accreditation process, which is voluntary, covers graduate, undergraduate, and two-year programs. Specific standards are applied to programs that provide a postprofessional master's degree, a first professional degree level education, or a pre-professional assistant level education.*

The FIDER Research Committee validates the accreditation process through studies and encourages research in interior design. The Standards

*The policies and procedures for the FIDER accreditation process have been developed in conformance with the guidelines and directives of the Council on Postsecondary Accreditation and the U.S. Department of Education and are subject to their review and approval.

Committee, composed of educators and practitioners, monitors the standards through periodic surveys. Standards are revised when significant developments in interior design education and the profession occur.

The Knowledge Base of Interior Design

FIDER outlines a number of areas which they term the *common base of knowledge for interior designers*. These include:

1. The basic elements of design and composition that form the foundation for creative design, and an awareness of the various media in the visual arts that assist in the understanding of the universality of these fundamentals.

2. Theories of design, color, proxemics, behavior, visual perception, and spatial composition which lead to an understanding of the interrelationship between beings and the built environment.

3. The design process; that is, programming, conceptualization, problem solving, and evaluation, firmly grounded on a base of anthropometrics, ergonomics, and other human factors.

4. Space planning and furniture planning and selection, developed in relationship to application to projects including all types of habitation, whether for work or leisure, new or old; for a variety of populations, young and old, disabled, low or high income.

5. Design attributes of materials, lighting, furniture, textiles, color, and so on, viewed in conjunction with physical, sociological, and psychological factors to reflect concern for the aesthetic qualities of the various parts of the built environment.

6. The technical aspects of structure and construction, building systems, that is, HVAC, lighting, electrical, plumbing, and acoustics, sufficient to enable discourse and cooperation with related disciplines.

7. Technical aspects of surface and structural materials, soft goods, textiles and detailing of furniture, cabinetry, and interiors.

8. The application of laws, building codes, regulations, and standards that affect design solutions in order to protect the health, safety, and welfare of the public.

9. Communication skills—oral, written, and visual—for the presentation of design concepts, the production of working drawings, and the conduct of business.

10. The history and organization of the profession; the methods and practices of the business of interior design; and an appreciation of a code of ethics.

11. Styles of architecture, furniture, textiles, art, and accessories in rela-
     tion to the economic, social, and religious influences on previous
     cultures.
12. Methods necessary to conduct research and analyze the data in order
     to develop design concepts and solutions on a sound basis.

The Standard Path to Professional Interior Design Practice Today

Although there are many fine interior design college level programs
throughout the country, your inexperience in evaluating them could lead to
an unfortunate selection. Any education today is a substantial commitment
of resources, time, physical and psychic energy, and, of course, money. It
would be wise for you to check with a reputable interior designer, if you
know of one, regarding their educational experience. Of course, a FIDER
accredited program would always be a safe, wise choice. FIDER publishes
lists of programs, organized by type of program—two-year, four-year, graduate level—as well as by school and state. Let's look at this accreditation system more closely.

The Schools and Accreditation   In 1989 FIDER upgraded its standards
and implemented new procedures for the interior design accreditation process. Because programs are accredited under specific categories as listed
below, and for set terms—now usually three years or six years—these new
standards and accreditation procedures may not be fully applied to all
currently accredited programs until later this decade. As the formerly accredited programs stand for renewal they will be required to follow the new
standards and categories. Do not be confused by these varying accreditation
categories when you review the FIDER listing.* You should not necessarily
attribute lesser quality to those programs accredited prior to the 1989
changes in standards and procedures.

There were nearly 100 college level programs accredited by FIDER in mid
1993. Under the new, post-1989 standards and procedures, these programs
fell into three classification levels:

Preprofessional Assistant Level Programs = 3

These prepare students for positions as design assistants, merchandisers,
and delineators. This education is generally considered a terminal level
not leading to practice as a professional interior designer. Requires 60

---

*Publications regarding the semiannual list of FIDER accredited programs may be obtained
from FIDER, 60 Monroe Center, N.W., Grand Rapids, MI 49503, (616) 458-0400.

semesters credit hours—approximately two years of full-time college study—including 15 credits devoted to the liberal arts, sciences, and humanities.

First Professional Degree Level Programs = 36

These provide academic preparation for the professional interior designer; the first component in a sequence including education, experience, and satisfactory completion of a qualifying examination. Requires a minimum of 120 semester credits—approximately four years of full-time college study—including a minimum of 30 semester credits devoted to liberal arts, sciences and humanities.

Postprofessional Master's Degree Level Programs = 1

These provide the opportunity to engage in research of creative design work and culminate with a graphics or written thesis. The common body of knowledge contained in the First Professional Degree Level is a prerequisite.

Below is a list of education levels which were used with the former FIDER standards. These levels are still in effect:

Paraprofessional (Terminal Education) Programs = 2

Provide concentrated, intensive preparation in interior design with less education in liberal arts than baccalaureate programs, but further experience in the field can prepare graduates to become professional interior designers.

Baccalaureate Programs = 46

Provide preparation that, with further experience in the field, will enable graduates to become professional interior designers.

Corresponding to these college program classifications, FIDER has developed definitions of practice at three levels:

1) Definition of an Interior Design Assistant
   The interior design assistant is a person who is qualified by education and experience to

   a. assist clients with the selection and arrangement of interior furnishings, materials and space planning;

    b. perform the basic skills necessary to implement a design, including taking measurements, providing cost estimates, preparing drawings and business documents, and consulting with workrooms, installers and other support specialists; and

    c. assist the professional interior designer

2) Pre-Professional Assistant Level
Accreditation at the Pre-Professional Assistant Level of education is directed toward those programs that, typically through a two-year time frame, prepare the students for positions as design assistants, merchandisers, delineators, estimators, etc. These standards reflect the needs of the various employment avenues open to the graduates. This education is generally considered a terminal level that does not normally lead to practice as a professional interior designer. However, individual institutions may grant some credits from these programs towards the achievement of the First Professional Degree Level.

3) Definition of an Interior Designer
This definition is internationally accepted by organizations of professional interior designers and educators. The professional interior designer is a person, qualified by education, experience, and recognized skills, who

—identifies, researches and creatively solves problems pertaining to the function and quality of the interior environment;

—performs services relative to interior spaces including programming, design analysis, space planning, aesthetics and inspection of work on site, using specialized knowledge of interior construction, building systems and components, building regulations, equipment, material and furnishings; and

—prepares drawings and documents relative to the design of interior spaces;

in order to enhance the quality of life and protect the health, safety and welfare of the public.

In planning a program to become a fully recognized interior designer, you might consider the following important issues:

1. Note the national examination requirements. Some state regulations require passage of the NCIDQ examination. You must satisfy the education and work experience minimum requirements to qualify to take the NDICQ examination.

2. Note the membership requirements for most professional interior design organizations in North America. While such membership is not

required to practice, nor to become certified/licensed in states with interior design statutes, membership is generally valued in most professions. It is a useful way to identify with your peers, pursue continuing education, and contribute to the profession.

3. In deciding upon the form and length of your education—if any—review the FIDER standards for various levels of accredited programs. Where do you fit in? Have you had any previous education or experience which may yield advanced standing toward an interior design degree? Contact one of the programs and ask for guidance.

Index